DISCOURSE ON POPULAR CULTURE

*This book is dedicated to the memory of
Raymond Williams*

DISCOURSE ON POPULAR CULTURE

*Class, Gender and History
in Cultural Analysis, 1730
to the Present*

Morag Shiach

Stanford University Press
Stanford, California
1989

Stanford University Press
Stanford, California
© 1989 Morag Shiach
Originating publisher: Polity Press, Cambridge
  in association with Basil Blackwell, Oxford
First published in the U.S.A. by
  Stanford University Press, 1989
Printed in Great Britain
ISBN 0–8047–1720–6
LC 88–63329

Contents

Preface

This book is based on research undertaken for a Ph.D. at Cambridge University. I would like to record my debt to Raymond Williams, whose intellectual and political acumen, and unfailing generosity and support, made the process of research both productive and pleasurable. His persistence in the face of theoretical difficulty and his insistence on the need to place theory within history were a constant source of inspiration. His influence is clear throughout this book. I would also like to thank my two Ph.D. examiners, Professor Marilyn Butler and Dr Alun Howkins, for their help and encouragement.

Many friends and colleagues have contributed to the writing of this book. I would like to thank Lisa Jardine, whose energy, kindness and clarity of thought have helped my research in many ways. Michael Moriarty has been both a critical reader of my work, and a constant source of support: for both of which I thank him. I would also like to thank Gillian Beer, Liz Bellamy, Teresa Brennan, John Caughie, Viv Gardner, Liz Guild, Lucy Dawe Lane, Paddy O'Donovan, Suzanne Raitt and Julia Swindells.

Finally, this book could not have been written without financial support from The Scottish Education Department; Jesus College, Cambridge and The Jebb Fund, University of Cambridge, all of whom I thank. I also thank my family, whose support in all sorts of ways has been greatly appreciated.

Acknowledgements

The author and publishers are grateful for permission to quote from the following:

Eliza Emmerson's Letters to John Clare, B.M. Egerton MSS 2245, by permission of the British Library;

Douglas Allen, 'Political Culture in Scotland: The Glasgow Workers' Theatre Group 1937–40', unpublished thesis material, University of Glasgow (held in the Scottish Theatre Archive, University of Glasgow), by permission of Douglas Allen;

J.W. Tibble, ed., *The Poems of John Clare*, Everyman's Library, J.M. Dent 1935, by permission of J.M. Dent and Sons Ltd;

Eric Robinson and David Powell, eds, *John Clare*, Oxford University Press 1984. Copyright Eric Robinson. Reproduced by permission of Curtis Brown Ltd;

Eric Robinson and Geoffrey Summerfield, eds, *The Shepherd's Calendar* by John Clare, Oxford University Press 1964. Copyright Eric Robinson. Reproduced by permission of Curtis Brown Ltd;

J.A. Gordon, Pamphlet containing poetry by William Thom, Aberdeen University Library MS 2304/4, by permission of Aberdeen University Library.

Introduction

Talking about popular culture is nothing new. As this book will demonstrate, interest in the cultural forms of the people, in cultural texts and practices outside the sphere of the dominant culture, has been a constant feature of literary, political and cultural debates since the eighteenth century. Although the concept of 'popular culture' was not fully developed until the nineteenth century, we can identify the emergence of distinctive ways of talking about the cultural role and significance of the people as early as the 1730s. Since then, the concept of 'popular culture' has remained as a powerful and pervasive element in cultural analyses.

'Popular culture' has now become an object of study in a variety of disciplines: literature, history, anthropology and communications all approach and constitute it in different ways. The tendency in all these disciplines, however, is either to assume 'popular culture' as an unproblematic term, and then to defend, or attack, its manifestations, or, alternatively, to construct 'popular culture' as rallying cry, usually preceded by 'truly', 'really' or 'authentically'. Neither of these approaches demonstrates any awareness of the historical emergence of debates about popular culture. They thus tend to accept uncritically the sets of attitudes towards 'culture' and 'the people' which the concept embodies.

What this book aims to do is to understand the emergence of the concept of 'popular culture' historically and to analyse the assumptions about class, gender and history which are part of that emergence. The aim is not to arrive at a definitive meaning of the concept of 'popular culture', to designate the authentically popular, but rather to explore the critical, literary and political positions which are expressed in historical debates about the culture of the people, and to examine the importance of these debates for the dominant culture.

This book is concerned less with producing an analysis of particular cultural artefacts than with developing an historical account of the assumptions about culture, history and 'the people' that lie behind analyses of popular culture. It does not, therefore, offer a definition of the nature and significance of folk music, or of 'peasant poetry', but rather looks at the reasons behind critics' discussions of these cultural forms, the languages with which they have discussed them, and the ways in which these languages affect the producers of popular culture. The focus of the book is, therefore, discourses about popular culture: continuities in the ways in which popular culture has been described and evaluated. In order to discover such continuities, however, it has proved essential to look in detail at specific cultural forms which have been seen as constitutive, or expressive, of popular culture. The analysis will, therefore, move between attention to the specifics of particular debates about popular culture and the development of a theoretical account of the concept of popular culture itself. Perhaps it is a useful generalization to say that when this book looks most historical it is, in fact, trying to get a new perspective on theoretical questions and that when it is most insistently posing theoretical questions it is, in fact, grappling with the limitations of existing cultural histories.

This book, then, has a double focus: it is concerned both with a series of cultural artefacts and with the development of discourses which render these significant as part of 'the popular'. My interest is neither in popular culture nor in 'popular culture', but rather in the historical interaction between particular cultural texts and practices and the discourses which circumscribe them and give them meaning. In this book, I will look at historical developments within a range of cultural forms which have been, for a variety of reasons, marginalized and excluded from the domain of the dominant culture. It is clear, however, that such developments cannot be understood without reference to the languages of cultural analysis, which produce judgements of cultural significance and value. Equally, in order to understand the substance, and the urgency, of debates about popular culture, it is necessary to see them in the context of changing social and cultural relations.

The development of the concept of 'popular culture', then, must be seen as a complex series of responses to historical developments within communications technologies, to increased literacy, or to changes in class relations. Such histories can only be demonstrated through an investigation of particular cultural forms, and an account of their emergence and development. It should be clear, however, that the recognition of those cultural forms which might be deemed 'popular' is not straightforward: it is crucially related to a broader series of discourses about culture and society. I am, therefore, not saying, 'here is a series of examples of popular culture; and these are the terms in which they were discussed'. I am trying, rather, to demonstrate the ways in which the very recognition of certain cultural forms as 'popular' is already bound up in a set of cultural and social discourses. For example, the notion that particular texts and practices form part of a recognizable entity, 'culture', whose state has implications for the social and cultural well-being of a nation, is a relatively modern one. My analysis, therefore, begins at the point where such conceptions of the role and nature of culture are beginning to develop, and to lead to an interest in a wide range of cultural production.

Clearly, this book cannot attempt a complete history of popular culture in Britain, nor can it indicate all the political, literary and theoretical questions about popular culture which have occupied critics since the eighteenth century. In choosing particular historical periods, and cultural artefacts, for analysis, however, an attempt has been made to identify historical moments where the state of popular culture became a crucial issue for theorists or practitioners situated within the dominant culture. The forms taken by these debates about popular culture depended, more generally, on the cultural and historical priorities of the time. Thus, in the eighteenth and early nineteenth centuries, poetry was a crucial site for definitions of authenticity, naturalness and cultural significance. Definitions of poetic writing, and practices of literary patronage, were two of the many forms in which the shift from feudal, hierarchical social relations to the more complex and diffuse power relations which characterize capitalism was negotiated. The conflict between 'the country' and 'the city' was a crucial part of this struggle. In looking at peasant poetry, in chapter 2, I thus try to place the phenomenon, and the discourses which constitute it, within this broader political and historical perspective.

The choice of the periodical press as the object of analysis in chapter 3 reflects the conviction that developments in communications technologies in the mid-nineteenth century were a crucial part of the constitution of industrial capitalism, and were perceived as such. The development of the radical press, and of penny fiction, were seen as metaphors for, and part of, the development of an organized working class. We can thus identify, in analyses of penny fiction, attempts to work out the relations between social and cultural transformations. Also, in this period, the powerful and persistent equation between technological progress and cultural decline, which is a recurrent trope in cultural analyses, was frequently and forcefully advanced in relation to the penny press, and in particular to popular fiction.

Later on in the century, arguments about popular culture became more broadly, and more significantly, arguments about the tenability of the social and cultural relations of capitalism. I have thus looked, in chapter 4, at a series of attempts in this period to re-evalute and to revive particular forms of popular culture, from folk music to pottery. I have tried to identify the terms of, and motivation for, attempts to rediscover 'traditional' forms of culture, and to examine the implications of such initiatives for culturally marginalized social groups.

By the beginning of the twentieth century, it is important to examine the contribution of socialist, and specifically marxist, traditions of thought to the analysis of popular culture. This reflects the extent to which recent analyses of popular culture have been largely produced from the Left, and in terms of class politics. Such analyses represent an important re-evaluation of the political implications of 'the popular'. Instead of seeing it either as a guarantee of social stability and unity, or as a dangerous threat to society, such analyses look to 'the popular' as a site of opposition, of resistance; as a demonstration of the possibility of developing new social and cultural relations. The Workers' Theatre Movement is thus examined as the site of a conscious exploration of the relation between political and cultural discourses of 'the people'.

Finally, in chapter 6, I look at the extent to which discourses of popular culture have been transformed by technological and social developments, particularly in relation to television, as medium and as cultural form. As a highly technological, widely available cultural form, consumed in the home, television has become the focus for much recent concern about the state of popular culture. I have thus analysed the origins of particular ways of theorizing the social and cultural impact of television, and related these to the positions and assumptions identified in earlier parts of the book.

It must already be clear that this book analyses a wide range of texts, from an extended historical period. This sort of scope seems unavoidable, if the transformations in, and complexity of, the analysis of popular culture are to be recognized and considered. It is, however, very hard to do justice to the ramifications of so many social and cultural debates, while still maintaining the focus and energy of the central enquiry. If the specificity of particular debates is insufficiently explored, it is to be hoped, at least, that their relation to the central problem of the book remains compelling.

Historical breadth, then, has proved to be an essential feature of the analysis undertaken in this book. This breadth must be set against the specificity of the political and geographical dimensions of the analysis, which have been limited to accounts of popular culture produced within Great Britain. The debates which are explored in the rest of the book certainly have their international dimensions: this is discussed specifically in relation to the poetry of Ossian, and the analysis of television. However, in order to relate developments in the sphere of cultural analysis to other social and political transformations it has proved important to specify the social and cultural relations that obtain at any particular period. If it is difficult to speak with any degree of accuracy about the development of class relations within Britain, to do so at a more international level is to risk meaningless generalization. This book attempts to relate cultural analysis to other social and political phenomena. It aims to demonstrate that assertions about culture, about national identity, about poetic value or about popular taste are part of the process by which historical and political developments are negotiated and made sense of. I have thus found it necessary to focus on the development of debates about popular culture within one particular society: in this case, Great Britain. The conclusions of such an analysis will, undoubtedly, be of relevance to debates about popular culture in other geographical and political contexts, but the analysis demands specificity.

The debates examined in this book do not always concentrate on the concept of 'popular culture'. I will examine the positions developed by theorists who talk instead of 'folk culture', 'mass culture' or 'workers' culture'. This is not to say that I am unaware of the different assumptions and positions that lie behind these terms. It has been argued by many cultural theorists that these terms should be clearly separated, and that they refer to different forms of culture, and make different assumptions about social relations. What I have found in writing this book, however, is that these terms are frequently used by different writers to refer to the same cultural forms. To nineteenth-century folk song collectors, Music Hall was debased mass culture. To recent historians, it is a vibrant and oppositional form of popular culture. I have thus treated these categorizations with a certain suspicion, and have focused instead on what is actually being said or claimed about cultural forms which have been marginalized, repressed or ignored by the dominant culture.

The historical material discussed in this book is not available to us in any unmediated form. It has already been selected, interpreted and 'made sense of' by historians and literary critics. This process of selection and interpretation is very instructive as to the assumptions and priorities with which critics have approached the analysis of popular culture. It does, however, make the task of reinterpretation and analysis more complex. The power of the theoretical models which have been brought to bear on this material makes it necessary at several points in this book to develop a critique of these models, before attempting an assessment of the texts and practices under consideration. This is particularly true in terms of the analysis of popular culture in the nineteenth century, which has been the object of sustained historical and political theorization since the 1960s.

My aim in this book, then, is to identify the assumptions about culture, history, gender and society which have underpinned analyses of popular culture since the eighteenth century. My thesis is that many of these fundamental assumptions have remained unchanged. This is not to say, of course, that the analysis, and indeed the conception of 'popular culture' have remained identical throughout this period. Debates about popular culture are always crucially involved with other debates or problems within the dominant culture. They thus take different forms, and address different material, in different historical moments. They do, however, rehearse many of the same arguments, and reproduce many of the same tropes. Rather than claiming that there is one continuous and coherent approach to the analysis of popular culture, I aim to show that there are sets of positions, on the nature of culture and of writing, on the relation between technology and cultural decline, or on the identity of 'the people' which are mobilized in different combinations at different periods. They are maintained by critics from different social and cultural positions, attempting to assert different sorts of claims about popular culture. This 'consistency in difference', powerful and theoretically disabling, is what this book will attempt to address.

The first consistency lies in the extent to which analyses of popular culture are always connected to, and motivated by, problems and perceived limitations within the dominant culture, rather that emerging from an engagement with the material forms of popular culture themselves. Thus, for example, the interest in 'peasant poetry' in the eighteenth century lay in the extent to which it could support particular theories about the relation between nature and poetic writing, rather than in any desire to re-evaluate the cultural and social role of the peasantry. The fascination with

Highland society which accompanied the 'rediscovery' of Ossian's poetry was produced by the search for authenticity, and for cultural forms untouched by modern civilization. The 'rediscovery' of this oral tradition was used to support an 'imaginary' of national unity and identity, and not to empower, or even recognize, those who had produced and preserved the tradition.

The articulation of the importance of popular culture for the dominant culture often involves notions of 'social control' and 'effects'. The anxiety is that the consumption of popular culture produces effects that will jeopardize the maintenance of social control. Thus, writers in the nineteenth century worried about the moral and social effects of penny fiction. From their own accounts, it is clear that this concern was not produced by a close study of this fiction, or an analysis of its readers' responses, but quite simply by the fact of its availability, its cheapness. Similarly, much criticism of television as a cultural form is occupied with the alleged destabilizing and debasing effects of the consumption of its representations. The concentration, in many studies, on the effects of television on children is illustrative of a theoretical paradigm which marginalizes the viewers of television, treating them as uncritical, immature and vulnerable.

The engagement with dominant culture is quite other in the case of popular theatre movements of the 1920s and 1930s. The relationship is centrally one of refusal, an insistence on the construction of new and vital forms which will marginalize and surpass the cultural manifestations of a decaying social and political order. This does not mean, however, that accounts of popular theatre are uncomplicatedly produced by, and focused on, their object. In the case of the Workers' Theatre Movement, for example, it is clear that many of the categories produced for cultural analysis are borrowed directly from political and economic analysis. This appropriation is not always productive.

My point is not to suggest that popular culture should be analysed without reference to other cultural, political and social spheres. Indeed, one of the other 'consistencies' of the criticism of popular culture which will be examined below is the desire to produce 'popular culture' as an autonomous and authentic space. What I want to suggest, however, is that many of the categories brought to, and conclusions drawn from, the analysis of popular culture reflect more about the state of the dominant culture than they reveal about popular culture.

The second consistency has been hinted at already: the perception of popular culture as corrupting. Penny fiction in the nineteenth century was represented as demeaning and dangerous. It was perceived as such not just by writers like Fanny Mayne, whose interest lay in the maintenance of capitalist social and cultural relations, but also by writers in the Radical and Chartist press. Radical writers were suspicious of penny fiction as feeding imaginary and romantic solutions to real social problems, and refused to discuss it in any detail. This worry about the distracting, depoliticizing and debasing impact of popular culture is also clear in the work of folk song collectors, who were deeply concerned about the harmful effects of Music Hall. This articulation of corruption often takes place under the label of 'mass culture'. As I have already mentioned, however, far from representing completely separate cultural spaces, 'mass', 'folk' and 'popular' are often used at different moments about the same sorts of cultural forms. These terms frequently amount to no more than a rhetorical attempt to seal off the category of 'popular culture'. Thus, if it is impossible to determine the specificity of folk song in terms of authorship, transmission or tradition, we can at least be sure that it is not Music Hall, not mass culture.

The same anxiety about the cultural forms which were actually being consumed by the people lay behind the popular theatre movement of the 1920s and 1930s. Numerous writers criticized the ideological nature of the cinema, the press, radio and West End theatre. What they sought to do was to create new cultural forms, by and for the people, which would produce representations that were of their lives, and in their interests.

The consistency of this refusal to engage with, or analyse, cultural forms that are seen as corrupting seems to me unfortunate. This is not to say that the extent to which cultural forms, which are produced and consumed as commodities, produce partial and interested accounts of social relations should be ignored. Indeed, Judith Williamson has demonstrated very convincingly the need to see popular culture in its dimension as ideology, as a space that is always contested and never won, as the cultural sphere of people who are constantly undermined and marginalized by the social relations in which they participate.[1] This sort of judgement can only usefully be produced, however, on the basis of a careful analysis of the forms and practices of popular culture. It is important, for example, to understand the power of narratives of romance and adventure, for ourselves as well as for others, and to realize the complexity of the ways in which they are consumed. The refusal and repression of cultural forms deemed inauthentic or corrupting does not greatly advance this project.

The analysis of popular culture is severely limited by the extent to which the rhetorical power of the concept of 'the people' far outstrips its descriptive specificity. The ambiguities and transformations in the concept 'popular' will be explored further in the first chapter. The effect of these ambiguities is to produce a particularly cavalier attitude in critics of popular culture to the sociological categories with which they are operating. There is little attempt to analyse who exactly is being talked about as 'the people'. Imaginary categories are produced: the illiterate 'folk', untouched by modern civilization or by social transformations. That the folk singers and performers who were discovered did not fit this description at all did not bother the collectors. They simply did not notice. They were uninterested in the real social relations of the 'folk', so they never discovered them. Similarly, the 'peasant' label attached to the poets in the eighteenth century should not be taken to imply that these writers were independent agricultural producers who still participated in feudal social relations. They were rural labourers, servants, washerwomen and pipemakers.

That the concept of 'the people' is never subjected to sociological or political analysis produces some interesting blind-spots in the analysis of 'popular culture'. The first of these lies in the absence of women from accounts of 'popular culture', which will be analysed in more detail below. Briefly, 'popular' emerges as a legal and political term at a period when most women had few legal or political rights. This gender bias never becomes obvious to cultural theorists, however, as their representation of 'the popular' remains abstract, and unchallenged by the facts of cultural production and consumption.

The abstract nature of conceptions of 'the popular' also leads to a very unsatisfactory ahistorical attempt to claim its meaning as constant from the Renaissance to the present day. Thus, theorists of popular theatre claim that theatre always has been popular, really. First of all this statement seems to me, if it means anything substantial, to be false. There are periods in our history when theatre was quite visibly the preserve of the ruling classes. More seriously, however, it seems to me that such a claim can only be made when 'the people' are reduced to a complete abstraction. The social, cultural and political relations of Elizabethan England and twentieth-century Britain are completely different. The economy of cultural production has been transformed. The social significance of a theatrical performance is totally changed. What sense, then, does it make to equate Elizabethan and contemporary theatre as 'popular'? I respect the political impulse behind the desire to make such an equation, the wish to claim cultural forms back from the selective and destructive histories of the dominant culture. I cannot accept, however, that abstraction and wishful thinking make for good cultural analysis.

Those who write about popular culture generally place themselves clearly outside its sphere. Thus the writing of 'peasant poets' is generally presented, mediated and made sense of by someone placed securely within the dominant culture. Their 'lives' of the poets are required before the poetry can be placed, rendered significant, and consumed with security. Similarly, the collectors of folk songs, though they valued oral tradition and illiteracy, were themselves educated and musically trained. They made little attempt to involve folk singers in the preservation and evaluation of their songs, and, indeed, generally excluded them from the societies founded to preserve their culture. Critics of television are equally clear that they are exempt from the mystifying and debasing effects of the form. They are able to bring a critical apparatus to bear, and remain untouched by the cultural and spiritual decline which television entails. Even in the case of popular theatre, whose theorists identified themselves politically as in opposition to the dominant social and cultural order, the place of the theorist in relation to popular forms is often in doubt.

Again, my point is not that theorists of popular culture should place themselves within the realm of 'the popular'. Such a gesture could only be rhetorical, or simply dishonest. The point is, rather, to note the constant slippage between speaking about, and speaking for. In order to legitimate their production of discourse on popular culture, theorists place themselves, culturally and linguistically, within the dominant sphere. At the same time, however, they frequently claim to represent the perceptions, nature and aspirations of 'the people'. Such an appropriation must be examined with care.

Perhaps the most notable consistency in the analysis of popular culture lies in the attempt to produce it as an autonomous sphere of authenticity, untouched by changing social and cultural relations. This is particularly visible in the work of folk song collectors, whose commitment to the notion of a continuous and coherent song tradition led them to a very selective and ultimately misleading account of the song culture of nineteenth-century England. The patrons of peasant poetry, however, were equally clear that they had discovered a completely natural form of writing that was uncompromised by sophistication and literary theory. The theorists of popular theatre also hoped to construct cultural forms that were untainted by the values and practices of the dominant culture. They tried to produce theatrical forms that were a completely authentic representation of the experiences and interests of the working class. All of these initiatives showed a reluctance to theorize, or even recognize, the negotiation between different cultural spheres, the extent to which writers, singers and actors produced themselves through forms available within the dominant culture, as well as in opposition to, or ignorance of, them.

The desire for an autonomous and authentic cultural sphere leads to a tendency in many cultural critics to repress, or mythify, history. The abstract nature of many of the 'histories of the people' offered by theorists of popular culture has already been mentioned. This is part of a general reluctance to recognize the implications of changing historical and social relations for cultural production. This reluctance is particularly visible in projects of recovery, such as the reconstitution of a tradition of rural pottery. Here the emphasis is on the rediscovery of techniques and forms of pottery which are both expressive of the vision of the craftsman and traditional. What is not considered, however, is the meaning that such a tradition has in an economic and cultural economy where flagons are for putting flowers in, rather than for serving cider.

This reluctance seems particularly significant given that the motivation for many cultural theorists to approach the domain of popular culture lies in their concern about cultural and political decline. It is not coincidental that the assertion of a continuous tradition of peasant writing in the nineteenth century was accompanied by a massive concern about the growth in the consumption and production of cheap literature. Similarly, folk song collectors campaigned against the cultural and economic developments that produced the debased form of Music Hall at the same time as they constituted a notion of folk culture which was unaffected by history. History becomes the 'repressed' of theories of popular culture, but it has a way of returning.

It is in the nineteenth century that we can first identify a clear and confident equation between technological progress and cultural decline. It was the cheapness and availability of fiction that was the basis of its corruption. This cheapness was directly attributable to developments in printing and paper-making technologies. This argument has proved remarkably tenacious, and is clearly visible in relation to analyses of television, as a technology. Thus, the danger of television, also, lies in its cheapness and availability. The technology of television, which produces moving images consumed by static viewers, is also held responsible for the passivity it engenders: the argument is that technological facts determine available forms of reading.[2] More recent research makes it clear that the 'reading' of television is actually a far more active and complex process than this model suggests.[3] But the model survives, and is mobilized in relation to comics, to cinema, to television and to video. The point here is not that technological developments are not part of cultural and social transformations, but rather that the immediate assumption of 'decline' is a barrier to the careful analysis of the cultural implications of technological change.

If the model of decline is persistent, so is the assertion of a Golden Age of cultural expression and significance, only recently disappeared. Cultural critics always seem to identify themselves as just a little too late: too late to find truly authentic texts, too late to escape compromise and fragmentation. For folk song collectors this perception is much repeated and clearly painful. From the late eighteenth century to the mid-twentieth century, collectors describe the vibrant and authentic forms of song culture which have recently disappeared. Even in a cultural form which is as relatively 'young' as television, the same sorts of judgements are made. A kind of nostalgia for television of the fifties develops, as somehow nearer to the essence of television, as opposed to the trivia and gloss of televison in the eighties. Again, my point is not to challenge the claim that cultural forms may decay, or disappear, but rather to draw attention to the persistence of this perception that things were, recently, so much better. This perception may say more about the imaginary terms in which recent history is available to us than it does about the vitality and power of any particular cultural form.

The final 'consistency' in the analysis of popular culture lies in the marginalization, or exclusion, of women. Accounts of peasant poetry, of folk song, of the Arts and Crafts Movement, or of popular culture in the nineteenth century all give women a very minor part in the production and the consumption of cultural forms. There are various reasons for this invisibility of women in popular culture. The first is methodological: the categories which are brought to the study of popular culture, and the cultural forms and artefacts which are deemed worthy of study, are already caught up in a gendered history which prioritizes the cultural activities and aspirations of men. The cultural activities of women were also marginalized at the moment they were produced. Thus women peasant poets were never allowed to escape from the double exclusion caused by their gender and their class position. They found patronage harder to come by, and financial independence impossible. The result of this and of the interests and preoccupations of later critics is that their poetic writing is now less available, less widely discussed, and thus assumed to be less significant. I will attempt in this book to redress the balance, but it must be observed that hundreds of years of cultural neglect cannot simply be wished away. The challenge of producing interesting and powerful accounts of poetic writing which has never before been part of critical discussions is daunting, particularly when set beside the proliferation of critical responses to the work of James Thomson, Stephen Duck or John Clare.

A similar process of marginalization of women is observable in the practices of the Arts and Crafts Movement. Women were kept within the less 'significant' spheres of cultural production, they were frequently excluded from Guilds and other craft associations, and their labour was often simply unacknowledged. Writers on the Arts and Crafts Movement have generally reproduced this marginalization, by focusing, for example, on the work of William Morris, and failing to take account of the political and cultural contributions of the women with whom he lived and worked.

So, women disappear from accounts of popular culture as a result of particular methodological preoccupations and practices. They are also constantly marginalized in the narratives of popular culture. Critics offer 'popular culture' as heroic narrative of authenticity and coherence versus triviality and decay. Such a narrative must have a hero, who is, of course, male. When women do appear, it is often as the embodiment of forces inimical to the great heroic adventure of popular culture: the peasant poets' wife, obstructive and stupid, or the clergyman's wife, repressing the spontaneity of all-male choirs. Such judgements are often implicit in the imagery of accounts of popular culture: as 'virile' and 'manly', as 'rigorous', as fighting against the 'sweetly pretty', the 'effeminate' and the 'namby-pamby'.

These, then, are the sorts of assumptions about, and accounts of, popular culture which I will examine in this book. The following chapters will examine analyses of popular culture at a number of different historical moments, and in the context of some very different debates: debates about poetry, cheap fiction, folk song, arts and crafts, theatre and television. Such a variety of objects of analysis makes the development of a consistent critical language very difficult. Each of these areas tends to generate its own vocabulary, which may seem mystifying or obscure to readers not familiar with its terms. I have tried to avoid 'technical' or misleading uses of language throughout this book. Nonetheless, I have found certain critical and theoretical terms, which have been developed by a range of cultural theorists since the 1960s, indispensable to the project of this book. It may, perhaps, be useful to clarify these at this point.

The concept of 'popular culture' itself may present the first difficulty for readers of this book. Since it is the aim of the book to explore the historical and theoretical dimensions of this term, no definition will be attempted here. I will start from the position that it is a persistent term in cultural analyses, which points us towards a consideration of cultural hierarchies and of the relation between the social and the cultural, whose history and significance have been insufficiently considered. In the first chapter, however, I do indicate the complexity of the concept of 'the popular', as well as trying to show the continuities, and the common political and cultural problems that are invoked by its use. The meanings and associations of 'the popular' in legal and political discourses turn out to be a crucial part of discussions of popular culture, as they have developed since the eighteenth century.

'Culture' is a notoriously complicated term. The history of developing uses and meanings of 'culture' and the relation of these to social and cultural transformations, has been most clearly described by Raymond Williams.[4] 'Culture' is a term which can denote a process of general cultivation, the state of moral and spiritual development of a particular group or individual, the whole way of life of a nation or group, or a collection of musical or literary texts. All, except the first, of these definitions will be implied by the accounts of popular culture discussed in this book. The ambiguity and complexity of the term 'culture' is an expression of important changes in, and choices about, ways of perceiving and representing social relationships. It will not be the aim of this book to arrive at one settled meaning of 'culture', let alone of 'popular culture': my interests are critical and historical, rather than prescriptive.

This book does, however, have a very clear commitment to the analysis of culture as a set of material forms and practices. It aims to identify the institutions in which cultural forms are produced, and by which they are rendered significant. It attempts to analyse the economic relations in which cultural production participates: patronage, commodity production or state subsidy. It tries always to understand culture as part of a set of social relations: relations between different nations, different social classes, and between men and women.

It may be objected that a particular meaning of culture is implicit in the choice of material to be analysed in this book, which is predominately literary. To some extent this is true, and overdetermined. First of all, the analysis, and constitution, of the concept of 'popular culture' has important literary antecedents. Even work as challenging as that produced by the Birmingham University Centre for Contemporary Cultural Studies, which has demonstrated a clear commitment to the analysis of culture as part of a whole way of life, as the expression through a range of forms and practices of competing definitions of social reality, has its origins in texts by Richard Hoggart and Raymond Williams, whose methodology and vocabulary are profoundly influenced by literary criticism. Literary criticism has been a crucial site for the construction of theories about the relations between history, national identity and the production of meaning, and has thus provided the space, methodology and motivation for many descriptions and analyses of popular culture. To focus on literary mediations in the analysis of popular culture is not, however, to say that 'culture' is equivalent to literary texts. It is, rather, to recognize the important role that literature and literary criticism have had in the development of categories and methodologies with which we analyse a range of texts: from pottery to poetry, and from tapestry to television. Anthropological and sociological discourses on popular culture are to some extent explored in this book, particularly in relation to folk song, to penny fiction, and to television. Generally, however, the book identifies literary accounts of, and interventions in, popular culture as dominant, and aims to explore the terms of this dominance.

The concept of 'popular culture' does imply a recognition of cultural hierarchy: the 'popular' is being contrasted to other forms of culture. The most obvious contrast is that between 'popular culture' and 'high culture'. The problems raised by the description of such cultural hierarchies are, of course, immense. As we shall see, the domain of 'the popular' itself is extremely fluid, and its relations to other forms of culture, described as 'high', 'traditional', 'folk', 'mass', or 'learned' are consequently unstable, and can only be described with any accuracy at particular historical moments. I am thus faced with a theoretical problem: the relations between cultural forms and social power emerge repeatedly throughout this book, and the domain of the 'popular' is repeatedly confirmed as secondary and marginal, yet, at the same time, any attempt to specify the content of cultural spheres, 'high', 'learned' or 'popular', comes up against the opacity of historical relations. I have thus used the concept of 'dominant culture' as a means to indicate the relation between social power and cultural production, without assuming that the cultural forms and practices which

constitute the 'dominant culture' are either unchanging or completely specifiable. Since part of my argument is to show the ways
in which texts or artefacts can move between 'popular' and
'dominant' cultural spheres, this should not constitute a problem.

I have derived my use of the concept of 'dominant culture' from
two different sorts of accounts of the relations between cultural
forms and social power. The first of these is to be found, for
example, in the work of the French social theorist Pierre
Bourdieu.[5] Bourdieu has explored the relations between the
possession of 'cultural capital' and the possession of wealth and
power. Certain cultural forms and practices have historically been
privileged, among other things by their position in institutions of
education, and by the critical practices that surround these
institutions. The possession of these forms or access to these
practices becomes both the expression, and the guarantee of social
dominance. 'Cultural capital' thus refers to the collection of
recognized and valorized cultural resources and powers, expressed,
for example, in educational qualifications, that can be 'invested' in
order to ensure a return of social power:

> . . . children of well-off families, who decisively consolidate their ad-
> vantage by investing their cultural capital in the sections most likely
> to secure it the highest and most durable academic profitability.[6]

Bourdieu does not equate the possession of cultural and economic
capital, indeed, he argues specifically that, within the dominant
social group, the structure of distribution of economic capital is in
inverse relation to the structure of distribution of cultural capital.
What Bourdieu does insist on, and demonstrate, however, is the
key role of cultural forms in the reinforcement and reproduction of
social hierarchies. He demonstrates the unequal distribution of
linguistic and cultural capital, between different social classes and
between men and women, and thus offers one particular account of
the construction of the forms and norms of 'dominant culture'.

Another important account of relations between cultural forms
and political structures can be found in the work of Antonio
Gramsci, particulary in his discussion of the nature of hegemony.[7]
'Hegemony' is a term which Gramsci uses to describe two different,
but related, phenomena: the maintenance of control by the state,
through organized consent rather than coercion, and the leadership
of one particular class or group in relation to other social classes or
political groups. Whether these two functions coincide is a matter
for historical analysis. Gramsci sees hegemony as covering many
aspects of relations between different social classes: he talks of

intellectual, ethical, moral and political hegemony. All of these terms refer to particular modes in which social relations are negotiated. What all forms of hegemony have in common is that they operate within 'civil society', that is the realm of 'the private', the domain of 'culture', rather than within the institutions of the state. Gramsci argues that social domination can only be maintained by both hegemonic and coercive activity, and, further, that any social group aspiring to social dominance must first assert its intellectual and moral leadership.[8] Thus, Gramsci offers us another explanation of the nature of the dominant culture. It can be understood as the site of hegemonic representations: those which 'foster forms of consciousness which accept a position of subordination'.[9] It is also, therefore, a sphere that must be won over by any social group aspiring to social leadership: struggles over the definition of culture can thus be seen as struggles for intellectual, moral and philosophical hegemony.

The dominant culture provides the norms in relation to which all other cultural production evaluates or describes itself. It produces both the terms of criticism and the rules of writing. There are moments, which will be examined in this book, of significant challenge to such power, especially by the theorists and practitioners of popular theatre. Such moments, however, do not detract from the basic model of cultural relations and forms as hierarchical: 'definitions of the emergent, as of the residual, can be made only in relation to a full sense of the dominant'.[10]

There are certain terms which are used in the book in a sense which might be described as metaphorical. Thus, for example, I talk of the 'investment' of certain social groups in particular cultural forms. This term does not necessarily refer to actual economic investment. Rather, it is meant to indicate the variety of forces which might reinforce the interest of different social groups in the sphere of culture. The investment might be economic, through patronage or subsidy; it might be psychic, a channelling of needs and desires into the consumption of a particular cultural form; or it might be political, a concession of elements of political control in order to secure a shift in cultural relations.

The metaphorical, or at least extended, use of terms such as 'economy', 'practice' or 'materialist' by cultural critics since the 1960s has caused quite a few writers some disquiet. It is, of course, true that the evocation of linguistic terms with a sound political pedigree does not, in itself, solve difficult theoretical or political questions. Nonetheless, I have found some of the terms developed by cultural theorist in recent years, such as 'investment', or 'stake', a useful way on indicating the dimensions of relations between the social, the individual and the cultural. Metaphors exist to extend our capacity for conceptualization: they are dangerous only when confused with the real.

Finally, the concept of 'mediation' is employed at various points in this book. By this, I mean quite simply to indicate that texts and practices from different historical moments or different cultural spheres are not available to us directly, but only through an active process of appropriation and reinterpretation. 'Mediation' implies an attempt to render a text meaningful and valuable in terms of the dominant culture. It refers to the movement of cultural texts within a hierarchical set of social and cultural relations, and signals the extent to which the meaning and significance of a particular text is related to its position within this hierarchy. The use of the concept of 'mediation' is thus intended both to indicate the complexity of the process by which cultural texts are made available and to preserve the dimension of power within this process.

1

A History of Changing Definitions of 'The Popular'

The historical and theoretical difficulties involved in a consideration of popular culture are not simply a function of the complexity of analysing culture. Certainly, the analysis of any cultural form involves questions of aesthetics, history and politics. It requires a theory which can account for cultural specificity as well as the social context which produces certain cultural forms. It also needs to account for the development and significance of the very category 'culture'. In the case of popular culture, however, the difficulties are compounded by the power and persistence of that other term, 'popular'. 'Popular' is not simply a cultural or aesthetic term. It exists in a range of political and legal discourses, and has been constantly redefined, refined and fought over. We can find debates over the definition of 'the popular' that stretch back over four hundred years: numerous attempts to win the term over for a particular theorisation of social and cultural relations.

Critics frequently represent the 'problem' of popular culture as a problem of definitions: 'If only we could clarify the precise meaning of "popular", and specify precisely what is meant by "the people", then the problem would disappear.' Thus, numerous books and articles about popular culture begin with a list of possible meanings, and an expression of frustration at the 'slipperiness' of the term. It is this desire for clarity that is addressed in this chapter, which will analyse different meanings of 'popular' in a range of political, legal and cultural texts. As we shall see, however, far from solving 'the problem' of popular culture, this analysis serves to confirm its dimensions. The ideological and practical struggles over definitions of popular culture are reproduced, or refought, in language, and not solved by it. We will see in later chapters the ways in which theorists and collectors of popular culture have always consciously tried to change the meaning of 'popular culture':

to legitimate certain meanings and to repress others.

The aim of this chapter is to rediscover the history of changing definitions of the concept of 'the popular'. This amounts to a 'return of the repressed' in analyses of popular culture. In investigating changing definitions of 'popular', we can identify significant changes in ways of talking or thinking about social relations and cultural production. We can reconstitute a history of political and cultural debates, and see the assumptions about power, class, gender and value on which they were based. It will thus become possible to understand the relations between different meanings of 'the popular' invoked by the critics and theorists discussed in later chapters, and to place these meanings in relation to other aesthetic and political discourses.

If we wish to establish the meaning of a particular word, our normal response, presumably, would be to look it up in the dictionary. The *New English Dictionary on Historical Principles*, commonly known as *The Oxford English Dictionary* (*OED*), does, indeed, offer an account of different meanings of particular words, supported by citation and a certain degree of analysis. It does, thus, represent a resource for uncovering the history of overlapping and changing definitions of 'the popular'. Before using the *OED*, however, we need to be aware of the particular history that lies behind it, as a way of organizing and presenting knowledge. The use of the *OED*, in fact, foreshadows some of the problems that will be encountered in later chapters. In order to produce a critical account of the analysis of popular culture, it is necessary to open out the history and the theoretical assumptions of such analysis. The texts that give us access to history, and to theory, however, are themselves caught up in particular social and cultural relations. These relations must be specified, before the operation of critical reassessment can begin. In the case of the *OED*, I will examine the historical development of the dictionary as a form, the role of the dictionary in the establishment of 'correct' English usage, and the constitution of the category of those most in need of the cultural authority of the dictionary: women and young boys.

The dictionary began as a medium to facilitate the introduction of new foreign words into the developing English language; it assumed certain pedagogical tasks, from a particular social position. The title page of Cockeram's *English Dictionarie* of 1623 makes this quite clear:

Enabling as well Ladies and Gentlewomen, young Schollers, Clarkes, Merchants, and also Strangers of any Nation, to the understanding of the more difficult Authors already printed in our Language, and the more speedy attaining of an elegant perfection of the English tongue, both in reading, speaking and writing.[1]

Initially, the dictionary merely provided synonyms and brief definitions. Cockeram's dictionary also included a section giving Latin-derived equivalents for vulgar words. Certain sorts of linguistic usage were being favoured and prescribed. Throughout the eighteenth century, dictionaries appeared, building on, and reacting to, previous etymological scholarship. By 1721, Nathan Bailey introduced a new stress on the historical derivation of words, in place of the mere statement of meaning. As the title page of *A Pocket Dictionary* of 1753 made clear, however, these histories of meanings were still being produced from a particular position, for a particular audience: from a learned man to the youth of both sexes, ladies and persons in business, and those without a literary education.[2] The dictionary thus appeared as an exercise in cultural hegemony: an attempt to win over subordinate and marginalized groups to particular linguistic usages. It was part of the process of defining and strengthening the dominant culture.

The dictionary developed, as an institution and a form of knowledge, on the basis of three different approaches. One was essentially pedagogical, giving aid in pronunciation and comprehension of hard words. The second saw the dictionary rather as a convenient reference book for classical historical and literary allusions. The third saw the dictionary as a practice and product of etymological research. When Samuel Johnson produced his dictionary in 1755, he attempted to combine all three of these, with attention to the complexities of definition, supported by quotation, in the context of an academic attention to the possibilities of a perfect English language.

Throughout its history, the dictionary has not merely recorded English usage, but has also prescribed certain linguistic forms, advocated the use of 'hard words' and proscribed regional dialects. It 'preserves the hierarchy of discourse in the very act of apparently trying to abolish it.'[3] None of this makes the *OED* unusable as an historical resource, but it does mean that we cannot use it as a neutral record of linguistic usage. It is both a record of, and part of, dominant cultural discourses. As such, we can learn a lot from it, but we should not be surprised if we occasionally find meanings or uses that seem to contradict the structure of significance it lays out.

The *OED* is a product of a particular historical and geographical context: basically, Britain between 1880 and 1920. There is a great redundancy in texts referred to, and an inevitable arbitrariness in the quotations chosen. Again, we are not being given a history of all the usages of a particular word, but rather a history filtered through the texts of a particular orthodoxy. In later supplements to the dictionary more recent texts are introduced, but this tends to reinforce rather than disturb the basic patterns of definition.

Despite these problems, the *OED* does at least allow us to begin to open out the history of a particular word, in this case 'popular'. We do encounter the meanings out of context, but by looking in some detail at the texts cited in quotations some of the contextual detail can be recovered. We will certainly be in the realms of the dominant discourse, but, since it is the ways in which the 'dominant' constructs the 'popular' that provides the focus for this chapter, we can safely proceed.

'THE POPULAR'

The first use which the *OED* cites of the word 'popular' is as a legal term. Here it denotes an action open to all people living under a particular government. J. Rastell says of an 'action popular' in 1579: 'This action is not given to one man specially but generally to any of the Queene's people as will sue'.[4] Or, again, Blackstone in 1766: 'accessible by all the King's subjects, but the acquired right of none of them'.[5]

William Lambard discusses the nature and implications of such actions in *Eirenarcha*, in 1581. Here he draws a distinction between two forms of social control: Suertie of the Peace, and Suertie of the Good Abearing. The former refers to the financial bond which a Justice of the Peace may force an individual to pay as a guarantee of peaceable behaviour. This bond may either be requested by another individual, or deemed appropriate by the Justice of the Peace. Suertie of the Good Abearing is also a financial guarantee of peaceable behaviour, but one that can be contravened without necessarily causing a disturbance. It refers to potentially disruptive meetings, or to the carrying of arms. It can be used against those disturbing a preacher, against poachers, against non-church-attenders, or those going to brothels.

Thus, Lambard argues, 'it seemeth more popular than the Suertie of the Peace'.[6] By this, he means that general social disruption is, by definition, detrimental to all those living within a particular state, whereas civil disturbance is more commonly aimed at particular individuals. Thus, 'the popular' seems to be identified with the interests of the state, that which disturbs social harmony being conceived as an offence against the people, although this identification is troubled by the complex mechanisms of social control which Lambard describes.

Rastell's example of the sort of event which might occasion an 'action popular' is also concerned with the stability of apparatuses of government. He cites the case of a corrupt jury member, who may, within one year of his offence, be sued by 'every man that will'.[7] The disruption of legal processes is construed as an offence to every person, or at least every man, living within a particular state, and thus necessitates an 'action popular'.

This legal definition of the concept 'popular' is thus seen to rest upon an equation of the interests of the people with the interests of the state, at least in some of its formulations. The resonances of this equation are picked up in the uses which the *OED* defines as: 'of, pertaining to, or consisting of the common people, or the people as a whole as distinguished from any particular class'.[8] The slipperiness of the term here becomes apparent. The common people can surely be distinguished from the people as a whole. The people as a whole might perhaps be seen as constituted by different classes, rather than as distinguished from any class. Or, indeed, the term 'distinguished' might be better replaced by some notion of exclusion. All of these positions are represented, explored and reworked within the texts cited by the *OED*.

In Strype's *Ecclesiastical Memorials* of 1721, we find considerable discussion of the relation between the people and the sovereign power, particularly in the appendix containing William Thomas's discourses to Edward VI (then aged eleven) entitled 'Whether it be better for a Commonwealth that the power be in the Nobility or in the Commonalty': the fundamental question of political legitimacy.

Strype himself seems caught between two different representations of the people. One is basically paternalist, as he argues against the social disruption caused by the enclosure of common lands. Criticizing the greed of the rich, he insists that the increased misery of the people is bad for the whole state. He advocates instead a benevolent interdependence of prince, nobility and people.

The instability of this political structure is apparent, however, as he introduces 'the Ignorant People, refusing to obey'.[9] This is the fickle multitude, with idle insinuations buzzing about in their heads. Here, the people emerges as a separate entity, dangerously in need of control.

It is to this dilemma that William Thomas addresses himself. He structures his discourse around several questions, including

1 Whether a Multitude without Head may prosper?
2 Whether is wiser and most constant, the Multitude or the Prince?
3 Whether it is better for the Commonwealth, that the Power be in the Nobility, or in the People?[10]

He ventures several answers, moral, practical and political, and the relations between these depend to a large extent on slippages in the notion of 'the people' or 'popular government'. At one moment 'the people' refers to all those ruled by a particular monarch, both nobility and commonalty, and the question becomes in which of these groups political power should rest. Thomas argues that stability and prosperity can only be achieved when power remains in the hands of the nobility. The nobility emerges through diligence, and must thus be maintained in ease, while those who lack material wealth must be constrained to work. Inherent human competitiveness and structural social inequality will then serve to maintain a stable and productive state. Thus, the theoretical justification, supported by metaphorical allusions to the natural basis of certain forms of power.

> For like as it becometh neither the Man to be Governed of the Woman, nor the Master of the Servant, even so in all other Regiments it is not convenient the Inferior should have power to direct the Superior.[11]

All this refers to economic, social and political relations within the people of a particular monarch. When he turns his attention more closely to 'the multitude', Thomas becomes increasingly uneasy. They are simply too numerous to constitute a government. They will never be able to agree: 'none is to be compared to the Frenzy of the People'.[12] Any popularly constituted government will fall apart, destroying both the nobility and the people themselves: 'what Popular Estate can be read that hath thirty years together eschewed Sects, Sedition and Commotions'.[13]

Both the people and popular government, then, take on a meaning that can only be seen as threatening. Despite his insistence that no popular government could survive its internal contradictions, Thomas devotes considerable energy to policies of social control. His debt to Machiavelli here is significant and acknowledged. He criticizes the nobility for excessive ambition and tyranny, not because these represent an assault on individual liberty, as Rousseau and Locke would later argue, but because they threaten the practical maintenance of power. He insists that the people must be kept in ignorance because: 'if they have but so much Liberty as to talk of the Princes Causes, and of the Reason of Laws, at once they shew their Desire not to be Ruled'.[14]

In North's translation of Plutarch's *Lives* (1579) we find the concept of benevolent interdependency brought into play once more in representations of the people. Popular government is here contrasted with the excesses of tyrannical power, and equated with liberty: 'Such . . . as misliked popular Government and liberty, and always followed the Nobility'.[15]

The term 'popular government' remains troubled, sometimes referring to government with the consent of the people, sometimes government in the interests of the people, and sometimes, though always with fear, to government by the people. Since 'the people' refers variously, and often within the same text, to all the inhabitants of a particular nation, the multitude, the commonalty, or the ignorant, the problem is compounded.

In Archibald Alison's *History of Europe from the Commencement of the French Revolution to the Restoration of the Bourbons in 1815* we find reference to 'completely popular' elections to the Legislative Assembly of revolutionary France.[16] It turns out, however, that by this he means that the vote was given to 'every labouring man of the better sort'.[17] 'The people' is thus both male and securely placed within dominant social and economic relations. Indeed, Alison discusses the need to limit the vote to those with property, that is with an interest in maintaining the stability of the state. He cites the parallel of different voting rights given to large and small shareholders in a particular company:

> Universally it has been found, by experience, to be indispensable to make the amount of influence in the direction of any concern to be in some degree proportional to the amount of property of which the voter is possessed in it.[18]

A popular government thus cannot include, or represent 'the least informed and most dangerous, but at the same time most numerous portions of the people', since 'the equal division of property . . . will, in every age, be the wish of the unthinking multitude'.[19] When this latter remark is contrasted with the claim 'Universal suffrage, or a low qualification for electors, has, in every age of democratic excitement, been the favourite object of the people', it becomes clear that at least one distinction between 'the people' and 'the multitude' lies in their perceived relation of threat to the social order.[20] As a self-conscious political unit struggling for the vote, they are 'the people'; as a self-conscious political unit struggling for economic power they are the 'unthinking multitude'. It would also

seem, in Alison's account, that 'the people' are remarkably
consistent, holding the same convictions 'in every age'.

All of these examples represent attempts to utilize the apparent
universality of 'the people' while simultaneously demarcating the
boundaries of 'the people' in relation to political power. At other
moments, however, 'popular' refers quite explicitly to one part of
the social formation: those 'of lowly birth; belonging to the
commonalty or populace; plebeian'.[21] Thus, in the mid-sixteenth
century, Harpsfield talks about the legitimacy of Henry VIII's
divorce, arguing that such a dispensation is different when it is
granted to the King than 'to any popular or common person'.[22]

'Popular' thus becomes associated with a cluster of themes
attributed to those of low social standing, as when Montaigne, in
Florio's translation, talks of 'popular or base men', who are to be
distinguished from men of taste, understanding and education.[23]
Naunton, in *Fragmenta Regalia*, written in the early seventeenth
century, having praised Queen Elizabeth as 'a most gracious and
popular Prince', by which he means that she acted in the interests
of, and with the support of, her people, then goes on to criticize
James's Parliament as being full of 'popular and discontented
persons'.[24] Here, 'popular' seems to indicate lacking in discretion,
reckless and opportunist. It is interesting to note the link made
between this term and the youthful nature of the Parliament: 'forty
Gentlemen, not above twenty, and some not exceeding sixteene of
Age'.[25] This theme is echoed later in Alison's attention to the
extreme youth of the members of the Legislative Assembly. This
relationship between 'the popular' and 'youthfulness' or immaturity
will re-emerge later in relation to the concept of popular culture.
For example, peasant poets are described as 'childlike in their
simplicity' and folk songs as produced by 'the children of society'.

In *Every Man out of His Humour* (1600) 'the popular' is clearly
what every aspiring gentleman must avoid. Sogliardo is given the
following advice: 'be sure you mixe your selfe still, with such as
flourish in the spring of the fashion, and are least popular; studie
their cariage and behavior in all'.[26] The advice is satirical, but the
resonances of 'popular' are, at least in this particular social
vocabulary, extremely negative. The negative connotations of
'popular' are picked up again in Milton's *Samson Agonistes* (1671).
Samson is subjected to the disturbance of a festival: ' . . . with
leave / Retiring from the popular noise, I seek / This unfrequented
place to find some ease'.[27] Here the 'popular' is associated with
chaos and vulgarity, with the multitude from whom Samson must
absent himself.

'Popular' has, at certain moments, come to mean simply 'full of people'. Thus Kirkton, at the end of the seventeenth century, refers to the west coast as 'the most popular part of Scotland'.[28] In a text such as *The Hermit: Or the Unparalleled Sufferings and Surprising Adventures of Mr Philip Quarll, an Englishman* (1727) the resonances of this use of the term 'popular' become clear. This text purports to be an account by an English merchant of the discovery of a hermit living alone on an island: ' . . . a second Garden of Eden, only here's no forbidden Fruit, nor Women to tempt a Man'.[29] The hermit is described as uniquely fortunate, having escaped the superficiality and hypocrisy that characterize 'busy Worlds and Trading-Peopled Towns'.[30] Quarll visits the island, sees the lifestyle of the hermit, eats with him, meets his monkey-servant ('subservient, loving, pleasing') and concludes thus: 'Oh! may I once more see that dear old Man, whose Habitation is free from all anxious Cares, from Oppression and Usury and all the Evils that attend this popular World'.[31] Thus the sense of 'popular' as meaning 'full of people' is stretched to include the notion of corruption and evil.

Thus far, we have seen the word 'popular' applied to governments, legal actions and social structures, but there is still another set of meanings of the word which refer to texts, language, argument and forms of knowledge: to what we might now call 'cultural forms'. Here, 'popular' refers to a cultural form which is 'intended for ordinary people', whether in terms of accessibility, of mode of address, or of the facts of reception.[32]

The earliest cited use of popular, meaning generally accessible, is from 1573, when Gabriel Harvey protests against the dilution of philosophical debate into 'popular and plausible theams'.[33] Later, we find 'popular language' and 'popular style'. The latter is Macaulay in 1849, who defines a popular style as one 'which boys and women could comprehend'.[34] Thus 'popular' is related to those excluded from the institutions of knowledge production.

The term begins to be applied specifically to certain forms of literature and to ephemeral publications generally in the early nineteenth century. In 1835, John Stuart Mill refers to the 'popular press'.[35] In 1841, T. Wright produces *Popular Treatises on Science*. By 1901, the concept of 'popular romance' is well established, and by the mid-twentieth century, phrases such as 'popular newspapers' no longer seem to demand any explanation.

At one level, the reason for this increasing confidence in designating certain publications as 'popular' is not hard to understand. Increases in general literacy throughout the nineteenth century, developments in communications technology allowing for the cheap reproduction of texts, and changes in patterns of ownership and distribution of printed texts brought about a distinctive shift in patterns of cultural production and consumption, which will be examined in more detail in later chapters. The existence of a growing body of texts which were both widely read and widely understood was indisputable. Once more, however, the attribution of the term 'popular' represents a telescoping of several debates.

Even if we look at 'popular' as meaning 'generally accessible', the supposed reasons for this accessibility obviously vary. There are directly economic reasons which are applied in a phrase such as 'all seats at popular prices'.[36] There are cultural and educational reasons: 'To an Esquimaux or New Zealander our most popular philosophy would be wholly unintelligible.'[37] There are also facts of general availability of particular texts, especially relevant in terms of a mass-produced 'popular press'.

In relation to cultural forms, however the term 'popular' commonly refers to a particular mode of address identified within the text as presumed to appeal to the 'common people'. This usage refers back to earlier meanings of 'popular' as 'studious of, or designed to gain the favour of the common people'.[38] Earlier uses of the word in this sense do not refer to texts, but rather to political strategies. Thus, in 1622, Francis Bacon describes Lord Audley as 'unquiet and popular', meaning that he is manipulative and untrustworthy in his political conduct.[39] Discussing the relations between Nobles and Commons in Athens and Rome, Swift refers to 'popular and ambitious Men who will, in the end, enslave the people.[40] Once more, 'popular' is associated with dishonesty and opportunism. Popular political actions are those which address the apparent desires of the people, but are, in the long term, ill-conceived and dangerous. This carries the necessary implication that popular political leaders practise some form of manipulation, deceiving the people as to their true interests.

It is worth pausing to note the importance of the 'popular' in Swift's *A Discourse on the Contests and Dissensions between the Nobles and the Commons in Athens and Rome, with the Consequences they had upon both those States*. It is a structuring category for much of his discussion of political, social and economic relations, although the tensions generated by its shifting significance now seem quite palpable. We have noted Swift's use of 'popular' to refer to the actions of ambitious and opportunist individuals. At another point, he refers to 'popular privileges', meaning the right of Roman plebeians to vote on laws and to discuss military policy. 'Popular tyranny' refers to the unmitigated exercise of democratic power, which Swift argues leads necessarily to arbitrary and totalitarian government, and 'popular commotions' is his term for political riots and demonstrations. These meanings are pulled together by assertions about the universal nature and function of the people: 'I think it is an universal Truth that the People are much more dexterous at pulling down and setting up, than at preserving what is fixt.'[41] Once more, this quality of 'timelessness' is an important stake in discussions of popular culture. Thus, for example, Ossian, a bard whose work supposedly survived for hundreds of years, is said to represent the 'timelessness' of Highland society.

From a notion of 'popular' as being a function of the mode of address of a political discourse or strategy we move to a definition of popular in terms of reception: 'finding favour with, or approved by, the people'.[42] This refers initially to individuals. Cockeram's dictionary of 1623 defines 'popular' as 'in great favour with the common people'. Swift, once more, writing in *The Tatler*, addresses an individual who desires to perform an action that will 'make me popular among my Dependants'.[43]

By the mid-nineteenth century, we find the term increasingly applied to aspects of cultural forms which appeal to, or are favoured by, people generally. Thus, Samuel Bamford, in 1841, observes that 'A hundred or two of our handsomest girls . . . danced to the music, or sang snatches of popular songs.'[44] Carl Engel, in 1866, discusses 'the peculiar character of the popular music of a nation'.[45]

In these cases, however, it is very difficult to specify the meaning of 'popular'. Reference is being made to its use in a number of different discourses. Thus Engel, in relating 'popular music' to nationalism is calling on a notion of 'the people' as a more or less self-conscious political and cultural unit. Aldous Huxley makes a similar connection when he argues that 'where popular art is vulgar, there the life of the people is essentially vulgar in its emotional quality'.[46] A claim about the specificity of popular culture is being made here which involves more than the facts of consumption. In these texts, popular culture is the expression of the spirit of a nation or a people. These are the terms which are developed in analyses of the poetry of Ossian, of folk music, or of forms of pottery.

At other times, the distinguishing feature of 'popular music' seems to be neither the authenticity of its production, nor its general consumption, but rather its exclusion from the institutions of cultural validation. In 1911, H. F. Chorley warns that, 'the large share . . . which popular . . . music has taken and takes in mourning for the dead in Ireland is a characteristic not to be overlooked'.[47] This takes us back to the notion of the 'popular' as common, lowly, or founded in ignorance.

Finally, the notion of hypocrisy and manipulation returns in the following description of popular art: 'By popular art we mean creative work that measures its success by the size of its audience and the profit it brings to its maker.'[48] 'Popular' is here a matter of debasing the product in order to maintain the audience. The increasing dominance of this definition is, however, challenged by the following claim made in 1966, 'popular culture . . . which is to be sharply distinguished from . . . commercialized "pop culture" . . . is the style of life of the majority of the members of a community'.[49] Here a definite attempt is being made to reinstate some of the reverberations of 'the popular' as an expression of national cultural identity, against an increasing tendency to dismiss popular forms as commercial and trivial.

There is one more set of meanings of 'the popular' which is of interest to us here. 'The popular' can also be understood as that which is prevalent among, or accepted by the people. Florio's translation of Montaigne mentions a 'popular sicknesse, which some yeares since, greatly troubled the townes about mee'.[50] The *Medical Journal* of 1803 talks of 'popular diseases'.[51] Here the emphasis is on the non-selective and uncontrollable element of the diseases concerned.

It is not simply diseases, however, which rage among the people. Ben Jonson makes the correlation between general acceptance and lack of discrimination when he writes, 'Sir, that's a popular error, deceives many'.[52] Again, in Ephraim Chambers's *Cyclopaedia, or an Universal Dictionary of Arts and Sciences* of 1727–41, popular errors are 'such as people imbibe from one another, by custom, education, and tradition'. Here, 'popular' seems to be equated with exclusion from the institutions of knowledge production. It signals a form of knowledge supported by tradition and superstition, rather than by reason, and thus one particularly prone to error. 'Accepted by the people' means non-legitimate and crude.

The *OED* lists another meaning of 'the popular' which is now obsolete. 'Popular' functioned in the sixteenth and seventeenth centuries as a noun referring either to the populace as a whole, or to the common people. David Lyndsay, in *The Monarch* (1552), offers a prayer for the spiritual improvement of the Church hierarchy:

> That they may be ane holy exemplair
> Tyll ws, thy pure lawid commoun populair.[53]

In the late sixteenth century, Sir Thomas Smith condemns the instability of democracy as 'the rule or the usurping of the popular', who are the 'rascall or viler sort'.[54] Smith is capable of giving within his text a very detailed social hierarchy. He is untroubled by notions of 'the people' as a unit of political legitimation, starting instead with the facts of existing political power and then reconstituting them structurally. Social distinctions thus appear both marked and natural: '. . . such as be exempted out of the number of the rascabilitie of the popular, bee called and written yeoman'.[55]

This obsolete usage returns us once more to the importance of 'the popular' as a term in political discourses of quite different historical moments and ideological positions. There is, however, a marked continuity in the uses we have cited so far. Basically, 'the popular' has always been 'the other'. The use of the term seems to imply a certain distance, a position from which 'the popular' can be evaluated, analysed, and perhaps dismissed. Writing from within the dominant culture, observations are produced about popular errors or beliefs. Thus, for example, in the nineteenth century, writers and critics condemn the evil and the excesses of popular fiction, while today, television critics write off large segments of television as popular, trivial, and addictive: an addiction from which they presume themselves to be immune. With the security of a legitimate culture, excursions can be made into the realms of popular culture. Folks songs can be collected and popular taste evaluated, without ever involving those who have preserved and transmitted such songs. From a position of political authority the instability and danger of popular government can be pointed out: something which the people could never be relied upon to understand.

All this, of course, is what we mean by a dominant discourse. We can, however, find uses of 'the popular' which trouble this consensus, which speak from a different position. One such use is cited by the *OED*, although, interestingly, attention is drawn to the surprising point of view. The *Saturday Review of Politics, Literature, Science and Art* of 8 November 1884 reports a remark overheard in a New York restaurant, 'I don't call this very popular pie', but quickly points out that 'they have come . . . to take popular quite gravely and sincerely as a synonym for good'.[56] Clearly an intolerable slippage. To find other examples of attempts to reappropriate the concept of 'the popular' we would have to look in other sorts of institutional sites. For example, in the Chartist *People's Paper*, we find 'popular action' as a form of collective strength against oppression. In 'Popular Front' politics, 'the popular' is the location of political legitimacy against fascism. It is the possibility of such oppositional meanings that is at stake in contemporary debates about the politics of popular culture. Such attempts to re-evaluate the concept of 'popular' are also clear in the popular theatre movement of the 1920s and 1930s, and in recent debates about the analysis of popular television.

This history of changing definitions of 'popular' as offered by the *OED* is now complete. It might, however, be useful to review the major historical shifts which we have detected in its use and significance. The earliest uses of 'popular' are as a term of legal or political thought. These depend on a notion of 'the people' as a constituted political unit. Popular government is the expression of the collective will, or alternatively a manifestation of the multitudinous confusion, of this unit. Popular legal actions are those that are accessible to all persons living within a particular state. They are applicable only in relation to offences judged dangerous to the fabric of the state. Later uses of 'popular' to mean 'accepted by the people', or 'favoured by the people' also refer initially to political strategies, with implications of manipulation and distortion, and only later to cultural texts.

Ambiguity as to who, or what, constitutes 'the people' is echoed in the shifting significance of 'popular'. It is generally applicable only to actions, or individuals, excluded from power, to the common, the lowly, the plebeian. It thus acquires a cluster of negative connotations: of crudity, ignorance, chaos and tyranny.

By the time that Johnson produced his dictionary in 1755, the relationship between 'the popular' and the legitimation of political power seems to have been diminished. He lists five meanings of 'popular':

1 vulgar, plebeian
2 suitable to the common people
3 beloved by the people, pleasing to the people
4 studious of the favour of the people
5 prevailing or raging among the populace

A tantalizing selection of definitions, whose conceptual relations are far from clear. Again, we see slippages from 'the vulgar' to 'the common people', to 'the people' and finally to 'the populace'. There is no notion here of 'popular' indicating generally accessible, except in the very patronizing sense of an action or text rendered 'suitable to' the common people. This patronizing linguistic recognition of hierarchy, the insistence that the people must be offered 'suitable' forms of culture, accompanied by a political discourse which occults the facts of political power in favour of a more harmonious conception of 'the populace', will be discernible in many texts of cultural analysis examined in this book.

From the late eighteenth century, we find 'popular' applied to cultural texts: to music, the press, art, science and fiction. These uses depend partially on the relationship between popular consciousness and national identity. They also reproduce notions of 'the popular' as that which is excluded from institutions of legitimation, either because of the material conditions of its production, or because its general accessibility lays it open to charges of debasement or simplicity.

When we look at definitions of 'popular' in recently published dictionaries, we can detect further shifts in its signification. Longman's *New Universal Dictionary*, published in 1982, lists four meanings for 'popular':

1   of the general public
2   suited to the needs, means, tastes or understanding of the general public
3   having general currency
4   commonly liked or approved

As we can see, the idea of 'the people' has completely disappeared, to be replaced by that of 'the general public'. Similarly, there is no indication of social hierarchy in these definitions, of differential power, of the lowly or plebeian. The notion of a calculated manipulation (studious of the favour of the people) gives way to personal choice. *Collins Concise Dictionary*, also published in 1982, gives a similar range of definitions. 'The popular' is that which is well liked by a number of individuals, or that which is accessible to the lay man.

All of this serves to evacuate the relations between social power, political democracy and cultural production which are so inescapable in the history of 'popular' constituted by the *OED*. A seemingly egalitarian discourse merely serves to shift the emphasis from social power to individual choice and taste. There is no reference to institutions, or to the facts of cultural production. The general public, a collection of discriminating consumers, linked only through opinion polls, designates 'the popular' according to individual tastes and needs. 'The people', in all its ambiguity, is now apparently out of date. This shift, which will be more fully explored in chapter 6, is clearly indicated in the untheorized, unified concept of 'the audience' invoked by many critics of television: an 'audience' whose identity is constituted solely in terms of television ratings.

But yet, 'the people' is still a recurrent concept in cultural analysis. The rest of this book will examine the power and persistence of the category of 'popular culture'. It will analyse the ways in which the relationship between 'the popular' and discourses of society, gender and value is constantly reworked in discussions of popular culture: from peasant poets to television. It will also examine some attempts to reconstitute definitions of 'the people' and 'the popular' in defiance of a dominant culture which would claim to speak for the people while denying the validity of cultural expression or political practice outside legitimizing institutions.

2

'Peasant Poets' 1730–1848: Consistency in Difference

PRELIMINARIES

Having established the shifting ideological terrain of definitions of 'the popular', I now want to look in detail at one particular example of a negotiation between the dominant culture and the culture of 'the people'. I will look at 'peasant poetry' and its patronage as a case study. Through it, I will explore struggles over the definition of popular writing, and the relation of this to economic dependency, institutions of literature and practices of social and sexual control. The tradition of peasant poetry is a particular manifestation of the troubled and contradictory discourses surrounding the development of the concept of 'popular culture'.

The period chosen brings some peculiar methodological problems. The years between 1730 and 1848 were a period of enormous transformations in social and cultural relations. The eighteenth century saw the consolidation of the bourgeoisie, the dominance of capitalist relations in agriculture and the expansion of mercantile capitalism. By the nineteenth century, the growth of urban centres, the development of new technologies of production and communication and, crucially, the establishment of an organized and articulate working class, had all changed the social relations within the British state. Yet, throughout this period, discussion of, and patronage of, the peasant poets remain remarkably consistent. Since my aim is to relate literary practice to changing social and historical relations, I am clearly faced with some difficult theoretical problems. These are further complicated by the difficulties of defining the categories of class within the eighteenth century.[1] Economic function and cultural manifestation are not always in harmony, and the perception and articulation of class by those living through it is, at best, opaque. For example, I have pointed to the consolidation of capitalist social relations within the sphere of agricultural production, but 'the aristocracy' continues to be a crucial category in the discussion of rural society throughout the century. This is overdetermined by the historical relation between the aristocracy and the economy of rural production. It is complicated by the aspirations of tenant farmers to the social and cultural capital of the aristocracy. It is not surprising that when John Clare attacks the causes of rural distress, he mixes attacks on 'Old Corruption' and representations of the aristocracy with satires on the power and pretensions of the bourgeoisie. These are not merely idiosyncratic confusions, but the result of the contradictory and painfully slow process of historical change.

In order to understand the historical developments discussed in this chapter, it will be necessary to break the rhetoric of 'peasant poetry' down into its constituent elements. As a whole, this rhetoric does remain superficially consistent, but its emphases and implications, as well as its relation to other literary and political discourses, change significantly. It is important to remember that John Clare and Stephen Duck were not writing within the same social or literary structure, but making sense of this fact will be the work of this chapter. We have to explain the emergence of the phenomenon of peasant poets in the early eighteenth century, its ideological purchase over the next hundred years, and its effective demise in the mid-nineteenth century. This analysis will necessitate an attention to the significance of representations of nature in the eighteenth century, an account of the power relations expressed and reproduced by the patronage of peasant poets, and an investigation of the models of social relations explored in the writing of peasant poets.

There is also a problem with the label 'peasant poet', as very few of those writers discussed have any claim to the title of 'peasant'. The poets I will look at include a weaver, a milkmaid, a pipemaker and a servant. Gustav Klaus argues that the label 'peasant poet' is a twentieth-century invention, and opts instead for the title 'plebeian'.[2] The term 'peasant poet' does, however, have a certain legitimacy. It represents a space into which a range of poets writing from educational and social backgrounds outside the dominant culture were placed, and the norm to which they referred themselves. Stephen Duck called himself 'a thresher', John Clare described himself as 'a peasant' and William Thom signed himself 'a serf'. This is an indication of the extent to which the various writers discussed in this chapter placed themselves within an economy of rural social relations, and placed their poetry within the pastoral and georgic traditions of the eighteenth century. This self-identification as 'peasant' or 'serf' may represent only one occupation out of several, or a partial source of livelihood. This fact in itself is of interest, however, as it already signals the imaginary nature of the relation between the dominant culture and the individuals who tried to insert themselves within the positions it offered.

The persistence of the appellation 'peasant' is in direct contradiction to the decline in real terms of the peasantry. Enclosure fundamentally altered the social relations of agricultural production, depriving peasants of their common rights. Peasants became agricultural wage labourers, whose social and economic position was precarious, and whose rights and powers were minimal. The drive for more efficient and more profitable agricultural production throughout the eighteenth century led to a huge reduction in numbers of the peasantry. The valorization of the peasantry in the eighteenth century is thus a feature of the cultural rather than the economic.

The term, 'peasant poet' also serves to distinguish these forms of writing which are all engaging at some level with the representation of natural scenery and rural labour from the broader category of artisan writing discussed by Brian Maidment or by Martha Vicinus.[3] Both these writers look at the work of nineteenth-century working-class poets, and their relation to developments in class politics and social protest throughout the century. Vicinus does discuss the patronage and writing of nineteenth-century self-educated poets, in the fourth chapter of *The Industrial Muse*, but they are clearly tangential to the argument of the book as a whole.

The poets examined in this chapter were operating within a very particular set of cultural and economic relations. Their work was crucially concerned with the representation of nature, of rural social relations and of agricultural labour. They were valorized in terms of the spontaneity and naturalness of their poetic voice, the 'wild vigour' of their rustic Muse. The peasant poets were almost totally dependent on some more or less direct form of patronage. This generally took the form of patrons arranging subscriptions to finance the publication of their verses, rather than granting them direct payments. The poets were, however, very significantly dependent on the support and approval of their patrons for financial success. The option, which increased throughout the nineteenth century, of publishing their work in the radical press, or of entering the literary market-place, was not available to the poets discussed in this chapter. The terms of the response to their writing within the dominant culture, and thus the terms of their patronage, were therefore absolutely central to the possibility of their writing.

The term 'peasant' does, however, have particular problems in relation to the (in)visibility of women. Our image of the peasant is not, it would seem, an image of a woman, and the term scarcely suggests the numbers of women writing in some sense within this tradition. I have, however, preferred to retain the term, and recover the women, in order to see what sort of tension this generates, and what this says about the categories of cultural analysis, rather than to discard the term completely.

PEASANT POETRY AND THE WRITING OF NATURE

In order to understand the extent to which the dominant culture invested in discovering a tradition of peasant writing, we must look at the relation between peasant poetry and other literary debates of the eighteenth century: debates which focused on the representation of nature, and the importance of simplicity and truth in literary style. John Barrell has demonstrated the importance of notions of 'landscape' and of 'nature' for eighteenth-century culture.[4] It was fashionable to collect landscape paintings, important to know the discourse of appreciation of natural scenery, crucial to go on the Grand Tour, pleasant to walk in landscaped gardens, and indispensable to read pastoral and nature poets. This engagement with 'the natural' led to the development of new theories of aesthetics and new forms of critical writing. The early eighteenth century, with the publication and proliferation of journals such as *The Tatler* and *The Spectator*, saw the consolidation of the profession of literary criticism. These journals became the site of a critique of essentially aristocratic notions of wit, complexity and self-conscious style as the marks of great art. They were an attempt to consolidate the production and criticism of literature round notions of rationality, nature, simplicity, and the universal passions and perceptions of man.

For Terry Eagleton, the relation between such cultural developments and wider social transformations is quite clear:

> the European bourgeoisie begins to carve out for itself a distinct discursive space, one of rational judgement and enlightened critique . . . The norms of such reason, while in their own way absolute, turn their backs upon the insolence of aristocratic authority.[5]

Richard Steele, writing in 1713, is equally explicit about the political implications of particular practices of criticism. He discusses the 'cautious' critic as one who needs to judge according to particular sets of rules, and says: 'the cautious Criticks are like the Subjects of an Arbitrary Prince . . . but the free Critick, like a free *Briton* is governed by the Laws which he himself votes for'.[6]

One important site for the construction of theories of literary style was the debate between 'ancients' and 'moderns' over the nature and function of pastoral poetry.[7] Alexander Pope argued, in 1713, that pastoral poetry should present the brevity, simplicity and delicacy of the actions and thoughts of a shepherd of the Golden Age. His model was Virgil, whose 'language is perfectly pure, and he often forgets he is among peasants'.[8] Pope found departures from the classical model, in the interests of realism or local reference, objectionable, and contrary to the true nature of pastoral. He insisted that the pastoral should construct ideal images of rural society and human relations within it, rather than showing real shepherds, with their lowness of vocabulary and moral appreciation. This was not just a question of content, but of style, vocabulary, form and moral tone.

Thomas Tickell, however, argued for greater realism and contemporary reference within the pastoral.[9] He explained the appeal of pastoral as a poetic form in terms of the natural goodness of rural characters, and 'our secret approbation of . . . goodness in others'.[10] This location of moral goodness in the unconscious and uneducated rural population is significant for later responses to peasant poets. Tickell saw the defining features of pastoral as simplicity and lack of reflection, and he advocated the use of proverbial sayings as guarantors of universal wisdom. He argued that differences of climate and soil should be respected, so that English shepherds could not behave as if they lived in the warm climate of southern Italy. The object, for Tickell, was not simply to reproduce particular pastoral forms and images, but to develop classical forms into a more powerful, indigenous and realist form of writing. This desire for an indigenous tradition of pastoral was to be a significant element in the patronage of the peasant poets.

John Hughes attempted a resolution of these two positions, although once more under the banner of realism. The crucial element of pastoral poetry, for Hughes, lay in its ability to represent relations other than those which dominated contemporary life. He insisted that it is: 'a wonderful amusement to the imagination to be sometimes transported, as it were, out of modern life'.[11] Pastoral poetry dealt with images of love and of country life, according to Hughes. It thus necessitated simplicity of expression, and freedom from the artificial cares of an over-refined society. At the same time, pastoral poetry did not need to represent the crude and the commonplace. Hughes argued that shepherds in ancient times had a quite different social role, and were individuals of standing. They were consequently capable of complex expression and considerable moral refinement.

All of these positions represent an imaginary relation to agricultural labour and its relations of production, but the implications of these representations are not all the same. 'The ideal' and 'the natural' may both be ideological constructs, but they nonetheless participate in quite different economies of social relations.[12] 'The ideal' represents an attempt to repress the existence of antagonistic social relations, 'the natural' seeks rather to render them transient, aberrant and unnecessary.

The privileging of pastoral in the critical debates of the early eighteenth century is in itself important, quite apart from the different positions taken up within this debate. Within strictly neoclassical terms, both the epic and tragedy should have been prioritized over the pastoral, which was, within classical writing, very definitely an inferior genre. The interest in pastoral was, however, overdetermined by other discourses of 'nature' and 'the natural' which predominated in eighteenth-century accounts of politics, economics and literature. John Husbands makes the connection between nature and poetic writing quite clear:

> As nations improved in knowledge and politeness, the sciences grew up gradually and flourished with them in proportion; systems in time were formed, methods of attaining to the knowledge of them proposed, and precepts established; so that what was originally natural became artificial. Hence poetry (as people grew more refined) was reduced to rules and became an art, whereas the writers of the first ages had no other guide than nature.[13]

This is a very clear statement of some of the investments in the concept of 'nature'. It is that of which we have knowledge, but also that which continually challenges that knowledge as artificial and over-refined. It is that which a powerful and rational society must aim to control, but it continually challenges the basis of such control. It is also seen as being the ahistorical grounding of all our passions and desires. As Samuel Johnson observed in 1750, although nature is infinite, 'its general effects on the ear are uniform and incapable of much variety of description'.[14]

There is something of a contradiction within Husbands's

position. He explicitly relates changing economic relations, the growth of empiricism and developments in poetry, but only the last of these is seen as being in decline. But this is no more of a contradiction than the general legitimation of ancient and peasant writing in a period of economic progress and enlightenment. Nostalgia is a frequent enough accompaniment to social transformations that render the very relations valorized quite impossible.

Accounts of the nature and importance of pastoral poetry were, then, an important source for the eighteenth-century interest in peasant poetry. The representation of nature as a source of universal perceptions and passions was not, however, adequate to the complex social transformations of rural society in the eighteenth century, nor could it provide the terms for a consideration of the social and moral importance of rural labour. In order to find a classical model for the representation of rural labour and social prosperity, early eighteenth-century critics and writers turned to Virgil's *Georgics*.[15]

The *Georgics* seemed to offer the possibility of writing about rural labour and the social relations of the countryside, and thus about the public sphere. Virgil certainly used the form not just to examine agricultural production, but to celebrate it as a model of public virtue, and of the health and viabiltiy of Imperial Rome. Addison wrote an enthusiastic account of the *Georgics*, which was included in Dryden's translation of the works of Virgil.[16] He saw it as powerful, varied and successful, giving information as well as pleasure, and avoiding meanness of expression. Thus, in 1757, when John Dyer wanted to write an account of the complexity of the relations of agricultural labour and commercial distribution in *The Fleece*, it was to the form of the *Georgics* that he turned. He in fact produced a very elegant elision of the pastoral and the georgic, beginning with shepherds and ending with the complex and thriving commercial relations of eighteenth-century England. James Thomson, whose writing was an important reference point for many of the 'peasant poets', also turned to the *Georgics* for writing which could celebrate rural labour, and naturalize the social relations of an increasingly commercialized England.[17]

Thomson was not, by any definition, a peasant. He was the son of a minister and was educated at Edinburgh University. His poem *The Seasons*, however, provided both a legitimation and a poetic style for writers within the peasant tradition. John Clare, for example, was to cite it as one of his favourite books.[18]

The Seasons was published between 1726 and 1730, although Thomson revised it constantly until 1744. The poem describes natural landscape, rural labour, the progress of the seasons, and their effect on plants, animals and mankind. John Barrell has demonstrated the influence of traditions of visual representation, as manifested in the landscape paintings of Claude, on Thomson's writing.[19] Thomson describes natural phenomena as an outsider, a sensitive and emotional observer. Thus his eye ranges widely, signalling powerful images and projecting their emotional and spiritual significance. He moves the reader through a plethora of natural phenomena in a highly structured landscape.

> Thus all day long the full-distended Clouds
> Indulge their genial Stores, and well-shower'd Earth
> Is deep enrich'd with vegetable Life;
> Till, in the western Sky, the downward Sun
> Looks out, illustrious, from amid the Flush
> Of broken Clouds, gay-shifting to his Beam.[20]

What Thomson is describing is nature in the abstract, as a focus for and point of production of moral and spiritual values. He moves from the tightly organized English estate to the wild expanses of the Alps with ease, positing their common bases in nature.

Thomson is not, however, unaware of the social dimensions and ramifications of natural landscape.

> So with superior Boon may your rich Soil,
> Exuberant, Nature's better Blessings pour
> O'er every Land, the naked Nations cloath,
> And be th'exhaustless Granary of a World![21]

Nature is here equated with the particular phenomenon of agricultural capitalism that will ensure that Britain has a dominant place as 'Granary of the World'. Thomson develops this idea in 'Summer', where a celebration of Britannia as the guardian of liberty is linked with the confident assertion that:

> Thy Country teems with Wealth,
> And PROPERTY assures it to the Swain
> Pleas'd and unweary'd, in his certain Toil.[22]

This 'certain toil' is described by Thomson in terms that were frequently to be reproduced in representations of rural labour. Haymaking is represented as a powerfully communal activity, of significance for all rural inhabitants. The empty village signals the common purpose with which everyone leaves to labour in the fields. Once there, the 'rustic youth', strong, healthy and bronzed,

works with the 'ruddy Maid, half naked'. The pattern is repeated
for the harvest.

> Soon as the Morning trembles o'er the Sky
> And, unperceiv'd, unfolds the spreading Day;
> Before the ripen'd Field the Reapers stand,
> In fair Array; each by the Lass he loves,
> To bear the rougher Part, and mitigate
> By nameless gentle Offices her Toil.[23]

Thomson clearly writes as an observer of, and not as a participant
in, rural labour. He naturalizes rural labour, within a paradigm of
the spontaneous bounty and fertility of the earth. He does,
however, include an exhortation to farmers, demanding that they
recognize that the 'God of Harvest', in offering abundance, also
requires charity: the gleaners must be treated with generosity.[24]
Social hierarchy can only be maintained in Thomson's poetry
through particular representations of 'the natural', through rhetorical strategies that render the swain 'Partners of your kind' and
through individual acts of generosity.

   Both the patronage of peasant poets and the language which
makes sense of it have complex social affiliations. In relating
peasant poets to the rise of professional criticism, to discourses of
individualism, of reason, and of 'the natural', we seem to be
establishing a certain consistency between the peasant poets and
the interests of the bourgeoisie. Yet, many of the patrons of the
peasant poets were, as we shall see, titled, landowning members of
the aristocracy. This is certainly less the case as the century
progresses, but it is important to note that discourses can be
appropriated and mobilized from a number of different positions.
Thus, investments in 'the natural' can be used by the aristocracy to
criticize the social relations of capitalism, by the bourgeoisie to
legitimate these social relations, and by Radicals to condemn the
excesses of capitalist exploitation of labour.

   Finally, the power of the concept of 'the natural' has particular
consequences for the representation of women. I have already
mentioned the apparent invisibility of women 'peasant poets'. This
is not just a fact about the marginalization of those women within
the eighteenth century, but is also something constructed by the
terms of more recent critical practice. The equation of the manly
and the natural is widespread. Leslie Stephen saw the positive side
of an interest in ancient poetry as being its capacity for 'exploring
emotions in a straightforward manly way'. He claimed that Burns
had 'strong manly blood coursing through every vein'.[25]

Time and again narratives are mobilized to account for the lives of peasant poets, which both marginalize women and hold them responsible for the alienation and isolation of the poets. The power and persistence of such narratives is something that will be explored in this chapter. They represent the last bastion of 'the natural'. The natural bases of gender relations and gendered language go unchallenged by critics who have long since consigned the idea of 'natural' social relations to the realm of ideology.

PEASANT POETS IN CONTEXT

The analysis of peasant poetry in this chapter will start in the 1730s with the career and writing of Stephen Duck. Despite Robert Southey's claim for William Taylor, the early seventeenth-century 'water poet', as the first uneducated poet, it is only with Duck that we find the beginnings of the insertion of the peasant poets into a system of patronage supported by the rhetoric of natural genius and stylistic simplicity. Although Duck was deemed to be exceptional, he was certainly not alone. His perceived success legitimated and provided a point of reference for the writing of others outside the dominant cultural institutions: 'When the late Queen patronised Stephen Duck, who was a wonder only at first, and had not genius enough to support the character he had promised, twenty artisans and labourers turned poets and starved.'[26]

There are two basic sets of assumptions about culture and society which interact to produce an investment in, and valorization of, peasant poets. The first concerns questions of literary style and realism, and their relationship to broader social transformations. The second involves representations of class difference, and the consequent strategies of social control. Both are essential ingredients in the rhetoric of peasant poetry, and indeed, arguments about the simplicity and naturalness of the peasant voice turn out to have a social dimension, while arguments about social relations turn on their relation to nature. Generally, however, it is the first of these which is mobilized in the eighteenth century, with the second having greater prominence as the tradition continues, and becoming dominant in discussions of John Clare and William Thom.

In this chapter, I will attempt to trace these developments, and to analyse their implications for the writing, and the patronage, of peasant poets, as well as for the development of theoretical and practical approaches to the study of popular culture. There were large numbers of peasant poets writing throughout the period covered by this chapter, and it will obviously be impossible to discuss them all. What I have done is to look at the writing of figures who came to sufficient prominence to generate debate and disturbance within the dominant culture, and at some of the poets who hoped to emulate their success. I have focused almost entirely on English poets, with the exception of William Thom, whose 'success' brought him to London. The interaction of discourses of nature with discourses of nation, which is inescapable, for example, in responses to Scottish poets, could not properly be explored within the confines of this chapter.

The interest in peasant poetry for the eighteenth century, then, lay largely in the extent to which it could strengthen particular accounts of nature and legitimate particular theories of writing. It represented the triumph of rationality, universality and nature over corrupt sophistication. What was valued in peasant poets was their simplicity of expression and honesty of emotion. Hannah More said of Ann Yearsley in 1784: 'she seems to possess the general principles of sound taste and just thinking . . . you will seldom find in her those inexplicable poetic sins, the false thought, the puerile conceit, the distorted image'.[27] There is reference in several discussions of peasant poets, from Stephen Duck to William Thom, to their 'spontaneous' good taste and their ability to recognize, if not exactly reproduce, good writing. Their judgement was apparently both constructed and guaranteed by their proximity to nature. Peasant poetry thus seemed to provide textual support for the development of nationalist and rationalist theories of writing.

At the same time, however, peasant poetry also served to demonstrate the gap which, necessarily, existed between primitive forms of language and thought and the abstract, self-reflective productions of the dominant culture. The writing of peasant poets is constantly mediated to its readers by a figure placed within the dominant culture. The point of this mediation is to draw attention to the gap between the learned and the vulgar, at the same time as signalling their common investment in 'the natural'. The writing of peasant poets is praised, but it is never raised into the realm of learned culture. The patrons of peasant poets are quite explicit in their demands that the poets retain their simplicity and refrain from reading too widely or thinking too abstractly. Hannah More praised the poet Ann Yearsley, saying: 'You will find her, like all unlettered poets, abounding in imagery, metaphor and personification.'[28] But, these are exactly the features of language that were increasingly being identified with primitive, unreflective and backward social groups.[29] Thus, peasant poets were encouraged, but their differences from, and inferiority to, the reflective, educated representatives of the dominant culture were constantly stressed.

This was the ideological context for the development of the phenomenon of 'the peasant poets'. Interest in such writing was widespread: 'It became almost a fashion amongst the patrons of letters to support at least one "untaught genius".'[30] Throughout the eighteenth century, individual writers were elevated by the good offices of a patron. Their position, however, and the reason for patronage, did not remain the same.

Hannah More's response to Ann Yearsley demonstrates the close relation between aesthetic and social judgements of the peasant poets. She commented on Yearsley's good taste, but she also examined her good behaviour. It was just as important that she be contented with her lot. The interest was still in nature but, crucially, specifically in the naturalization of social relations.

The concentration on the social implications of writing from outside the dominant culture becomes quite acute by the time John Clare is writing in the 1820s and 1830s. Eliza Emmerson and Lord Radstock constantly complained to Clare of his 'radical and ungrateful sentiments'. Octavius Gilchrist, however, writing about Clare in *The London Magazine* in 1820 was anxious to assert that Clare was aware of, and content with, his station: 'Nothing could exceed the meeknes, and simplicity, and diffidence with which he answered the various inquiries concerning his life and habits.'[31]

Peasant poetry was also seen as a source of information about the working classes. Many patrons were, by the nineteenth century, Radicals. They saw in the poetry of the uneducated lower classes representations of suffering and injustice, vindications of the attack on 'Old Corruption' and of the fight for suffrage and egalitarian social relations. Even those who were not in sympathy with working-class organizations used the representations of suffering to argue for benevolence and charity. Poetry was a medium in which the working classes could be confronted as unique, even deserving, individuals, and not as a mass.

By the time that Southey came to legitimize this peasant tradition in the 1830s, it was already disintegrating. Rayner Unwin argues in *The Rural Muse* that such writing continues into the twentieth century. By then, however, it functions in the context of such different relations of cultural production that we cannot really argue for a continuity.

The reasons for the demise of peasant poets are several. Firstly, patronage became less of a norm, and indeed less of a possibility.

Although Duck was significantly different from poets of the mainstream, the fact of being patronized was in no sense unusual. By John Clare's time, he was an oddity in the economy of cultural production. Cheaper printing technology and increased literacy allowed for the development of literature as a commodity form. Writers exchanged their work in the market-place rather than the salon or country house.

Further, the growth of a Radical and Chartist press shifted the grounds of patronage of working-class poets. Mary Leman Gillies argued in 1846 that the people should be their own patrons.[32] She deplored the fact that 'genius and skill become the drudges of luxury', and urged the people to unite and take control of their own writing. The Radical and Chartist press regularly printed and criticized poetry. This signalled the breakdown of certain rhetorics of class collaboration and unity of interests. The writing of those outside the dominant culture became something to be controlled rather than encouraged. The developing languages of class sat uneasily with ideas of a common and universal culture.

THE PEASANT POETS

Stephen Duck was an agricultural labourer. Born about 1705, he attended school only long enough to learn to read and write. The 'Life' of Duck appended to the pirated edition of his works in 1730 claims his mother removed him from school so that his excess of learning would not render him unfit for his station in life. Since this observation was made after Duck had become marked as a 'natural genius' who had risen above his lowly station through personal merit, the temptation to irony must render this account of his mother's motivation a little dubious. However, it is clear that he had minimal access to institutional education.

He started to write soon after leaving school, although none of his earlier compositions survives. He studied with a friend, whose identity is unclear, reading *Paradise Lost* and Addison's critical essays in *The Spectator*. He also taught himself arithmetic. Spence, whose 'Life' of Duck was attached to the 1736 edition of his work, emphasizes, however, that 'Stephen is all simplicity': his mind was neither spoiled nor improved by his acquaintanceship with literary works. He was still writing directly from his own experiences. Spence further stresses Duck's 'natural' good taste and his sound moral principles: 'he seems to have an excellent moral Turn in his Thoughts'.[33]

Spence's account of Duck is important, because it was the form
in which he was mediated to his prospective patrons. Spence
realized the basis of Duck's fascination for the dominant culture:
'A Poet from the Barn, tho' not so great a Man, is as great a
Curiosity, as a Dictator from the Plough.' Spence's knowledge of
Duck is based on a week's conversation, but he takes on himself
the task of representing his life, his character and his morals. He
makes it clear that Duck's exceptional talents do not constitute a
threat to the social order. Stephen was careful never to neglect his
work while acquiring an education: never has there been 'so strong
an instance of Honesty and Industry mix'd together'.

This preamble giving assurances as to moral and political
character is one of the consistencies within the tradition of peasant
poets. These accounts are, as we shall see, gendered. Different
emphases emerge, and different limitations are imposed in the
treatment of women writers. Nonetheless, the need for some form
of mediation is constant. Both reassurance and legitimation are
required before the peasant voice can be heard, or heeded, in its
natural simplicity.[34]

Duck's early patrons were mostly local gentlemen – the Rev.
Mr Stanley of Pewsy, and Dr Alured Clarke. They encouraged him
to write on particular subjects. His first poems include an account
of poverty and of 'the thresher's labour'. 'The Thresher's Labour'
was one of Duck's most successful and interesting poems. In this
poem, Duck explicitly rejects images of shepherds idly musing
against a rural background: his representation of labour is as
localized, subjective and painful experience. The form of this poem
is difficult to specify. It is not a pastoral poem, although much of its
descriptive vocabulary is drawn from the pastoral tradition. Nor is
it really a georgic, since it does not celebrate the productive power
of labour, and it falls foul of Addison's insistence that 'the precepts
of husbandry are not to be delivered with the simplicity of a
ploughman, but with the address of a poet'.[35] Its use of the
collective pronoun, 'we' also signals its problematic relation to lyric
traditions of poetic writing. It is, perhaps, best understood as 'anti-
georgic'. For Duck, there is no beauty and no leisure:

> Our Eye beholds no pleasing Object here,
> No chearful Sound diverts our list'ning Ear.
> The Shepherd may well tune his Voice to sing,
> Inspir'd with all the Beauties of the Spring.
> No Fountains murmur here, no Lambkins play,
> No Linnets warble, and no Fields look gay:

> 'Tis all a gloomy, melancholy Scene,
> Fit only to provoke the Muse's Spleen.[36]

The labour of threshing corn is described in detail. The bounty of
the earth is very painfully and slowly brought forth in Duck's
poetry. Haymaking sees the men of the village 'quite o'erspent with
Toil' and scarcely able to eat. The farmer in Duck's poem has not
heeded Thomson's call for charity.

> Behind our Master waits; and if he spies
> One charitable Ear, he grudging cries,
> 'Ye scatter half your Wages o'er the Land'
> Then scrapes the Stubble with his greedy Hand.[37]

Duck continually insists on the farmer as heartless, as cruel and
censorious, a person before whom, 'we just like School-boys
look, / When angry Masters view the blotted Book'.[38]

Even the harvest feast turns out be a piece of deception. Hard
work is forgotten in revelry, but returns the next morning. He
describes the psychology by which the workers convince themselves
the worst toil is past, only to find the afternoon twice as hard. The
poem is a celebration of skilled labour, from the position of
labourer, but also a complaint against its arduousness. About
women's labour, Duck is completely scathing. He describes the
contribution of the 'prattling females': 'Ah, were their Hands so
active as their Tongues, / How nimbly then would move the Rakes
and Prongs.'[39]

In 'On Poverty' Duck once more registers a complaint, against
the excesses that individuals are driven to by the fear of poverty.
This does not lead, however, to any sort of critique of social
inequality: 'Contented Poverty's no dismal Thing / Free from the
Cares unwieldy Riches bring.'[40] It leads rather to an emphasis on
individual moral rectitude and forbearance: 'Tis nobler chearfully
to bear our Fate / Than murmur, and repine beneath its Weight'.

These two poems and 'The Shunamite' made his early reputation.
He was supported by Spence, who also patronized James Thomson.
Through the offices of Mrs Clayton, Mistress of the Robes to Queen
Caroline, his poetry came to the attention of the Queen. Furnival
suggests that Queen Caroline's lack of facility in the English
language, her enthusiasm for the arts, and the difficulties of patronizing individuals with clear party political affiliations accounted for
this phenomenon.[41] The suggestion is not exactly flattering, but
seems nonetheless a fairly accurate account of the contingent
factors which led to this particular individual's success at this

particular time. The appearance of 'the peasant poet' was overdetermined by a certain literary and critical history, but the appearance of Stephen Duck was, arguably, just good luck. It was certainly to be resented, both by those such as Swift and Pope who felt their position within the dominant culture deserved greater recognition, and by later writers in the peasant tradition.[42]

Duck was brought to Court in 1730, and given a salary of thirty pounds and a house. By this time, his first wife had died. Successive writers on Duck seem to have invested heavily in representing her as both obstructive and stupid: 'His wife, a simple rustic wench, did not understand either poetry or her husband, and her lack of sympathy must have been trying, to say the least, for Duck.'[43]

Rayner Unwin's account also reproduces the claim of the pirated 'Life' that Duck's wife presumed him to be insane. It may be that his wife is here used as a condensation of the stupidity and lack of education assumed to attach to her class: Stephen's exceptional nature being constructed in opposition to his wife's. It is, however, notable that this gender stereotype has been so uncritically reproduced as a marker of Duck's early suffering. There is no evidence about these claims in regard to Duck's wife, apart from the 'Life' which was published as part of the pirated editions. Other evidence, from Dr Alured Clarke, suggests that Duck's domestic relations were very happy: 'He speaks so well of his wife, that I believe it would give him pain to see so indifferent a character of her in writing.'[44]

Once at Court, Duck's social status became increasingly ambiguous. His value lay in his 'otherness', which his insertion into dominant social and cultural structures negated. A satire on his writing, and on his social position, was published under the title of *The Thresher's Miscellany*, which claimed to have been written by a thresher, who had once been a scholar at Eton.[45] Rumours that he was being considered for the Laureateship exacerbated his dilemmas.

Throughout all this, Duck continued his project of self-education, in learning Latin. His early insecurity about the value of his poetry was not resolved: 'Gentlemen indeed, he said, might like 'em, because they were made by a poor Fellow in a Barn but . . . he knew, as well as any body, that they were not really good in themselves.'[46] His attempts to imitate Pope and Spence were met with little enthusiasm. He began writing occasional poems, dedicated to members of the aristocracy such as 'To a Young Lady who had a Cupid given her', but, once more, these did nothing to mitigate the contradictions in his position.

It is a critical commonplace that, once removed from their original social position, peasant poets were incapable of any significant work. If this claim is taken to imply that literary production is somehow 'naturally' associated with a certain position in the social structure then it must be resisted. Nonetheless, given the construction of Duck as 'natural', 'speaking directly from his own experience', his encounter with the norms of educated eighteenth-century literary style could not but destroy the basis of his appeal for the dominant culture. Duck had been removed from his social, geographical and cultural space, which was now perceived by him as marginalized and ridiculed through the very process of valorization, and was thus left in a social and cultural limbo.

The extent to which Duck found his social and poetical space undermined is illustrated by the difference between his account of rural labour in 'A Description of a Journey' and his earlier representation in 'The Thresher's Labour'. 'The Thresher's Labour' had attacked the hypocrisy and delusion of paternalism, in the collective voice of rural labourers. In 'A Description of a Journey', Duck describes, from outside, the labour of 'the swains' and describes their grateful response to a harvest supper:

> Full twenty *Threshers* quaff around the Board;
> All name their toast, and ev'ry one, *my Lord*.[47]

Duck was, for a period, employed in the Queen's library, which was housed in a building known as Merlin's Cave. This building contained works of art as well as books, and constituted something of a curiosity. It was Duck's job to show visitors round, receiving tips for his trouble. This employment provides a powerful metaphor for the contradictions of Duck's position: he was taken up by the dominant culture, but not taken inside it.

After the Queen's death, interest in Duck subsided. By the 1740s his name scarcely appears in any of the literary periodicals. He took Holy Orders in 1746, and was eventually given a living of £130 a year at Byfleet, in Surrey. He kept on writing, although he represented this as an incurable weakness. He eventually committed suicide in 1756.

Duck's initial success encouraged other poets to seek publication and patronage. As *The Gentleman's Magazine* noted in 1739, 'the story of Duck's rise did not fail to arouse optimism, even in the humblest among the opposite sex'.[48] Mary Collier published *The Woman's Labour: An Epistle to Mr Stephen Duck* in 1739. At the beginning of this volume, it is made clear that Mary Collier makes no claim to the 'Genius of Mr Duck', but a hope is expressed that 'the Novelty of a *Washer-Woman's* turning Poetess' will procure her some readers and a small income. In 'The Woman's Labour' Collier takes issue with Duck's representation of women: 'But on our abject State you throw your Scorn, / And Women wrong, your Verses to adorn.'[49]

Her poem is clearly constructed in response to Duck's poem. She describes the routine of daily labour:

> Heaps of fine Linnen we before us view
> Whereon to lay our Strength and Patience too,
> Cambricks and Muslins which our Ladies wear . . .
>
> Pots, Kettles, Sauce-pans, Skillets, we may see,
> Skimmers and Ladles and such Trumpery
> Brought in to compleat our Slavery.[50]

She stresses the particular hardship suffered by women workers. She protests that Duck is unreasonable in expecting women to be silent while they work. She denies his suggestion that their work is less arduous. She describes agricultural labour, laundry work, and also the domestic labour that women must perform before their husbands return from work.

> And our domestic Toils incessant ply
> Against your coming Home prepare to get
> Our Work all done, Our House in order set.[51]

Duck had described the men's arrival home for supper, but the labour involved in preparing it was quite invisible to him.

Mary Collier represents her poem not simply as a personal account, but rather as an attempt 'to vindicate the injured Sex'.[52] She explicitly allies herself with other women:

> My Life was always spent in Drudgery:
> And not alone; alas! With Grief I find
> It is the Portion of poor Woman-kind.[53]

There is a certain coyness in her writing, as she remembers earlier poets and the homage they paid to women. There is also a very conscious polemic against Duck, for his misrepresentation of woman's labour, and for his social ambitions: 'Deign to look on one that's poor and low, / Rememb'ring you yourself was lately so.'[54]

These two features seem to have rendered later critics' responses to Collier's writing less than enthusiastic. Unwin insists that *The*

Woman's Labour 'neither has, nor claims, literary merit'.[55] The basis of this judgement remains mysterious, although it is clear that Unwin does not take the politics of Collier's project very seriously. The difficulty with fitting Collier into a tradition of spontaneous and natural peasant verse may lie in the degree of intertextuality her first poem displayed. The degree to which 'The Woman's Labour' depends formally and structurally on Duck's poem renders the discourse of unmediated creativity a little problematic.

Nonetheless, Collier's poem was widely read, and in 1762 she published a volume of *Poems on Several Occasions*. There were about 120 subscribers to this volume, including a significant number of women. Those subscribing were mostly from the professional classes, lawyers and clergy, rather than from the aristocracy.

The volume begins with the obligatory 'Life', although on this occasion written by the poet herself. She describes her parents as 'poor, but honest'. They taught her to write, but after her father's death she had to go to Petersfield where she found work as a washerwoman and in a brewery. The heterogeneity of her various employments is significant, although she presented herself in *The Woman's Labour* under the sign of 'washerwoman'. By the time of the publication of *Poems on Several Occasions* she has retired 'to pass the relict of my days in Piety, Purity, Peace, and an Old Maid'.[56]

Several poems in this volume involve an exploration of gender relations. One is presented as a dialogue between 'The Happy Husband and the Old Bachelor'. When asked to write another poem showing the unhappy maid and the happy wife, she writes:

> Most Men are now so viciously inclin'd
> That happy Wives are very hard to find;
> And as for discontented Maids, I own,
> Any such Persons are to me unknown.[57]

Mary Collier mobilizes humour, and the disturbance caused by her gendered voice, to good effect in deconstructing certain stereotypes of gender relations. She demonstrates the ways in which descriptions of labour have excluded, or removed to the realm of erotic spectacle, the labour of women. She thus adds a different, and largely unacknowledged, dimension to the 'peasant voice'.

Robert Tatersal, who published *The Bricklayer's Miscellany: Or Poems on Several Subjects* in 1734, was also writing 'in Allusion to Stephen Duck'. The title page demands: 'Since rustick Threshers entertain the Muse, / Why may not Bricklayers too their Subjects chuse?'[58]

He describes himself as deprived of both the means and the opportunity of addressing the Muse in a becoming manner, and also as a 'mean Mechanik'. His poems include several dedicated to patrons, 'To Christopher Lowe', and 'To the Honourable John King', but also one written explicitly to Stephen Duck. Here he once more pleads his case:

> Yea, modern Times afford a Rustick Flail,
> Whose threshing Lays cou'd over Queens prevail
> And why not Bricklayers exercise their Quill,
> Whose Art surmounts a country Thresher's still.[59]

He complains that his conditions of labour give him little opportunity for reflection, and contrasts them with Duck's comfortable situation of Royal patronage. His poem 'The Bricklayer's Labours' also owes much to Duck. This is a description of the minutiae of his daily routine:

> When up I start and view the eastern Sky,
> And by my Mark find Six o'Clock is nigh,
> Then hanging on my Thread-bare Coat and Hose
> My Hat, my Cap, my Breeches and my Shoes. . .[60]

He points to the physical excesses that characterize his life.

> Full five Hours Space to toil without Allay:
> Now parch'd with Heat, and almost chok'd with Dust
> We join our Pence to satiate our Thirst.[61]

He also describes the insecurity and suffering brought on by seasonal unemployment and poverty. Tatersal clearly suffers from the absence of any poetic tradition for the representation of his labour. He cannot appeal to nature as a moral force, as poets of rural labour can do. He offers us very little description of the physical setting of his labour, except for the movement of the sun which indicates the passing of time. Once more, he lacks a poetic tradition which would render his landscape meaningful. Indeed, Tatersal seems more confident of his poetic voice when he describes the easy lot of the agricultural labourer than when he tries to render his own experiences of labour into verse:

> Your menial Slaves, bles'd by thy gen'rous Pay,
> With Pleasure spin the sultry Toils of Day.
> By thee sustain'd they sing in rural Lays
> Delightful Sonnets to your Honour's Praise.[62]

Mary Leapor's *Poems Upon Several Occasions* was published in

1748. Leapor was the daughter of a Northamptonshire gardener. Her family background was poor, and she received little formal education. She worked for some time as a cook–maid. Her poetic talents were discovered by a local woman called Bridget Freemantle, who determined to raise a subscription in order to publish Leapor's poems. Unfortunately, Leapor died, aged twenty-four, before the volume appeared. There were about 700 subscribers to the volume, including a significant number of the aristocracy. The volume is prefaced by a short description of Leapor's life. She is described as 'a young unassisted Genius' and her poems as fine 'in their native Simplicity'. The preface also considers her character: 'her Conduct and Behaviour entirely corresponded with those virtuous and pious Sentiments which are conspicuous in her Poems'. She is described as 'contented in the Station of Life in which Providence had placed her'.

Her favourite author is said to have been Pope, whom she tried to imitate in her own writing. Her 'Pastoral Complaint' and 'The Beauties of Spring' are highly stylized evocations of the countryside as a place of peace and tranquillity, a distillation of the finer emotions: 'Grief flies from hence, and wasting Cares subside, / While wing'd with Mirth the laughing Minutes glide.'[63] She represents the spontaneous bounty of nature, offering forth its fruits to a grateful world:

> Sagacious Bees their Labours now renew,
> Hum round the Blossoms, and extract their Dew:
> In their new Liv'ries the green Woods appear,
> And smiling Nature decks the Infant Year.[64]

Her poetry is mostly concerned with classical models of pastoral, and with moral essays. Only when the bounty of nature is in question, that is during winter, can she represent rural labour as in any way arduous:

> Poor daggled Urs'la stalks from Cow to Cow,
> Who to her Sighs return a mournful Low;
> While their full Udders her broad Hands assail,
> And her sharp Nose hangs dropping o'er the Pail.[65]

Her 'Essay on Happiness' articulates a similar position to Stephen Duck's 'On Poverty'. Regardless of rank, she argues, happiness lies within the sphere of the individual. Riches can lead to unhappiness, but individual moral virtue will lead to contentment. Obviously, this is a message her patrons were not disappointed to hear. It is also, perhaps, the only one that could be produced in a poetic voice so wedded to classical tradition: punctual complaint was possible, but not sustained analysis.

Ann Yearsley's *Poems on Several Occasions* was published in 1785. In this volume she describes herself as 'A Milkwoman of Bristol'. She was patronized by Hannah More, who organized over a thousand subscribers, most of whom were women. Hannah More opens the volume with a letter to Mrs Montagu, describing Ann Yearsley's life, writing and morals.

More admits that Yearsley's poetry is 'incorrect', but nonetheless finds 'a certain natural and strong expression of misery'. Yearsley's reading has consisted of *Paradise Lost*, *Night Thoughts*, Shakespeare and the *Georgics*, although More suggests she also look at the Bible in order to enlarge her vocabulary of images. It is claimed that she exhibited 'the general principles of sound taste and just thinking' and thus avoided the worst excesses of over-refined and stylized poetry. More is keen that she should not be encouraged to study: Shakespeare, after all, did not look to critical texts in order to determine his writing. More 'should be sorry to see the wild vigour of her rustic muse polished into elegance'.

A gentleman writing to the *Gentleman's Magazine* in 1784 is equally clear about the appeal of her writing, of which, at the time, he knew only one poem: 'She warbles wild notes in a style that makes me believe (though, indeed, I am no judge) that, with instruction, she might have become a Siren.' He comments particularly on her 'real humility'.[66]

More is keen to stress that Yearsley is 'active and industrious in no common degree', and that her morals are sound. She is also clear that patronage is intended only to alleviate her suffering and not to transform her social position:

> It is not intended to place her in such a state of independence as might seduce her to devote her time to the idleness of Poetry . . . as a wife and mother, she has duties to fill, the smallest of which is of more value than the finest verses she can write.[67]

She is, then, to remain dependent, marginal, and constrained by her domestic relations. And so, indeed, she did. She eventually parted company with Hannah More, who refused to allow her to act as a trustee for the money made by her book. The disagreement between Yearsley and More was public and prolonged. Yearsley published her account of it in the fourth edition of her *Poems on Several Occasions*, including the claim that More had called her 'wretched', 'ungrateful' and 'base'. The economic and social relations in which she participated were clearly untenable for

Yearsley. The contradiction between the valorization of her literary production and the stigmatization of her social position is explored in several of her poems. Her volume of *Stanzas of Woe* of 1790 is prefaced by an account of the maltreatment of her sons and herself by local gentry. This foregrounding of her treatment at the hands of the ruling classes has not always been appreciated by critics. J. M. S. Tompkins remarked that 'she lacked altogether the docile subservience that makes charity a pleasure'.[68]

Yearsley's poetry perhaps owes as much to Edward Young's *Night Thoughts* as to the poetic tradition discussed so far. Her first volume, *Poems on Several Occasions*, contained a poem called 'Night' and one called 'Thoughts on the Author's own Death'. 'Night' is addressed to Hannah More, in the person of Stella, and demonstrates a clear awareness of the significance of 'peasant' writing for the dominant culture.

> Accept the wild and untaught rapture, form'd
> From simple Nature, in her artless guise;
> Yet in its wildness charming to excess
> To souls like thine . . .[69]

The same volume includes a poem called 'Clifton Hill', which makes extensive use of the pastoral tradition. It describes a landscape in winter, where: 'The Swain neglects his Nymph, yet knows not why / The Nymph, indifferent, mourns the freezing sky.'[70] Its representation of rural labour is, again, marginal and written in the third person. Yearsley does not have the collective, confident voice of the rural labourer as expressed by Duck. She refers to her own work, in the person of Lactilla, 'Lactilla, shivering, tends her fav'rite cow / The bleating flocks now ask the bounteous hand.'[71] But the emphasis is, generally, on the spontaneous bounty of nature, and the movement of the seasons: 'the laughing hours / Advancing swift, shall strew spontaneous flowers.'[72]

In this volume, she does not challenge the organization of rural society. She calls on the rich to exercise their paternal role,

> Awake, ye rich, that sleep! awake to save!
> And infants, yet unborn, in choral song,
> Shall bless the hand which form'd a social father.[73]

and represents the organization and struggle of the oppressed as unnatural and dangerous.

> What pen, tho' dipp'd in horror's deepest dye,
> Can justly paint the poor unletter'd tribe
> Assembled in a groupe?[74]

Her later writing does, however, represent a very clear commitment to a critique of tyranny. She published, in 1788, *A Poem on the Inhumanity of the Slave-Trade*, where her attack on those who profit from the slave-trade is quite explicit:

> Curse on the toils spread by Christian hand
> To rob the Indian of his freedom! Curse
> On him who from a bending parent steals
> His dear support of age, his darling child.
> . . .
> Behold that Christian! See what horrid joy
> Lights up his moody features, while he grasps
> The wish'd for gold, purchase of human blood.[75]

The poem describes in detail the sufferings of those who are removed from their family and deprived of their liberty. It ends with an invocation of 'social love' as the necessary antidote to the selfishness and greed which support the slave-trade. This critique of arbitrary power and tyranny was carried over into *The Royal Captives*, her gothic novel of 1795, which was a treatment of the story of 'The Man in the Iron Mask'. Her criticism of tyranny was certainly strong enough to provoke a response from Richard Polwhele in 1798:

> Ann YEARSELEY (*sic.*), who had warbled, nature's child,
> Midst twilight dews, her minstrel ditties wild
> (Tho' soon a wanderer from her meads and milk,
> She long'd to rustle, like her sex, in silk)
> Now stole the modish grin, the sapient sneer.[76]

Yearsley's powerful response to tyranny, and her advocacy of liberty, is never really addressed by most of her poetic writing. Her accounts of nature remain at a symbolic rather than a social level, with flowers as the representation of death. Her account of her own social position is only fitfully present in her verse, and moves between frustration at the charge of ingratitude and a confident insistence that she has worked out what the dominant culture wants from her:

> I've patient trod the wild entangled path
> Of unimprov'd Idea. Dauntless Thought
> I eager seiz'd, no formal Rule e'er aw'd.[77]

Hannah More's predictions about Yearsley's social position were, however, largely fulfilled. She did open a bookshop in Bristol, published several volumes of poetry, a novel and a play, but never obtained financial security. She died in 1806.

Responses to John Bryant's writing focused, once more, on the 'naturalness' of his poetic voice and vision. The preface to his volume of poetry describes his verses as 'being intended for the perusal of those who may be desirous of seeing the gradual progress of natural poetic genius, unassisted by education'.[78] John Bryant obtained about 300 subscribers for his *Verses* published in 1787.

The 'Life', written by Bryant, which appears in this volume articulates Bryant's increasing social dislocation. He appears under the label of 'Tobacco Pipe Maker', but after the collapse of the tobacco trade, following the American Stamp Act, in fact worked in the docks, in a foundry, as a labourer and for the Press Gang. The narrative of his literary success is pleasingly melodramatic: he was overheard by a gentleman while 'singing for his supper'. His poems sit uneasily between sycophancy and self-pity. His attack on the arrogance of the rich is too ritualistic to produce very much conviction: 'O black Ingratitude! O shameful Pride! / Whose cold contempt insults the honest poor / To whose humility and toil ye owe / . . . For all you superfluity and state.'[79]

He deals in abstractions, within which he seems unable to find a place. Similarly, his reproduction of the natural as a moral repository removed from the contradictions of urban social relations is uneasy and forced.

> To breathe fresh air, and view the sylvan scenes;
> To taste the various sweets of rural life,
> The bounteous gifts of Nature, and in part
> Recall the bliss of man's primeval state,
> I quit the smoking city's busy strife.[80]

Bryant does stress the fact that only labour produces wealth, that riches depend on the sufferings of individual workers. When he comes to represent that labour, however, Bryant falls back on the poetic representations of cheerful peasants which we found in James Thomson:

> . . .with chearful brow
> Her early task the ruddy-featur'd maid
> Begins, and each full udder to her pail
> Resigns its burthen, sweetly while she sings
> Her simple song of some inconstant swain.[81]

Robert Bloomfield wrote *The Farmer's Boy* at the beginning of the
nineteenth century. Like *The Seasons*, this poem was critically
successful, widely read, and influential for later 'peasant poets'.
Bloomfield himself mentions his reading of *The Seasons*, while
John Clare was to record the importance he attached both to *The
Seasons* and *The Farmer's Boy*.[82]

The Farmer's Boy is an intense and detailed representation of
rural life in Suffolk, an investigation of the social and moral
economy of rural relations, and an argument for responsible
paternalism. By the time of writing it, Bloomfield was no longer
working as an agricultural labourer, but as a shoemaker in London.
It is a text of memories:

> It recalled to my mind those ages and those countries in which the
> poet and the shepherd were more naturally united . . . They please
> us because they breathe the language of nature and speak the
> language of the heart.[83]

Bloomfield moved to London at the age of thirteen, and *The
Farmer's Boy* is as much a poem about childhood as about rural
society. He writes 'ecstasies of praise / for all the blessings of my
infant days'.[84] The emotional force of the poem comes from the
representations of organic society, natural scenery and useful
labour combining to produce a sense of identity and liberty. Of his
protagonist, Giles, Bloomfield writes: 'No stripes, no tyranny his
steps pursued; / His life was constant, cheerful servitude.'[85]

Bloomfield's description of rural labour, like Bryant's, owes
much to Thomson:

> Hark! where the sweeping scythe now rips along:
> Each sturdy mower emulous and strong,
> Whose writhing form meridian heat defies,
> Bends o'er his work, and every sinew tries.[86]

It is the same sense of the anonymous labourer, at one with the
season, and fulfilled in his work. Once more, Bloomfield offers the
reader the lovely maid, 'Her hat awry, divested of her gown'. The
lunchtime beer is refreshing, the farmer and his wife are generous,
and the gleaners are happy: 'Children of want, for you the bounty
flows.'[87]

After the publication of *The Farmer's Boy* in 1800, Bloomfield
became a curiosity for literary London. He was given a job at the
Seal Office with a salary of fifteen pounds by the Duke of Grafton.
He was inundated by callers, letters and critics. His success was
extremely double-edged, however, as the financial demands of his

new social position proved overwhelming, and he suffered from very poor health. Rayner Unwin conjectures, however, that he did find occasional relief: 'Now and then he would escape from his wife and explore the countryside.'[88]

John Clare has been more written about than any of the other poets discussed so far, and has even been admitted into the literary canon, albeit in a minor role. Yet, it was as 'A Northamptonshire Peasant', or, in one of Clare's early letters, 'A Northamptonshire Pheasant',[89] that he was introduced onto the literary scene, into the tradition of peasant poetry that he was inserted, and as an 'untaught genius' that he was praised. Octavius Gilchrist represents Clare in 1820 as 'the rustic poet who had just now returned from his daily labour'.[90] Clare's first volume of poetry, *Poems Descriptive of Rural Life and Scenery* was published in 1820, and met with immediate success. It was published through the mediations of Edward Drury, a bookseller in Stamford, who drew the attention of John Taylor, the publisher, to Clare's writings.

Clare was a poor and little educated rural labourer. It was largely because of Clare's curiosity value that Taylor interested himself in his writings. The introduction to Clare's first published volume insists that 'Clare is most thoroughly the Poet as well as the Child of Nature', and argues that poverty is essential to the protection of his poetic abilities.[91] This volume brought Clare the patronage of Lord Radstock and the Bishop of Peterborough, who established a fund out of which Clare drew an annual income of thirty pounds. This was to prove totally inadequate, and financial insecurity remained a dominant feature of Clare's life.[92]

Clare was never happy with the form in which he was mediated to the dominant culture. He rejected the special pleading implied by the label 'peasant': 'I hope my low station in life will not be set off as a foil against my verses'.[93] He knew that visitors who came to seem him at Helpstone did not always find what they expected:

> to prevent dissaapointments I will describe the spot and the sort of company and cheer you will meet here with us . . . we have a many woods on one hand and a many nightingales, but no Chloes or Phillises worth the mention.[94]

He was also aware of the ambiguity of the response of many critics to the voice of the peasantry, and criticized Southey, in particular, for his poor opinion of uneducated poets and his 'sneering way'.[95] Likewise, his patrons were never completely comfortable with their ability to assimilate and appropriate his writings.

Clare was 'adopted' by Mrs Eliza Emmerson, who seems to have

acted as a mediator between Clare and Radstock. Her correspondence with Clare gives us an interesting articulation of the series of
dependencies and insecurities which marked Clare's career as a
writer. Eliza Emmerson first introduces herself in a letter dated
21 February 1820, where she says she has read his poems and has
persuaded Lord Radstock to act as a patron.[96] She tells Clare he is
a 'superior genius' and regrets his 'lowly situation'. She gives her
reasons for favouring his poetry, which is 'at once simple, beautiful,
affecting and occasionally sublime', saying 'you prove yourself in
your scenes from Nature to be truly Nature's child'.

Her support is, however, neither unqualified nor disinterested.
Two months later she is presuming on her position sufficiently to
reprimand him for not writing: 'True friendship, like true love is
ever attendant with feelings of jealousy.' She also foregrounds the
importance of his political profile, in this instance in relation to
gaining the support of the Bishop of Peterborough. Lord Radstock,
it would seem, had

> to convince the Bishop of the purity of your political principles [and]
> read some extracts from a letter which you wrote . . . and your
> sentiments of Loyalty and attachment to your King and Constitution
> with which the Bishop expressed himself much *Pleased*.

In her next letter, Eliza Emmerson moves from suggestion to
direct intervention, reminding Clare of his dependence. Lord
Radstock has suggested the removal of

> passages wherein his then depressed state hurried him not only into
> error, but also into the most flagrant of injustice, by accusing those
> of pride, cruelty, vices and ill directed passions who are the very
> persons by whose truly generous and noble exertions he has been
> raised from misery and dependency.

Eliza Emmerson suggests to Clare that he ask John Taylor to
remove passages 'conveying *Radical* and ungrateful sentiments'.

Far from suggesting, it then turns out that she has actually
promised Lord Radstock that the offending passages will be
removed, in particular the ten lines in 'Helpstone' beginning
'Accursed wealth'. She then reminds him of the gratitude he should
feel, and promises he will be sent a dictionary so he can improve
his English.

By November of 1820, Eliza Emmerson is clearly worried. Clare
has not been writing to Radstock. She asserts somewhat desper-
ately, 'your political sentiments quite agree with mine, and they
must be those of every rational and good man'. Yet, she can

scarcely have found Clare's poetry reassuring evidence for this claim.

The politics of Clare's writing has long been a point of critical debate. Some writers, like Elaine Feinstein, see Clare as a social critic of a rather muted and simplistic kind, with a fear of real change.[97] Others, like Eric Robinson and Geoffrey Summerfield insist that, 'the true extent of Clare's radicalism has never been disclosed from his own time down to the present day', because of the mediations of successive editors.[98]

This claim raises a more general problem for anyone studying Clare's writing: the lack of availability of, and even the impossibility of, a 'standard edition' of his works. Clare often sent his poems to Taylor unfinished, asking that Taylor render them fit for publication. Taylor himself often made substantial changes, far in excess of what Clare had asked for, or could readily accept. In the case of *The Shepherd's Calendar* Robinson and Summerfield make a very convincing argument that such changes were not made simply in the interests of 'clarity', but also in order to remove subject matter considered 'low', attitudes that appeared too radical, and expressions that were judged too provincial.[99] Later editions have therefore turned to Clare's manuscripts for elucidation, hoping to find there the true John Clare. But this operation is, in itself, unsatisfactory. The manuscript poems were often, in Clare's own opinion, unfinished, and it is unclear whether they were intended to be published in their existing form. The editions of Clare I have used therefore depend on the questions I am addressing. If the interest is in the form in which Clare was available to his patrons in the early nineteenth century, then Taylor's edition is clearly the most important. The Tibbles' edition, though criticized by Robinson and Summerfield, is an interesting part of a twentieth-century impulse to rediscover Clare and make his writings more generally accessible, particularly through the addition of punctuation. Robinson and Powell's recent edition represents an attempt to assert the real voice of Clare, free of all mediations. For the purposes of analysis below, I have decided, with some reservations, to use the most recently published version of each poem, adding Taylor's version where the discrepancies seem particularly interesting.

The lines of Clare's poetry which so upset Eliza Emmerson are from 'Helpstone', one of Clare's earliest poems. The poem is a lament for the loss of organic social relations, nature's freedom, and 'Peace and Plenty'. Clare writes:

> Accursed wealth o'er bounding human laws
> Of every evil thou remainst the cause
> Victims of want those wretches such as me
> Too truly lay their wretchedness to thee.[100]

and the indictment seems quite specific. Yet, out of context, the passage is misleading, or at least misrepresents the argument of the poem as a whole. John Barrell has demonstrated the close relationship between this poem and Goldsmith's *The Deserted Village*, although in doing so he perhaps underestimates the importance of the social dimension in Goldsmith's poem. *The Deserted Village*, written in 1770, celebrated a rural life of innocence, decency and benevolence, which had been destroyed by luxury, wealth and excess. Goldsmith insisted on the documentary evidence of his poem, 'all my views and enquiries have led me to believe those miseries real, which I here attempt to display'.[101] His poem describes the decay and degeneration of a rural community, caused by a concentration of wealth and the erosion of old farming practices. The innocence and ease of village life are linked to childhood, to youth, 'Dear lovely bowers of innocence and ease / Seats of my youth, when every sport could please.'[102] The poem often seems to move to an articulation of regret for the loss of youth. It also proposes, but simultaneously contradicts, the thesis that social degeneracy and unnaturalness render poetry impossible. In the nexus of psyche, poetry and society, it is not clear which wins out.

In 'Helpstone' we find the same uncertainty of focus. Clare attacks wealth, but also risks treating it at a purely metaphorical level, as simply part of an inevitable process of decay and disaffection:

> When weary age the grave a r[e]scue seeks
> And prints its image on my wrinkl'd cheeks
> Those charms of youth that I again may see
> May it be mine to meet my end in thee
> And as reward for all my troubles past
> Find one hope true to die at home at last.[103]

Social change is here undone by an effort of desire, an image of peace.

The relationship between Clare and Goldsmith's writing seems to raise a more general problem about the forms of writing available to Clare. The need to discover a lyric voice constantly sent him back to traditions of writing where the psychological and the individual articulate the social, rather than vice versa. Clare read Milton, and Goldsmith, and Bloomfield, and Beattie: all creating a poetic voice which was resolutely individualistic The tension here can be found at several points in Clare's writing. His voice is occasionally social, where he seems to speak from, and for, a particular group or class.

> What thousands now half pin'd and bare
> Are forced to stand thy piercing air
> All day, near numbed to death wi' cold
> Some petty gentry to uphold,
> Paltry proudlings hard as thee
> Dead to all humanity.[104]

Yet Clare also rejects such identification. His description of, 'the dull and obstinate class from whence I struggled into light like one struggling from the nightmare in his sleep', is merely a more extreme example of the coupling of poetic sensibility and social alienation to be found in Clare's 'The Village Minstrel'.[105] Lubin, the protagonist in this poem, is represented as singular and suffering. Like Beattie's 'Minstrel', he prefers solitude, avoids the company of others, and finds inspiration in nature.

'The Parish' is often held to be Clare's most radical poem, and it was certainly too much of a threat for anyone to publish it in the nineteenth century. It is a satire on the pretensions of rural capitalism, and a complaint against its excesses.

> That good old fame the farmers earnd of yore
> That made as equals not as slaves the poor
> That good old fame did in two sparks expire
> A shooting coxcomb and a hunting Squire.[106]

But here, too, many of Clare's moves amount to what Barrell describes as the language of 'nostalgic radicalism'.[107] The critique is of specific developments in nineteenth-century rural relations, particularly the social effects of enclosure, but the available language is the radical individualism of Paine's the *Rights of Man*.

'The Shepherd's Calendar' also sees Clare engaging with traditions of representing rural labour, most obviously with Spenser and Thomson. The relationship to Spenser's poem is less significant than the coincidence of titles might suggest. Clare is little concerned with allegorical readings, his shepherd is almost a minor character in relation to the multiplicity of activities and seasonal developments of rural life. The engagement with Thomson is more productive. Clare's poem offers much greater detail than Thomson's abstraction of 'Nature'. Again, Clare offers some apparently uncompromising observations, 'And where enclosure has its birth / It spreads a mildew oer her mirth.'[108]

Yet, the poem often seems to negate the sort of representations of social hierarchy, of the pretensions of wealthy farmers, and of the real power that supports these pretensions, that can be found in 'The Parish'. The representation of rural labour is of harmony of purpose, personal fulfilment, and natural sexuality:

> Stript in his shirt the hot swain drops adown
> And close beside him in her unpind gown
> Next to her favoured swain the maiden steals
> Blushing at kindness which her love reveals
> Who makes a seat for her of things around
> And drops beside her on the naked ground
> Wearied wi brambles catching at her gown
> And pulling nutts from branches pulld adown
> By friendly swain the maid wi heaving breast
> Upon her lovers shoulder leans at rest
> Then from its cool retreat the beer they bring.[109]

or, as Taylor preferred it:

> Next to her favour'd swain the maiden steals,
> Blushing at kindness which his love reveals;
> Making a seat for her of sheaves around,
> He drops beside her on the naked ground.
> Then from its cool retreat the beer they bring.[110]

This basic harmony is confirmed in the pleasure of the harvest supper 'which rustics welcome with delight'.

The other aspect of Clare's writing to which critics have responded is his representation of love, another 'natural' emotion. Clare's own emotional history is complex, and much speculated on. He fell in love, at a very young age, with Mary Joyce, the daughter of a local farmer. Mary Joyce's responses to this are unknown, although Clare asserts that, 'I fancyd her eyes told me her affections.'[111] The friendship came to an end. Clare speculates this is because she thought herself above him. Again, there is no evidence, but the Tibbles rally to Clare's defence, condemning Mary Joyce for having 'no word of kindness for Clare'.[112]

Mary Joyce's name haunts his poetry, however, rather than the name of his wife, and by the time of his entry to a mental asylum he had convinced himself that Mary, too, was his wife. The critical tendency has always been to blame this on his wife: 'His marriage to Patty was not an unhappy one, but she can never have understood what he was trying to do.'[113] It is, however, as well to resist this temptation to biographical criticism, which is as best conjectural, and accepts uncritically a certain history of gender relations. The fact is that Clare chose to represent desire and sexuality in his poems under the sign of fantasy:

> Say What Is Love – To Live In Vain
> To Live And Die And Live Again. . .

> Say What Is Love – What E'er It Be
> It Centers Mary Still With Thee.[114]

The significance of this can only be produced through a reading that takes account of the history of poetic representation of love, the relationship between Clare and his poetic voice, and the history of literary objectification of women.

Once inside a mental asylum, Clare continued to write for over twenty years. His poems became more visionary and less grounded in the details of his environment. These poems articulate the desire for escape, for peace and tranquillity, but never fall into the convention of equating this with the rural.

> I long for scenes, where man hath never trod
> A place where woman never smiled or wept
> There to abide with my Creator, God.[115]

But Clare could not construct this as a pastoral Utopia.

As a 'peasant poet' Clare was caught in a series of contradictions. His patrons wanted him to speak simply, but not uncouthly. They wanted him to express his individuality, through a very particular construction of nature. Clare himself was trying to find a distinctive voice that was both 'poetic' and yet authentic. He was trying to write poetry that was both lyrical and social. In the middle of it all he went insane.

Finally, at the point of disintegration of the system of patronage, we come to William Thom, the Inverurie Poet. Thom began his working life as a weaver in Aberdeen. By 1837, the weaving trade was in crisis, and Thom was out of a job. He tried to make a living as an itinerant bookseller but found the financial hardship intolerable. During this time his daughter died of hunger and exhaustion. He went back to weaving, although wages were low. His financial and domestic situation was precarious. He eventually submitted his first poem, 'The Blind Boy's Pranks' for publication in the *Aberdeen Herald* in 1841.

Response to this poem by 'a serf' was enthusiastic: 'the genuine spirit of poetry pervades "The Blind Boy's Pranks"'.[116] He came to the attention of J. A. Gordon of Knockespock, who gave him money and tried to arrange for the publication of a volume of his poetry. Gordon was an enthusiastic collector of ballads, and a scholar of local dialect. He counselled Thom to stick to the landscape of Aberdeenshire, which he had evoked in 'The Blind Boy's Pranks':

> Twas just whaur creeping Ury greets
>   Its mountain cousin Don,
> There wandered forth a weelfaur'd dame
>   Wha listless gazed on the bonnie stream
>   As it flirted an' played with a sunny beam
>   That flickered its bosom upon.[117]

From the very beginning, the relationship between Gordon and Thom was not an easy one. In a letter to Gordon, Thom apologizes for not having written sooner to thank him for his generosity: 'my lowly breeding has hid from me those nice and proper distinctions recognized by people of education and superior training'.[118] Gordon made detailed enquiries about Thom's education, age, means of living and religion. It is clear, from Thom's account of his life published in *Rhymes and Recollections*, that this enquiry caused some resentment. A footnote, added by Gordon himself, however, assures us that he had no object in mind other than to determine whether or not Thom might be suitable for a schoolmaster's position. Not only does Gordon have the right to pose his questions, he also has the right to explain his motives within Thom's own account of his life.

The interest in Thom's poetry was a function of his marginal social position: he was an exception, a natural genius. His patrons and supporters seemed to invest less energy in discussing his poems than in unpicking the details of his life. The facts of his poverty, his toiling for 'fourteen hours out of the four-and-twenty' were endlessly retold. He seemed to stand for the 'superiority of mind over matter': a curiously anti-materialist twist for a discourse that represented itself as interested in the representation of the material fabric of everyday life.[119] For Thom himself, this 'natural genius' was both a curse, in that it marked him as different, and a blessing, in that it offered the chance of escape from the necessity 'to battle lip-deep in poverty, with a motherless family and a *poetical temperament*'.[120]

Thom went to London in 1844, where he was set up in business as a weaver. The venture had something of the air of a charade, and it is clear that Thom spent more time with patrons and admirers than he did 'at his loom'. In London, he met Dickens, W. J. Fox of the Anti-Corn-Law League, and Douglas Jerrold, editor of *Punch*. Jerrold had already expressed himself interested in a study of 'The Songs of the People'.[121] Thom also met Harney, the Chartist leader, and spoke at meetings organized in support of the Charter, arguing for 'a broad bannock and a brief parliament'.[122] He presented a tablecloth to the Anti-Corn-Law League bearing the inscription, 'If Heaven intended corn to be the property of *one class* only, corn would never have been permitted to grow but in *one* land only'.[123] The logic is precarious, but the sentiment is clear. Thom also expressed his criticism of social inequality in a poem entitled 'Whisperings for the Unwashed'. In this poem he first of all describes the farmer and the Laird as well fed, lazy and happy. He contrasts their lot with that of the weavers:

> The stately stalk of Ceres bears,
> But not for you, the bursting ears;
> In vain to you the lark's lov'd note,
> For you no summer breezes float,
> Grim winter through your hovel pours –
> Dull, din, and healthless vapour yours.[124]

His poem urges the demands of justice and reason to right the condition of the poor.

Thom's success was short-lived. His patrons grew less and less comfortable with his domestic affairs and his politics: 'He thought he deserved charity . . . which made him despise the honest labour of his hands.'[125] His finances were disastrous, and his health poor. He also drank heavily. There were delays over the publication of his second book. The 'poet serf' had lost his appeal. Thom died of lung disease in 1848.

The contradictions of Thom's position had, by the end, become uncontainable. The discourse of philanthropy and common interest which had sustained the tradition of 'peasant poets' was being undermined by the development of analyses, and languages, of class. Certainly, Thom had had his radical patrons, who looked to him to provide representations of suffering, and an indictment of the unnatural and oppressive features of industrialization. Thom's financial and physical distress were seen by such patrons as a marker of the selfishness of the profit motive, and his poetry an indictment of the capitalist class:

> Has God disown'd them, the children of toil,
> Is the promise of heaven no more?
> Shall industry weep – shall the pamper'd suppress
> The sweat-earned bread of the poor?[126]

Yet, Thom's writing oscillated uneasily between evocations of rural peace and condemnations of urban squalor. His identity as 'rural serf' seemed to constrain the forms of writing, or types of identification available to him. He produced representations that were critical of the ruling classes, but remained locked in their definitions of poetry, and dependent on their charity.

The polarization of class politics throughout the 1840s, however, meant that such criticisms as Thom did produce could not readily be appropriated, or valorized, by the dominant culture, which grew uneasy with unmediated expression. The growth of the Radical and Chartist press increasingly provided an alternative space for the publication of the works of the 'uneducated poets', although, as Brian Maidment has shown, this space was far from liberating for the poets concerned. Fictional representations, within the dominant culture, of the lives, perceptions and struggles of the working classes became the business of the novel. Elizabeth Gaskell and Charles Dickens provided different sort of mediations and spoke from significantly different positions, which served further to marginalize the 'peasant poets'.

So, with William Thom, we arrive at the effective end of the tradition of peasant poetry. What has been discovered is the complexity and power of the investment by the dominant culture in certain forms of popular writing, which were perceived as natural, simple, unmediated and containable. Throughout the period examined, there were increasing numbers of individuals who wrote from positions that were marginal and precarious. They did not, however, write in complete isolation from, but always in negotiation with, the texts of the dominant culture. They did not write from the heart, but through the text, reproducing, rewriting and representing a set of discourses on nature, labour, gender and class. It is this tension between the aspiration towards simplicity and transparency, and the actual facts of contradiction and negotiation, which produces the energy and persistence of the concept of popular culture.

3

Popular Culture and the Periodical Press 1830–1855

In the previous chapter various transformations in the field of cultural relations in the nineteenth century were noticed, which must now be explored in more detail. In relation to the phenomenon of 'peasant poetry' we noted the almost total disappearance of patronage, the increase in publishing outlets, and the emergence of a critical discourse about popular culture which simultaneously addressed political and class position, moral propriety and literary merit. In this chapter, the implications of such transformations for the theorization and criticism of popular culture in the mid-nineteenth century will be examined. This will be done through a reading of accounts of, and reactions to, increasing literacy and the growth of penny fiction, as registered in a wide range of periodical publications. Since these periodical publications are, themselves, part of the cultural and economic transformations described, contributors to them are particularly keen to map out the hierarchy of cultural forms, and to specify their own place within such a hierarchical structure.

The importance and specificity of cultural changes in the mid-nineteenth century has long been recognized. In some form or other the story is usually one of decline: the dangers of mass culture, the disappearance of regional cultures, increasing practical and ideological control of leisure time. As Louis James would have it, the nineteenth century provides 'a blueprint of many cultural problems that face modern society'.[1] If this is taken to imply an inevitable continuity in problems of cultural decline, then it is a claim that has to be challenged, but the metaphor is nonetheless a useful one: a blueprint is a coded representation which constrains the development of a final product. In this sense, the cultural relations and theories of nineteenth-century Britain have, indeed, provided a blueprint for contemporary accounts of popular culture.

The 'nineteenth century' is available to us only in a highly mediated sense, through a range of texts and representations, in this case specifically texts about popular culture. It is, thus, an ensemble of texts, varied and often contradictory, which construct the 'blueprint' for contemporary cultural analysis. What we have inherited is not just the cultural 'problems' of the nineteenth century, but also distinctive ways of theorizing them.

The point is important, because it means we cannot simply go to nineteenth-century texts and read off the nature and problems of popular culture. There has to be a continual negotiation with an already constructed history, an engagement with inherited definitions of 'the popular', and a questioning of the absences and emphases we have inherited in relation to nineteenth-century culture.

CULTURAL TRANSFORMATIONS IN THE NINETEENTH CENTURY

The years between 1800 and 1870 saw changes in the forms, relations of production, and patterns of distribution, of cultural artefacts and processes in which as literary critics, or cultural analysts, we have an investment. These changes include the perception of popular culture as something to be controlled, and as something in decline. The proliferation of literary forms and their increasing availability to the working classes become both the focus of anxieties about social transformations and a metaphor of social decline and disintegration. This, in turn, signals the beginning of an argument about the relationship between technological development and cultural decline, which continues to structure discussions of popular culture to the present day.

Generally, throughout the nineteenth century there was a shift from cultural forms and practices based on communal and regional observation and celebration of seasonal or work cycles and towards the development of cultural commodities which were consumed in a more individualistic way:

> What was involved, was, above all, a reshaping of the entire field of cultural relationships between classes, the newer forms of popular culture occupying a position within that field which was different from that which had been occupied by the popular recreations of the past.[2]

Within the ruling classes, the crucial shift, which solidifies during the nineteenth century, is from an attitude to popular cultural forms based on a mixture of tolerance and direct repression of excess to one based on attempts at control grounded in ideological intervention and analysis. The complex of economic, social and cultural transformations which go under the name of 'industrial capitalism' brought new forms of class division, which both allowed and required an extension of control in relation to culture. This was manifested in a gradual shift in attitude rather than a sudden transformation. As Eileen Yeo argues, there are plenty of examples of intervention, particularly in the early part of the nineteenth century, which still take the form of 'a pitched battle, with each side fighting for the totality of the culture, even for its physical spaces'.[3]

The argument that capitalist relations of production required direct intervention in cultural forms in order to destroy traditional notions of seasonal work and extended holidays is a cogent one, and in many cases clearly correct.[4] The need to establish a work discipline in order to allow for the development of centralized industrial production did overdetermine attempts to repress traditional fairs, holidays and sporting events.[5] However, such direct intervention is not the story of this chapter, which is concerned instead with the shift throughout the nineteenth century from periodic but direct repression to attempts at ideological intervention in the field of popular culture. It is thus concerned with theories and practices which attempted to engage with the potential of cultural forms as mechanisms of social control.

The claim that interventions in popular culture in the nineteenth century were crucially concerned with *social control* is a controversial one. Some, like Golby and Purdue, claim that such politicization of the cultural is in itself misplaced.[6] Others, like Gareth Stedman Jones, worry about the term's origins in functionalist sociology, and its tendency to minimize elements of struggle and resistance within cultural relations.[7] Golby and Purdue's position will be discussed in more detail below, but it must be said at this point that their rewriting of cultural history in terms of individual choice and the free operation of market forces leaves too much unexplained. For example, within a few years of riots in the rural area of Bossenden Wood in the early part of the century both a church and a school were provided for the inhabitants. Those investigating the unrest were quite clear about the links between illiteracy and social unrest.[8] Again, in 1841, *Chambers's Journal* quotes the attitude of a factory owner towards the educataion of the working classes, 'I find that those who are best educated see their own interests the most clearly . . . I have the fewest disturbances, and manage the most easily with them'.[9] Similarly, R. K. Webb notes the determination of the ruling class to provide schools and libraries in mining areas in the 1840s in the aftermath of a long strike.[10] In 1834, however, 87 out of 540 contributors to the Report of the Poor Law Commission gave the radical press as a reason for riots and civil disturbance.[11] The conclusions may seem opposed, both ignorance and knowledge being seen as dangerous, but the common factor is the positing of a direct link between cultural consumption and political action. Both reflect a conviction that exposure to specified cultural texts can directly affect political actions and attitudes. The crucial difference is between exposure to texts regulated by institutions of education, and those produced outside the sphere of the dominant culture, by the radical press. We may now be rather squeamish about arguing for such causal relations between cultural consumption and political behaviour, or about attributing monolithic structures of control, but the ruling classes in nineteenth-century Britain certainly were not squeamish about trying to construct them.

For Gareth Stedman Jones, or Eileen and Stephen Yeo, the difficulty over 'social control' is quite other. All argue that 'social control' suggests an achieved state of domination, and thus tends to minimize the importance of struggle and resistance. Stedman Jones objects particularly to the attempt to graft the term onto marxist accounts of the history of popular culture. He argues that the use of the term leads to an overly mechanistic account of the relation between economic and cultural power, tending to see 'control' as something achieved, rather than seeing the elements of struggle within cultural production and consumption. He claims that 'social control' is an organic metaphor, which posits society as a natural self-regulating entity. But, if we decide to take on the term, surely the first step is precisely to *denaturalize* the control, rather than to deny its existence. Control is not equal to power, but suggests rather a struggle, tension and checking: 'keeping something under control' involves labour, whether ideological or practical. Social control is always something being worked towards: the exercise of hegemony rather than the imposition of ideology.

Richard Johnson expresses anxiety about the concept of 'social control', seeing it as 'a concept in search of a theory', but he does also acknowledge its importance in allowing us to separate accounts of cultural relations from the 'self-evaluation' of those involved in the production and theorization of culture and education in the nineteenth century.[12] In using the term, I aim to foreground the extent to which debates about popular culture in the nineteenth century were also debates about the nature of society, and about the necessity of extending the scope and the forms of power within cultural relations. I do not aim to suggest that the theorists and legislators of popular culture succeeded in destroying the cultural forms to which they objected so strenuously, but rather that, in seeking to intervene in cultural production and consumption, they sought also to assure the working classes of their interests in the maintenance of existing social relations. 'Social control' was an aspiration, the avowed object of debates about 'the dangers' of popular cuture. That there was active resistance to attempts to control the forms of popular culture is clearly detailed in this chapter. So, too, however, is the extent to which nineteenth-century cultural critics succeeded in establishing powerful equations between cultural significance and the existing forms of the dominant culture. The marginalization of penny fiction, and the banishing of large sections of the population to the realms of the 'loathsome and depraved' remains a problem for those who aim to theorize the possibility of resistance and struggle in the fields of politics and of culture.

In insisting on the importance of 'class relations', and 'social control' as explanatory terms for an analysis of nineteenth-century accounts of popular culture, I am challenging the sort of conclusions about nineteenth-century cultural relations contained in J. M. Golby and A. W. Purdue's book, *The Civilisation of the Crowd: Popular Culture in England 1750–1900*. Golby and Purdue criticize the politicization of accounts of popular culture in the nineteenth century. In a claim which echoes that of E. P. Thompson in his *Making of the English Working Class*, they argue that 'urban popular culture of the mid nineteenth century was, to a considerable degree, created by the people themselves'. This formulation is repeated with varying degrees of conviction: the culture which emerged 'owed much to the tastes and aspirations of the mass of the populace' and 'we would . . . question whether the popular culture of the day, however commercialised, does not broadly express the aspirations and desires of most men as most men are'.[13] Nonetheless, it is clearly challenging claims that the people were merely subjected to cultural forms in the interests of capitalism, in much the same way that Thompson challenged the historical argument that the working classes were completely subjected to the economic structures and interests of capitalism. The parallel is, however, both mischievous and misleading. Thompson was trying to rethink the categories of marxist historiography in order to theorize both social control and resistance to it. Golby and Purdue, however, play with concepts derived from marxist historians in order to demonstrate the repressive missionary basis of these concepts, and to refute arguments about social control.

The assertion that popular culture was, 'to a considerable degree, created by the people themselves' is not really tenable. The evidence of direct intervention by the ruling classes, as well as the history of ideological intervention in cultural forms which Golby and Purdue themselves describe makes the notion of the working classes as free agents in the construction of their own cultural forms insupportable. It is predictable that their attempts to modify the claim should resort to the denial of agency, the introduction of 'the mass' and the identification of the people with 'most men'.

But these are rhetorical strategies, interesting for what they reveal of Golby and Purdue's gender and cultural politics, but inadequate to the problem. The problem of 'agency' versus 'social control' is solved rather by changing the definitions of agency and choice. Instead of seeing capitalist relations of production as something that had to be imposed, or the wage contract as a modified form of exploitation, Golby and Purdue insist that capitalism was eagerly welcomed since it raised standards of living, that the desire for commodities was enough to ensure transformations in work routines, and that wage labour was fundamentally emancipatory. It is beyond the scope of this chapter to refute each of these in turn, but their implications for Golby and Purdue's view of cultural relations must be addressed. Firstly, they deny the importance of social control as a motivation for interventions in culture: that is to say they deny culture as a locus of power. Secondly, they argue that, as culture partook increasingly of the commodity form, individual choice increased and cultural forms reflected needs and desires more adequately. Thus they reject culture as a site of resistance.

Both of these conclusions will be challenged in the rest of this chapter by an analysis of writings about popular culture in the periodical press. The terms in which popular culture is discussed by the ruling classes, by Radicals or by trade unionists makes it clear that for them, at least, the relation between culture, politics and the state was crucial. The press was subjected to various determinations and forms of control. The Stamp Act, which aimed to keep news as an expensive commodity, led to long years of struggle, with sellers of 'the Great Unstamped' facing imprisonment as they defended their right to knowledge, which they equated with power. Radical journals faced financial crises as advertisers refused to buy space in publications whose aims were so contrary to their own interests.

Golby and Purdue would, presumably, see this as the free play of the market, a natural part of the commodification of leisure: 'its expansion into a mass industry was as natural a response to increased spending power as Thomas Lipton's shops'.[14] The notion that a particular form of retailing commodities is the archetype of nature is hard to accept, but it is part of Golby and Purdue's rhetoric to remove politics and replace it with nature. Thus they argue that 'blood sports were the natural focus for the energies of rural people'.[15]

Golby and Purdue argue quite precisely and provocatively against the conclusions of most recent studies of popular culture. Their strategy is to undermine one premise of an argument, and then to claim that this invalidates the conclusion. Thus they show that theorists of popular culture since the late eighteenth century have tended to repress the contradictions and forms of exploitation inherent in agricultural production, because of their hostility to industrialization. However, even if we accept this critique it does not follow that industrialization is then immune from criticism. To show that the eighteenth century was permeated by the commodity form does not diminish a critique of the production and distribution of cultural commodities in the nineteenth century.

Golby and Purdue set themselves up against all forms of moralizing, all attempts to criticize existing forms of culture. They lump together missionaries and marxists as 'killjoys' who seek to intervene in individual free choice. The result is that Golby and Purdue both naturalize and legitimize the cultural, political and gender assumptions which underpin existing cultural forms. 'If this book has a hero,' they say, 'it is Punch': Punch who has already been encountered in the book 'in the act of beating his wife to death'.[16] The veneer of depoliticization has worn very thin.

It is, then, in response to Golby and Purdue, and in order to foreground the relation between discussions of penny fiction and attempts to strengthen and naturalize existing power structures that I use the, admittedly problematic, concept of 'social control'. I do not use the term to describe an achieved state, but rather to indicate the extent to which debates about popular culture in the nineteenth century involve one (dominant) class knowingly acting so as to modify the behaviour of another in its own interests.

Of course, the patness of this formulation should already arouse suspicion. I seem to have been tricked by the oppositions and positions offered or ignored within 'the debate on social control' into repressing the very ambiguities and difficulties which are of interest to me. The general formulation above has nothing to say of the relation between class formation and gender division, or of the terms of the interaction between these and the economic, the political and the cultural. To some extent, it will be the work of this chapter to raise such questions, but the fact of their seeming so secondary, the difficulty of finding a place in the argument where they 'fit', must lead us back to some of the sources of the debate on social control, and to a questioning of their priorities and premises.

Although issues of gender are rarely foregrounded in histories of popular culture, the gender politics of some accounts are quite transparent. J. F. C. Harrison, in *Learning and Living*, gives an account of the development of institutions of adult education. This account is premised both on the authenticity and deep-rootedness of earlier forms of popular culture, and on the decay of judgement in the face of mass culture: 'the weakness of popular taste'.[17] These are familiar enough concerns in the field of cultural analysis. They are, however, linked to gendered accounts of cultural production and consumption. Thus Harrison speaks with approval of an editor who produces cheap editions of Milton, Burns and Pope, but warns that 'there was also a lower class of fiction published such as Miss Cummin's *Lamplighter* and Mrs Roche's *Children of the Abbey*'.[18] This casual identification of cultural decline with the literary production of women goes unnoticed, and unjustified.

Harrison describes the political writings produced for 'working men of the metropolis' but also mentions 'an ample provision of fiction and anecdote for the mental regalement of their wives and the rising generation'.[19] Now it may be said in Harrison's defence that he is merely reproducing the divisions already found within Victorian popular culture, and to an extent this is true, if unhelpful. When we look more carefully at the periodical press, however, we will find that women did participate in political debates and organization, and that men both wrote and read cheap fiction. Harrison is reproducing ideology as fact. The political and gender categories he brings to bear on his 'facts' are finally unavoidable as he describes the differences in cultural aspirations of the working class 'from the West Riding pantheon of self-educated working men to the Bradford mill girls who signed the marriage register with a mark'.[20] What happened to the self-educated women?

The difficulty of answering this question in any detail suggests the extent to which the cultural struggles of women disappear from accounts of popular culture. When we look at histories of education in the nineteenth century we will find it requires a constant effort to work out what girls and women were doing, and how they felt about it. This fact is of importance not only for feminists. In ignoring the ways in which working-class and middle-class women participated differently in the production and consumption of cultural forms, historians of popular culture are working with incomplete concepts of class, which cannot adequately account for the complexities of class relations in the nineteenth century.[21]

From nineteenth-century sources we can discover that women were involved in cultural production: worryingly so as far as some writers were concerned. Thus we find Dixon Hepworth, writing about popular fiction in the *Daily News* in 1847, 'sorry to have to say that the great majority of these scandalous stories are written by females'.[22] Henry Mayhew's accounts of the streetlife of London, written in 1851, include an account of the active involvement of women in the publication of cheap literature. Many of the 'improving' periodicals of the day were edited or written by women. Yet most accounts of popular culture are silent on the participation of women.

Walton and Walvin, in *Leisure in Britain: 1780–1939*, admit the silence, but preserve it anyway. David Vincent's chapter in this book explores 'Reading in the Working Class Home' and shows the ideological and political investments of both the ruling classes and working class radicals in literacy. He provides some useful insights into the range of political concerns focused around education and the consumption of literature but, surprisingly for an account focused on the home, the domestic, assumes that the self-improving reader must be male. 'The reader', it seems, 'needed free time from the demands of his family', and if the male reader 'required, as he often did, help and encouragement, he looked not to his family but to other working men in the community'.[23] Since Mechanics' Institutes generally did not admit women to membership it would seem here, at least, he was free from distraction.

What seems like a surprising omission in Vincent's account, elsewhere appears as a structured absence. If we look at the cultural forms discussed in Eileen and Stephen Yeo's *Popular Culture and Class Conflict* the reasons for the invisibility of women become much clearer. Chapters in the book deal with 'the rise and suppression of popular church music' (largely plebeian and all-male choirs and bands being supplanted and suppressed by the clergy and the clergy's wives and sisters), 'the suppression of street football in Derby in the first half of the nineteenth century' (a recreational form which women struggled to retain, but in which they did not participate) and 'the culture of working class movements'.

'Working class movements' is a term with its own gender history. Trade Union activity, political organization, even Temperance movements are included, but with an inbuilt set of priorities which always privileges the major institutions and parties of male political organization. This has particular implications for the analysis of penny fiction. As we shall see, both Radicals and Chartists generally despised and ignored penny fiction, and saw it as a distraction from political activism, of interest only to women. This attitude has been reproduced in much recent writing on the popular culture of the nineteenth century. Availability of sources, an implicit concept of history as progress and a particular definition of the working class coincide to marginalize the political and cultural activities of working women. This marginalization is exacerbated by the tendency of historians of popular culture to focus on public and communal activities, in which women generally did not participate.

There are, of course, very good reasons for concentrating on the public and the communal in popular culture. These are the cultural forms devalued by a philosophy of individualism, and the decision to take them seriously is an important one. Also, as an attempt to broaden definitions of political struggle, to see a range of activities in their dimension as struggle over time and space, it is both historically and theoretically useful. But, over and over again, this concentration foregrounds cultural forms which are exclusively male, and then redefines these as 'an essentially common working class situation'.[24]

One reason for the concentration on literary forms of popular culture in this chapter, then, lies in the fact that these forms were both produced and consumed by women, as well as by men. There are, however, also very good historical reasons for such an emphasis. As both Webb and Vincent argue, the expansion of written texts, and the degree and terms of access to them were crucial areas of concern for the Victorian ruling classes. Reading was a peculiarly problematic activity. Much of it, although less of it than one might suspect, took place in the home. The home, which was identified with 'the working class family as the last remaining social structure capable of nurturing and sustaining habits of discipline and rational behaviour', was also worryingly removed from observation and control.[25] The very place which was valorized as the site of social control was simultaneously dangerous in its privacy and invisibility. The concern over literature and reading is very often a concern about the state of the working-class family, and ultimately about the social relations of the state.

As well as worrying about the fact of reading, there was a lot of concern about the matter of reading. We will see when we examine responses to the increase in cheap publications that by far the greatest concern was over fiction. Fiction was identified with irrationalism and with excess. Fanny Mayne and Dixon Hepworth hold it responsible for political radicalism, while writers in the radical press hold it responsible for political ignorance and apathy. Poetry, on the other hand, was almost always thought of as improving. The extent to which the Radical and Chartist press accepted judgements about the worthlessness of fiction and the transcendence of poetry meant, however, that they were unable to challenge dominant accounts of literary quality and value.

This widespread concern about reading was not just a concern about literacy. The nineteenth century did see a qualitative and quantitative change in printed texts and in their availability. The material causes of this expansion are readily identifiable. In the case of the newspaper, for example, the development of the iron press allowed for the production of newspapers in broadsheet form. The steam-powered printing machine, developed in 1817, led to faster print runs. By the 1860s type revolving machines allowed for print runs of 18,000 copies per hour. The invention of a machine to convert woodpulp into paper meant cheaper paper, as well as reducing the disease and distress which had been endemic to the production of paper from rags. Finally, the telegraph made possible a national system of news gathering, and the development of the railways reduced the cost of distribution by 80 per cent.[26]

Other literary forms were similarly affected. I am using 'literary' here in the broad sense we will find in nineteenth-century periodicals, rather than the narrower sense of particular fictional texts. There was a massive increase in the production of all forms of literature throughout the century: periodicals, biographies, scientific texts, cheap editions of 'classic' fiction, almanacs, and a range of penny publications. By 1840 there were approximately eighty cheap periodicals circulating in London, of which 'twenty-two contained nothing but romances or stories'.[27] Literacy increased throughout the century. Libraries, Mechanics' Institutes and pubs became the centres of both individual and communal consumption of texts. The printed word became a problem in a new and urgent way as the century progressed.

In order to understand how this problem was conceived, and analysed, in relation to forms of literary producion variously called cheap, or popular, or low, it is important to look at how the dominant culture defined itself, and at how it theorized the production and consumption of texts, particularly in relation to the possibilities of education. If we are to argue that 'popular culture' was a political, social and gender problem, we must recognize that it was also, precisely, a cultural problem. That is to say that arguments about the role and function of culture must be taken quite seriously in themselves, before their relation to other sorts of arguments and practices can be established. Throughout the century, the area of 'the cultural' was delineated, debated, defended and transformed. In order to assess the implications of this for analyses and definitions of popular culture we will now look at perhaps the archetypal theorist of culture in its relation to the state and the individual: Matthew Arnold. Arnold was writing about culture some twenty years after most of the cultural critics we will examine in this chapter. Nonetheless, a careful reading of his analyses of cultural forms will be useful, since such analyses represent a sedimentation, a systematized account, of the sorts of judgements about culture and politics which we will find in the periodicals of the 1840s and 1850s. By comparing his writings on culture and society with earlier accounts by Coleridge we can more easily analyse the shifts that are taking place, at a less theorised level, in the period examined in this chapter.

Arnold is known as a poet, a cultural theorist and an educationalist, and it is the fusion of these three concerns that is of interest here. His practical involvement in institutions of education, as a Schools Inspector, as well as his descriptive and analytic accounts of education abroad, place him within a certain rhetoric concerning the potential, necessity and priorities of education in its relation to the state. His work as a poet, and his prioritizing of the poetic form among other forms of cultural production, reflects a judgement about the improving qualities of poetry. His attempt to claim for culture a central role in the establishment and maintenance of hegemony marks a qualitative shift in textual and artistic criticism. Arnold's definitions of culture are far from precise, though whether this represents confusion or a comfortable belief that his readers will have no doubt about his meaning is not clear. Perhaps it comes to the same thing. Nonetheless, 'culture' is variously described in *Culture and Anarchy*, first published in 1869, as 'the disinterested endeavour after man's perfection', as 'reading observing, and thinking', as making 'the will of God prevail', and as 'the study of perfection'.[28] The emphases and implications are clearly different in each case. The discourse is, however, resolutely moral.

Arnold sees culture as both constituting and permitting a moral imperative. The pursuit of culture is the act of making God's will prevail. The propagation of culture is the means for a general expansion of humanity. His discourse functions through the construction of social and spiritual oppositions: he favours knowing rather than doing, the communal rather than the individualistic, and culture rather than anarchy.

The politics of Arnold's project is, in a sense, inescapable, but few accounts have taken on the complex class mediations involved in his analyses of culture. The charge of elitism must stand. Although he condemns the production of 'popular' texts aimed at the assumed interests of the masses, he is completely unable to imagine 'the masses' producing their own texts or cultural forms. His observation that 'the sterner self of the populace likes bawling, hustling and smashing; the lighter self, beer', is a patronizing and rather self-conscious bad joke.[29]

Similarly, his insistence that the 'raw and unkindled masses of humanity' must be touched with sweetness and light frequently slips into a suggestion that they could reasonably be forced into doing what is best for them. Arnold claims that culture 'seeks to do away with classes', yet later insists that it is only when 'the Populace', rather than the middle classes and aristocracy, try to do as they like that the social fabric is in danger.[30] There is quite a lot of substance to Chris Baldick's claim that Arnold advocated the influence of poetry 'upon the masses . . . to wean them from class conflict'.[31]

It is, however, important to notice the ambiguity of the class position from which Arnold spoke, in order to appreciate the novelty and the power of his elision of the cultural and the political. At a structural level, this ambiguity is quite clear: Arnold divides society into three groups, and the individual psyche into two parts, with none of which he identifies himself. *Culture and Anarchy* is a critique of the cultural capital of the aristocracy. His attack on the worthlessness of a classical education which panders to nothing but curiosity is taking on a long history of aristocratic culture. He also insists that the aristocracy is not fit to supply social authority. Arnold specifically rejects culture as an engine of class distinction, and argues instead for culture as 'a desire to leave the world a better place'.[32]

His relationship to the middle classes is in some senses equally problematic: they, after all, are the Philistines. He criticizes the equation of greatness with wealth or with industrialization. He has thus taken on two fundamental tenets of capitalism, and he goes on to criticize individualism, and the desire to do what one likes. His prioritizing of knowing over doing was likewise unlikely to lead to his adoption as a spokesman of the Victorian capitalist class.

What Arnold is proposing, however, is nothing less than a new form of hegemony: a formulation of social and cultural relations which will command general assent. Thus, when Arnold talks of culture in its relation to the state he does so not in the name of one particular social class, but in terms of supposedly universal perceptions about the nature of culture and society. Culture is, he argues, intimately connected with the state. It establishes the legitimacy of the state, indeed 'suggests the idea of the state' as a representative of communal values of humanity.[33] Culture further allows the development of our 'best selves' or 'right reason' which makes us condemn tumult, demonstrations and disorder. Thus it both justifies the existence of the state and shows the need to repress any dissent from it.

At this point the precariousness of Arnold's position becomes apparent. Repression is in tension with the maintenance of moral and intellectual hegemony, indeed it signals its breakdown. It is a vulnerable point in the argument of *Culture and Anarchy* when Arnold both claims to speak for all humanity and insists that riots must be forbidden and repressed. Here, in this difficulty, the ultimate nature of Arnold's class investment shows through: 'without order there can be no society, and without society there can be no human protection', but that society must, and will, be Victorian capitalism.[34]

This, then, is the way in which culture is politicized in *Culture and Anarchy*. It is not just the rather obvious elitism of his language, or the optimistic wishing away of class, but the construction of a discourse in which culture is centrally implicated in the maintenance of hegemony. It is also a discourse with a very shrewd understanding of history, which might otherwise be characterized as a fear of following through its own implications. The time is not yet right, Arnold insists, for the man (*sic*) of culture to achieve power.

Finally, it is worth noting the resolute empiricism of Arnold's project, and the consequent paucity of its theorizing of cultural consumption. Arnold insists that he is opposed to abstract systems of theorizing. He looks instead for texts which will serve the practical and moral purposes he desires. The list is substantial: philosophy, poetry, history, science, religion. The mere immersion in these texts will lead to a civilizing effect. Thus, 'Effects Theory', which argues that the stimulus of a particular text operates in observable ways upon discrete individuals, and which underpins later accounts of the workings and dangers of popular culture, particularly of television, can be seen to have its grounding in accounts of the dominant culture.

Arnold was not theorizing and writing in isolation. His account of culture and of its social dimension owes much to the political writings of Coleridge. Coleridge had drawn a distinction between 'civilization', which was the material progress of civil society, and 'cultivation' which was 'the harmonious development of those qualities and faculties that characterize our *humanity*'.[35] In his *Lay Sermons* and in *The Constitution of the Church and State*, Coleridge developed a critique of the moral, political and spiritual bankruptcy of a social system which addressed only the imperatives of civilization. He argued for the need to establish a Clerisy, 'a permanent class or order' which would be responsible for the development of speculative thought and the dissemination of culture. Such a group was to be financed by the nation, since it alone could guarantee to mediate between the competing social forces of permanence and progression, and thus to ensure a viable and significant form of society.

Coleridge's project involved a complete reformulation of the relations between social structures and philosophical and cultural categories. In this sense, it was far more radical than Arnold's project which, despite its gesturing towards philosophy and history, was relatively narrow in its conception of the cultural transformations implied by its implementation. In another sense, however, Coleridge's project was more limited. It relied on the notion of the Clerisy as a particular class, who were to hand down the benefits of culture and philosophical thought to those below them. Arnold moved beyond this model to the extent that his account of the spiritual and political effects of culture attempted to demonstrate a general applicability. He diminished the scale of Coleridge's project, but offered instead a relation to culture which was available to all subjects.

This difference is also manifest in Arnold's positioning of himself outside the social categories he constructs, while Coleridge clearly identifies himself with the Clerisy, and addresses his texts '*ad clerum*'. Coleridge's Clerisy was a class, while Arnold's cultured minority were individuals with no class loyalties. All subjects could, and should, aspire to the benefits of culture, in Arnold's model. What was a social project in Coleridge has become, in Arnold, a seemingly individual project with social implications. As I have argued, the absence of class in Arnold's account cannot be sustained. He does have a particular notion of the state, and of its role in maintaining the social relations of nineteenth-century Britain. Culture is to play a central role in this process. It is, however, the apparent universality of Arnold's model which explains its hegemonic role in the theorization of culture and society.

The differences between Coleridge and Arnold can usefully be related to changing political responses to mass literacy between 1790 and 1870. Coleridge's model of an educated class, handing down the benefits of its knowledge to those below it, corresponds quite closely to interventions in mass literacy in the 1790s. Olivia Smith, in *The Politics of Language 1791–1819*, describes the work of Hannah More in producing *Cheap Repository Tracts* which were distributed to the poor. These tracts argued the case for social stability, and for moral and spiritual improvement. This sort of initiative was accompanied by more direct attempts at repression: Paine's *Rights of Man* was banned, and its readers were persecuted.

Throughout the nineteenth century, however, critics and politicians were increasingly confronted, not just with the fact of working-class literacy, but with working-class writing, or at least with forms of literature over which they had no control. This required a more complex response. It was not enough just to hand down suitable texts and bits of knowledge. What was required was a general model of the effectivity of culture. Even Fanny Mayne, by 1852, was forced to recognize the importance of understanding the power of the narrative forms of penny fiction. The project thus moves from repression coupled with patronage, to a more thorough intervention in the forms of reading matter being consumed by the working classes. This project is still partial by 1855, and the older responses remain very much in evidence. Its emergence is, however, clearly visible in the texts discussed in this chapter.

There was a range of texts throughout the nineteenth century addressing the relation between culture and the political fabric of the state, with particular reference to education. In the 1830s the Central Society of Education was campaigning for governmental intervention in elementary education. Its prospectus made the stake in this quite clear: 'to learn by what means individuals may be best fitted in health, in mind and in morals to fill the stations which they are destined to occupy in society'.[36] They were concerned precisely about the inadequacy of existing forms to this task. They opposed Charity Schools, since these merely taught dependence. They were unhappy about both the National and British and Foreign Schools Societies, since both taught minimal skills of literacy using texts, chiefly the Bible, which were largely incomprehensible to their readers. In 1837 B. F. Duppa complained that there was no system in elementary education 'for the formation of habits of patient industry'.[37]

In 1858 James Augustus St John was still concerned about the failure of educational institutions to involve the great majority of the population in the pursuit of culture. He advocated the education of women as a means to civilize the whole family. He also advocated cheap editions of history, poetry 'and even good novels'.[38]

By the end of the century, J. C. Collins had appropriated this rhetoric of civilization and control specifically for English literature: 'as an instrument of political education it is to warn, to admonish, to guide'.[39] The study of literature was to provide instruction for the individual in that which pertains to his or her relations to the state, and duties as a citizen.

This discourse of education and social control was, inevitably, fragmented by class and gender. As Margaret Bryant argues, the middle classes felt particularly neglected in relation to the reforms which restructured elementary education throughout the 1840s and 1850s, and much of this concern focused on the education of women. As early as 1838, the Central Society of Education had expressed concern over the vacuum in the education of middle-class women. Lady Ellis complained that they were trained for nothing other than teaching, and that a broader education would qualify them for more occupations, as well as assuring a right direction of the affections.[40] All of the major battles over access for, mainly middle-class, women to secondary and higher education were fought in the years 1845–95.

Of course, this account of education as social control was not the whole story. There was always a tension between the real potential for power gained through knowledge, and the attempt to use knowledge to naturalize the political impotence of large sections of the British population. David Vincent makes it clear that, 'useful knowledge was seen by self-educated working men as a means of arming themselves to do battle with the established order which the Central Society was striving to protect'.[41] The argument that access to knowledge brings the possibility of social transformation should be treated with caution, however, and the testimony of one working woman, writing in 1892, makes the difficulties in such an account apparent. Mary Smith struggled to educate herself, as a means both to spiritual improvement and social advancement. At elementary schools she learned little apart from needlework. Largely through her own efforts she gained sufficient, or rather excessive, knowledge in order to become a governess, but the dangers this knowlege implied were inescapable: 'I was shrewd enough to know . . . that whatever incidents of knowledge or reading I might display, would rather tell against than for me.'[42] Mary Smith was clear that the expansion of her spiritual or critical faculties was of little use to her employers, whose interest lay, rather, in docility.

ATTITUDES TO POPULAR FICTION IN THE PERIODICAL PRESS

Arguments about the social implications of increased literacy and greater cultural accessibility achieve one sort of focus in accounts of the dangers and effects of penny fiction. My analysis of accounts of popular fiction in the periodical press will begin with the 1830s. In the early 1830s, there was a huge expansion in 'improving' periodicals, which carried very little fiction. What cheap fiction was available tended to be reprints of existing material. By the end of the 1830s, however, there was a significant and thriving trade in the production of popular romances and adventure narratives for the working classes.

In the early 1830s, we can still identify the survival of many of the most salient features of the discourse of 'the peasant poet': an assumption of common cultural objectives, and an attempt to assert universal cultural values. Yet, at the same time, there are radically different cultural expectations and presuppositions which are articulated across a range of publications. Class relations and mediations are inescapable in accounts of the cultural forms which were, or 'should have been', consumed in the 1830s. The early 1830s saw some crucial transformations within the class structure of Britain. The middle classes were brought more directly within the apparatus of the state. The working classes remained excluded from both political and economic power, and began to develop their own forms of organization and resistance which very gradually and complexly moved from the language of late eighteenth century Radicalism to the language of class struggle. Culture, as the site of values, perceptions, and practices which represented themselves as universal, became an important element in the attempt both to repress and to transform class relations.

The Society for the Diffusion of Useful Knowledge, in its *Penny Magazine*, seemed both confident and optimistic about the possibilities of expanding literacy leading to social harmony. They advocated general literacy for the working classes, or at least for working men, since, 'the more he knows, the less hasty and the less violent will be his opinions' or, more explicitly, 'the intelligent [working classes] will not be the dupes of demagogues or incendiaries'.[43] The *Penny Magazine* did also express its concern over the inadequacy of much elementary teaching, particularly in terms of its failure to provide sufficient guidance about moral and political behaviour, but these doubts did not undermine the *Penny Magazine*'s commitment to the extension of literacy and the increasing availability of cheap texts.

The confidence expressed by members of the society for the Diffusion of Useful Knowledge in the efficacy of knowledge as a means of social control was based both on their own position as mediators of that knowledge and on a genuine attempt to construct a cultural tradition that included, or perhaps appropriated, the articulated experiences of writers from different social classes. The two, as in the case of 'the peasant poets', are closely related.

The Society for the Diffusion of Useful Knowledge was essentially interested in what the working classes could be taught, or brought, to read rather than what they actually were reading. There is little mention of the penny press, or of fiction generally. The *Penny Magazine* was convinced that 'there is a great need of raising among the people a sentiment of admiration for what is beautiful'.[44] They sought to inculcate standards of literary appreciation, and to make available information on a wide range of scientific and historical subjects. The *Penny Magazine* published a number of moral fables and short tales, but the bulk of its 'imaginative' content was poetry. Nature poets were heavily favoured, suggesting the accessibility and manageably oppositional position which were valued in 'the peasant poets'. Burns and Wordsworth appear in the *Penny Magazine*, which also published poems like 'The Weaver's Song' by Barry Cornwall, which argued for class harmony on the basis of common humanity:

> There is not a creature, from England's king
> To the peasant that delves the soil,
> That knows half the pleasures the seasons bring
> If he have not his share of toil.[45]

The Society for Promoting Christian Knowledge was also basically confident about the implications of increased literacy. The *Saturday Magazine*, in 1833, argued that cheap editions should be welcomed. Far from impairing the capacity for hard manual labour, a frequent enough charge, it was held that mental improvement actually led to greater diligence and a reduction in criminal behaviour: 'intellectual culltivation will, in many instances, call men off from gross and vulgar gratifications'.[46] Since both Established and Dissenting religions were central to the institutions of elementary education it is not surprising that the *Saturday Magazine* contained numerous articles both defending the expansion of education and proposing the forms in which such an expansion should take place. They had both an ideological and practical stake in the increase of literacy. Nonetheless, looking back on the 1830s in an article published in 1844, the *Saturday Magazine* is less sanguine about the nature and implications of increased cultural consumption, 'week after week there poured forth, in various shapes and in countless thousands, low-priced publications, teeming with licentiousness and sedition, with impiety and blasphemy. . . . This state of things proved the necessity of meeting the demand for popular literature with a supply of such as might fairly be permitted to circulate in a Christian country'.[47] The *Saturday Magazine* saw itself as an important part of the attempt to move the reading matter of the working classes from sedition and blasphemy to piety and Christian morals.

The *Saturday Magazine* also paid attention to poets writing outside the dominant tradition. Charles Crocker, the shoemaker poet, was praised for his ability to represent his experiences and perceptions 'without contracting a single habit unsuitable to his station in life'.[48] The *Saturday Magazine* also took an interest in the preservation of 'pre-literate' cultural forms: 'popular legends and fictions'. Once more, the interest was in the construction of a continuity of interests and of cultural reference between dominant and popular cultures, rather that in any attempt to assess the implications of existing forms of penny fiction and popular literature.

W. J. Fox, writing in *The London Review* in 1835, has, to a certain extent, similar preoccupations. He is trying to introduce Ebenezer Elliott to 'the nation's muster-roll of bards', as someone who not only speaks for the people, but from them.[49] Fox argues for both the necessity and the desirability of the people having 'a literature of their own', although he does not scruple to set himself up as an arbiter of its authenticity, consistently valuing those texts which demonstrate 'sturdy straightforwardness'. He does, however, also see the institutional and political changes such a transformation would require. He attacks patronage as a crude means of controlling popular articulations, claiming that it tends to honour individual writers, while denying the socially determined nature of their writing. He also criticizes Stamp Duty, which made newspapers either unaffordable by the majority, or illegal, because such a tax represents an attempt to deny the necessary and important social changes brought about by popular literacy.

The *Poor Man's Guardian* was published 'contrary to "Law" to try the power of "might" against "right"' in the early 1830s.[50] As a newspaper selling at one penny, and paying no Stamp Duty, it was illegal. Hundreds of men and women were imprisoned for selling copies of the *Poor Man's Guardian*. Its slogan 'Knowledge is Power' provided the focus for a range of political groups and individuals, who saw the *Poor Man's Guardian* as a crucial element in the struggle against a repressive state. Clearly the possibilities for education perceived by the *Poor Man's Guardian* were not the same as those predicted by the Society for the Diffusion of Useful Knowledge. The *Poor Man's Guardian* had little time for imaginative literature: 'as for literature, of course, *that* also is made to suit the taste and views of the wealthy'.[51] They saw it as giving false charm to an unnatural society. The texts which were advertised in cheap editions in the *Poor Man's Guardian* included algebra, natural history, philosophy, French grammar and poetry. The *Poor Man's Guardian* was thus committed to a project of self-education as the means to acquiring the cultural capital to challenge the existing social order. Penny fiction, or humorous publications, were not mentioned in its pages. They were presumably seen as a distraction and an irrelevance in relation to the struggle for a free press and a free people.

Since the *Crisis* was an Owenist publication, it is not surprising to find considerable discussion of cultural politics within its pages. Owenism always argued for the importance of ideology and representation in determining political behaviour. The judgements about cultural production in the *Crisis*, however, seem to endorse many of the presuppositions of the dominant literate culture.

A significant amount of poetry was published in the *Crisis*, much by poets who are now unknown although, once more, Wordsworth is given a privileged place. Articles in the journal argue the need to expand the numbers of cheap editions, and criticize the system of patronage as evil. They do thus challenge existing relations of cultural production and consumption. The implications of the transformations they suggest, however, seem to take fairly contradictory forms. On the one hand, the aim seems to be to make existing cultural forms more accessible, and they note: 'the gradual advancement which the wealth-producing part of the population are making in the acquirement of a taste for those refinements of knowledge and art, which enamel the surface of society, and contribute so much to the happiness and comforts of life'.[52] On the other hand, a letter to the *Crisis* published in 1832 seems to confront the limits of such a conception of inevitable and gradual democratization of culture.[53] It argues that the arts survive only because the rich have the time, the education and the money to support them. Thus, greater equality would inevitably lead to cultural decline. What the article goes on to say is that it would also lead to the production of forms of art better suited to human need, but it lacks the theoretical vocabulary to use this insight to subvert existing judgements about the value and function of art. The argument seems to be trapped by the power of certain definitions of the aesthetic into seeing the democratization of society as the cause of inevitable cultural decline. This correspondent is reprimanded by the *Crisis* for failing to realize the amount of general wealth that would be created by a truly rational and democratic society, but the fundamental relation proposed between the ruling classes and cultural production is never properly challenged.

The *Pioneer*, a Trade Union publication, was highly critical of aristocratic patronage of the arts. The journal carried a column on literature, 'as the working-men are now forming libraries'.[54] It also published a number of poems, each representing the experiences of a particular trade: 'Builders' Union' and 'The Labourer's Prophecy'. Its interest, however, was not just in the extension of cultural forms but in their transformation. An article published in 1834 criticizes street football in Derby. It sees it as time-wasting and degrading. It encourages Trade Unionists to give up the sport, so that 'men will bless your virtue, and women love your soul'.[55] Again, the impetus behind this lies in the conviction that such forms of popular culture are merely distracting and depoliticizing. The result of such judgements, however, is the further fragmentation of the working class into the 'serious and politically significant' and the 'frivolous and politically irrelevant'.

By 1840, the Chartist publication, the *Northern Star*, shows clear evidence of an expectation that its readership will involve itself in a broad range of literary texts. The 'Literature' section examines recent publications on the political structure of North America, on English proverbs, and also on the poetry of Ebenezer Elliott and Eliza Cook. Advertisements in the *Northern Star* include 'Cheap Illustrations of Boz', Robert Southey's 'Drama of Wat Tyler', Byron, and Godwin in the list of titles. An interesting development in the split between groups such as the Society for the Diffusion of Useful Knowledge, which sought to assure social control through an extension of education, and radical politicians who sought to increase the power of the 'working man' through access to knowledge, can be found in the *Northern Star*'s column, 'Chartism from Shakespeare'. The column uses extracts from *Coriolanus, Julius Caesar* and *Antony and Cleopatra* to criticize oppressive government. It thus seeks to reappropriate dominant cultural representations in order to criticize the very group which has perpetuated them. It tries both to make the writings of Shakespeare accessible, and to mobilize them for the Chartist cause. It therefore seeks to bring the people to the site of dominant culture, in search of cultural capital. Once more, however, there is no discussion of the nature, or implications, of penny fiction. The aim is to encourage the working classes to claim their share of the cultural capital of their rulers. There is no attempt to account for the power or the potential of the fictional forms which were being consumed by the working classes in ever greater numbers.

In the 1840s there were a number of 'magazines of popular progress' which used the language of philosophical Radicalism to argue for transformations in social and cultural relations which would lead to greater harmony and equality.[56] William and Mary Howitt's *People's Journal* was consistently concerned with the analysis of cultural production, and with the humanitarian basis of literature. An article by Mrs Percy Sinnett in 1848 tries to establish the relation between cultural forms and national identity. The article addresses the dangerous consequences of the fragmentation and mutual hostility observable within both cultural and political spheres. It acknowledges the difficulties of the concept 'popular' and explores its different meanings, although in the end settling for a formulation which is, at best, mystificatory: 'that which springs spontaneously from the heart and inner life of the people'.[57] The article argues for the need to encourage and create a popular literature, in order to heal the split between high literature and national culture. Dickens and Eugène Sue are both praised as writers who fulfil the possibilities of literature as a focus of 'class understanding'. Because of its use of mechanisms of identification, and its descriptive powers, the novel is the best possible agent of class mediation: 'the popular novel has often sent an electric thrill of common human feeling from Buckingham Palace to the mechanics' institute and the milliner's back parlour'.[58] Mrs Sinnett concludes that critical and political interventions aimed at controlling popular literature are permissible precisely because literature is such a powerful medium for the transformation of class relations.

It is interesting that Mrs Sinnett is as concerned about the milliner as the mechanic. The *People's Journal* had many women

contributors, as well as female readers. It published the poetry of
Eliza Cook as well as Ebenezer Elliott, in a general attempt to give
a place to writers outside the dominant tradition. Indeed, as Brian
Maidment says, 'women were prominent as editors, as well as
contributors, to the magazines of popular progress in ways quite
unparalleled in the period'.[59] Women were beginning to establish
an expertise and an institutional position from which to embark on
cultural and literary criticism which was not to be seriously
challenged until the institutionalization of the study of literature at
the end of the century.

By 1847, the confident optimism which characterized the publications of the Society for the Diffusion of Useful Knowledge and
the Society for Promoting Christian Knowledge had been shaken
by the apparent ineffectiveness of these organizations, and the
increase, in particular, of penny fiction. Dixon J. Hepworth wrote a
series of articles on 'The Literature of the Lower Orders' in the *Daily
News* in 1847. He attacks the penny press, in particular Lloyd's
Penny Miscellany. Literature, he argues, has a 'vast influence for
good or evil in the education of the masses'.[60] It is a powerful force
in the determination of national character. Hepworth describes the
heroes of Lloyd's fiction as robbers, pirates and murderers and the
tales as grotesque and horrible. The most worrying feature is that,
as romances, they excite sympathy and identification among an
ignorant readership, 'for the greater part females'.[61] As women
were increasingly being represented as the moral focus of family
life, this aberrant and uncontrollable consumption of romantic
fiction was seen as dangerous. Women writers also come in for
Hepworth's criticism. Mrs Reynolds is singled out for attack in
relation to her novel *Gretna Green*, which Hepworth insists
inflames the passions, although he later agrees that, actually, the
novel shows no impropriety. The ease with which Hepworth
contradicts himself, without changing his argument, is an indication
of the paucity of textual example or analysis in his criticisms. He
insists that 'we denounce the impurity, but we cannot soil our pages
with it'.[62] The argument thus proceeds with innuendo and
generalizations which say more about the level of Hepworth's
anxiety over penny fiction than they do about the contents of that
fiction. He concludes, however, on a fairly optimistic note,
arguing that such fiction will inevitably diminish as more cheap
books become available, and the working classes become better
educated.

The publications which caused 'a problem' for cultural critics are
exemplified by Lloyd's and Reynolds's *Miscellanies*, both published

in the 1840s. Lloyd's *Miscellany* was almost completely devoted to fiction, particularly romance. The stories are usually set in an aristocratic social milieu. They are stories of love, treachery, betrayal and murder. The *Miscellany* also included articles of 'general interest', for example, one by Susan Clifford which detailed the mythological descent of the passions from Satan! Despite the force of moral revulsion from Lloyd's publications, most of the stories now seem positively moral, oppressively so in their mobilization of 'just retribution' for women gone astray. 'The Tale of Louisa Barton' describes a woman who married against her father's will. This disobedience is punished by divorce, financial ruin, drunkenness, prostitution and disease.

Reynolds's *Miscellany* carried a broader range of material. Fiction was, once more, absolutely central, but there were also 'improving lessons', recipes, and 'letters to the industrious classes'. Reynolds became an active Chartist after 1848. His *Political Instructor*, which was mostly devoted to political analysis, failed after a year. In the *Miscellany*, however, he tried to combine his fictional and political interests. The attempt is interesting, particularly since the Chartist press generally was extremely wary of fiction, seeing it as a dangerous distraction from the business of politics. Reynolds, however, tried to use the appeal of his fiction to gain an audience for his political analyses. In 1847 the *Miscellany* had a circulation of 30,000. Reynolds's *Mysteries of London* sold over one million copies within a decade of its publication.[63] *Mysteries of London*, although a fictional text, contained many references to contemporary social and political life. Its heroine was one of the many female characters in popular fiction who was allowed to demonstrate courage, stamina and strength, even, in a clearly transgressive gesture, disguising herself as a boy. At the same time, however, the merging of these fictional and political interests does raise some difficult political questions. What sort of 'imaginary' was being supported by romantic representations focused so clearly on members of the aristocracy? Did these representations leave any space for critique? There is something peculiarly unsettling about the juxtaposition of an advertisement for a Chartist meeting and an advice column on etiquette. Fanny Mayne, for one, found it deeply unsettling.

The *Englishwoman's Magazine* was seriously interested in the analysis of 'popular literature'. In 1850, Fanny Mayne wrote an article complaining of the dangers of unchecked literary production. She was emphatic about the dangers of the working classes consuming violent and morbid tales:

Can a man touch pitch and his hands not be defiled? Can he take fire in his bosom, and his clothes not be burned? Surely not. As certainly as we read a glowing description of any transaction – be it what it may – we throw ourselves into the situation of the describers or of the actors in that transaction. Man, by nature, is a being of imitative sympathy. Facts testify to this; witness the well known truth, that when one person had, not long ago, thrown himself from the monument, others tried to do the same; that poisoning, begets poisoners; a murder, murderers; down to the fact of our every-day experience, that one *yawner* in a company will produce several.

Tales of imagination, then, that deal in murders, and in other species of iniquity, lead to the actual commission of similar sins.[64]

Her rhetorical comparison between reading material circulating in the penny presses and 'Satan and his agents on earth' is meant to be taken quite literally. She poses it as a political and moral duty of the 'higher classes', having allowed the spread of literacy, to control the texts that are actually being consumed:

Those who *love their country*, will try to assist in this work; for the lawlessness and chartism disseminated by the penny press, is undermining the foundations of our tranquillity. Those who *love the souls* of their fellow-creatures will be up and doing in providing a substitute for the atrocities and impurities described and rendered attractive in this pernicious literature. Those who desire *the glory of their God* will do all that in them lies to hinder the circulation of blasphemous and shocking works against the Most High and his Word.[65]

Fanny Mayne thus combines political, literary and religious discourses in her insistence that the ruling classes must understand the power of popular fiction, and intervene to 'provide a substitute'. This attempt to address problems of politics, morality and religion through intervention in one particular form of popular culture is echoed in many of the responses to television which will be examined in chapter 6.

Fanny Mayne frequently refers to the consumption of literature as a kind of perverse sexuality: 'reading is a sensual gratification'.[66] After a series of articles in the *Englishwoman's Magazine* laying out the scale and nature of the problem, the particular danger to women and youths, the political dangers of mixing socialism with the fascination of fiction, she eventually founded the *True Briton* in 1852. This magazine was meant to provide reading matter which would not only interest and educate the working classes, but also 'reach their hearts'. She wanted to use the power and appeal of romantic narrative to argue a very different case. Viscount Ingestre, writing in the *True Briton* in 1852, declared 'our end then is to wage war to the knife against the pernicious literature of the day'.[67] Again, the scale of the problem, its power, is signalled by the use of sexual imagery. Ingestre says of the readers of popular fiction, 'whilst they peruse it [they] may derive a morbid excitement from it, but afterwards suffer'.[68] He compares the effect of such publications on the mind to the effects of opium on the body. In a later article in the *True Briton* the battle is waged once more, against writing which, 'produces uneasiness and tumult in the minds of common readers . . . and leaves nothing behind but a sense of weariness after unworthy occupations'.[69] The unconscious irony of his reference to 'unworthy occupations' deserves note. The working classes often did have 'unworthy' and alienating occupations, but this is not addressed by the *True Briton*.

Several authors in *Chambers's Edinburgh Journal* take on Fanny Mayne's insistence that forms of literature must be provided which entertain as well as instruct. The people must be given '*innocent amusement*' since they mostly show little interest in lectures and reading rooms.[70] The failure of Mechanics' Institutes and reading rooms to involve all sections of the working classes, can, of course, be attributed to other causes than innate frivolity. Such institutions were mainly frequented by male artisans. They were often run by the middle classes. They generally demanded fairly large subscriptions, payable in advance, which suited neither the level nor the form of mid-nineteenth-century wages. They also tended to refuse education which was perceived as political, concentrating instead on science, history and, occasionally, literature. The easy, dismissive tone with which *Chambers's Edinburgh Journal* described the working class as simply uninterested in self-improvement is, however, depressingly familiar. The conclusion they drew from this observation was that the common people must have suitable literature provided for them, preferably in the form of *Chambers's Edinburgh Journal*.

The *Westminster Review*, a journal founded by Bentham in 1824, was the organ of the philosophical Radicals, the freethinkers and the liberal reformers, which tried to establish the cultural bases of social progress and constitutional equality. In 1855, it approached the 'problem' of popular culture in a way reminiscent of earlier parts of the century. It did not deal with penny fiction, but looked instead to re-establish a tradition of ballad literature. Ballads were described as accessible, and as an expression of 'natural feelings common to the whole human race'.[71] Its discussion of the work of Thomas Hood or of Ebenezer Elliott was part of an attempt to 'improve the popular ballad literature', and thus to provide the terms for a reassessment of the cultural and political role of the people.[72] The *Westminster Review* thus tried to mitigate the effects of transformations in cultural production by insisting on a form of cultural continuity. Uneasy about the recognition of difference, which looked like decline, they repressed it. They denied the extent of cultural transformations, in order to avoid the effects of class polarization in both cultural and political spheres.

When *Blackwood's Edinburgh Magazine* looked at transformations in cultural production in the 1850s the political implications were quite different. *Blackwood's* was a Tory publication, which opposed the extension of the franchise, and argued that the working classes were politically and culturally unsuited to any active role in government. *Blackwood's* argued that education could never really succeed in enforcing social control, and that the extension of literacy represented a positive social threat: 'At the schools a boy is taught to read and write, but he is not taught, and never can be taught, what he ought to read and what he ought to abstain from reading hereafter.'[73] *Blackwood's* was particularly concerned about the content and the volume of penny fiction. The argument was that the reading matter of the working classes, 'utterly loathsome and depraved', rendered them unfit for the vote.[74] The characters and narratives within penny fiction were objected to on political grounds: the villain who was inevitably a nobleman, the heroine a 'daughter of the people'. In particular, *Blackwood's* objected to representations of the aristocracy in brothels and gaming clubs, apparently squandering the wealth produced by the labouring classes.

The Chartist press was also concerned about the production and consumption of cultural texts. Ernest Jones, editor of the *People's Paper* and *Notes to the People*, was himself a poet and novelist. Both publications celebrated and advertised schools and libraries founded and run by the working classes themselves, and carried short stories, theatre reviews and poetry, sometimes styled as 'democratic song'. *Notes to the People* was also interested in the material base of cultural production. It described with conscious irony how the women who bind the bibles meant to civilize Britain's Empire were themselves driven to prostitution by low wages.[75]

The stated aim of *Notes to the People* was 'to make the reader better acquainted with some of these . . . English poets whose works have circulated but little among the general public – the working-classes especially', although the canon represented was certainly not orthodox.[76] Jones's own fictional writing was consciously polemical. His novel 'Woman's Wrongs' combined representations from melodrama with a consistent analysis of the oppression of women at all levels of society. Jones also published 'De Brassier: A Democratic Romance' in *Notes to the People*, arguing that it represented an important attempt to communicate political and social truths to the people. Of 'truth', Jones wrote, 'the more attractive you can make her, the more easily she will progress'.[77] Thus, like Reynolds, he attempted to address the possibilities of producing representations that were both fictional and politicized. In engaging thus with the forms of popular literature, in an attempt to win them over for the representation of oppression and inequality, Jones's writing looks forward to some of the work in popular theatre which will be explored in chapter 5. His publications, like much of the nineteenth century periodical press, were financially precarious. *Notes to the People* ceased publication after two years, and the *People's Paper* after six. Nonetheless, Jones's work does represent an important point of difference in responses to the cultural transformations of the mid-nineteenth century, an attempt to construct different sorts of responses to the cultural production and consumption of the working classes.

Harney's *Democratic Review*, *Red Republican* and *Friend of the People* acknowledged the importance of cultural politics, insisting 'that knowledge and Freedom go hand in hand'.[78] Harney also published lengthy reviews of Ernest Jones's writings, as well as those of working-class poets like Gerald Massey, who published a volume entitled *Voices of Freedom and Lyrics of Love*. He did therefore, to some extent, support the development of socialist cultural forms, and the move towards a more politicized notion of popular literature. Harney seemed reluctant to follow through the implications of this at any level other than the political, however. He argued that truly national education was only conceivable after popular sovereignty, thus essentially postponing cultural struggle until 'after the revolution'. Although his journals carried significant amounts of poetry, they did not seem interested, or able, to intervene directly in the forms of popular literature. There is an interesting attempt to reappropriate Milton from a history of Royalist distortion, but mostly cultural critique is left at the level of advocating some very general political principles.

Whether this is to be seen as a failure of the Radical and Chartist press is a difficult question. They certainly recognized the importance of cultural capital, and tried to make certain aspects of the dominant culture more accessible and to demystify them. They also published a whole series of fictional and poetic writings which criticized the social relations of capitalism, and articulated the perceptions of a range of different individuals from different class positions. Perhaps the most powerful of these were the songs which were to have both ideological and practical significance for working class organization. In the end, however, they did leave the criticism of popular literature detailed above unchallenged. That was to concede a lot. It allowed for the development of a discourse of the relation between technological progress, increasing democracy and cultural decline, and a consequent 'writing off' of the cultural forms widely favoured by the working classes, which has remained remarkably consistent to the present day.

4

Poetry, Pottery and Song: The Mediation of 'Popular' Forms

Rather than concentrating on a particular historical moment, this chapter will focus on a process. It will look at the process of cultural re-evaluation, whereby a set of texts, or practices, lose their marginal, subordinate status and become an important stake or element in the dominant culture, under the sign of 'the popular'. It is the process referred to, inadequately, by the term 'incorporation'. 'Incorporation' suggests a simple one-way process, where texts which are vibrant, oppositional and authentic become essentially meaningless and debased. What will be looked at in this chapter, however, is a more complex set of processes. The entry of certain 'popular' texts and practices into the dominant culture is always a site of struggle: over form, meaning, ownership and history.

Initially, the intention was to look at three different moments in this process of incorporation, or construction, of the popular. Firstly, the debate over the publication by Macpherson of Ossian's poems in the 1760s. Secondly, the development of folk song collecting in the nineteenth century, and, finally, the Arts and Crafts Movement, from its origins in the nineteenth century to its development in the work of St Ives potters and painters, particularly Bernard Leach. The first two of these moments turned out to be very closely linked, and the second to comprise at least two significantly different phases. The neat division of historical moments was therefore impossible to maintain, but the resultant series of references from one moment to another, the recurring themes, questions and issues, do seem to do more justice to the difficult category of 'popular culture'.

As well as continuities, there are also very significant differences and transformations. Basically, the debate over the poems of Ossian focused on the question of authenticity. Were the poems really as old as they were claimed to be? Could the Scots have been capable of such poetry in the third century? Were the poems all written by one man? Were they forgeries? The interest in all this seemed to be the search for answers to questions about the origin and nature of social organization. The poems of Ossian, if authentic, provided evidence about the nature of savage society, and furnished a model for natural forms of writing, which could then provide the means to develop national forms of writing.

The folk song collectors of the nineteenth century were less immediately concerned with authenticity than with the significance of particular cultural forms. They used the survival and continuity of folk song as the basis of a critique of the social and cultural relations of industrial capitalism. In contrast to the fragmentation, decay and change, which the collectors felt characterized nineteenth-century Britain, folk songs seemed to represent tradition and social and cultural coherence. The hope of nineteenth-century collectors was that tunes, songs and other forms of folk culture could be revived as part of the living culture, thus mitigating the worst effects of industrial society.

The folk song revival which took place from the 1950s on, in Britain, was concerned less with the significance of folk songs for contemporary culture than with their ability to contribute to a wider understanding of working people's history and experience. The concern was with the power of cultural forms to transform people's identifications, their 'common-sense' understanding of history.

Even these very broad categorizations are open to question. Elements of each area of concern – 'authenticity', 'significance' and 'history' – are clearly present at each moment. Yet it is an attempt to sketch out how cultural debates, even when they seem to be more or less continuous, can actually mean quite different things. We have to grasp the continuities as well as the differences, but also the differences that can look like continuities.

First, it is perhaps necessary to explain the concentration on 'folk' song in a book which is examining the constitution of the concept of 'popular culture'. It has been argued, very convincingly, that the terms 'folk' and 'popular' refer to different forms of cultural hierarchy, and could usefully be kept separate.[1] We would then use 'popular' to refer to cultural forms which depend on mass production and consumption, which are essentially urban and industrial, and the term 'folk' to refer to cultural forms which are predominantly rural and oral in their creation and transmission. However useful this distinction might be to the project of cultural classification, it does not reflect the proliferation of terms which are constantly competing with each other, undermining each other and replacing each other in the texts which try to define, or transform, cultural relations. The process of validation of forms of popular culture has often involved an attempt to insert them within what is seen as a more authentic folk tradition. Thus A. L. Lloyd developed the idea of 'industrial folk song' in the 1950s and 1960s.[2] Nineteenth-century collectors wrote about 'folk songs' and 'the literature of the people' without theoretical, or even practical, distinction.[3] Often, the term 'folk' is used quite consciously to suggest cultural forms which are untainted by the effects of literacy or urban life. But, as we shall see, this purity is basically always imaginary and ideological rather than actual. Refusing to discuss forms that describe themselves as 'folk culture' would run the risk of accepting these definitions, and thus failing to examine what is an important element in the process of cultural stratification.

All this is to say that cultural analysis is not easy. Terms cannot be accepted uncritically: we must deconstruct the concept of 'folk' culture and see what assumptions about history, culture and gender lie behind it. At the same time, the attempt to discover 'the real' behind these terms, to say 'this is not truly popular but that is', is ultimately futile. This chapter will attempt to steer a middle course: taking the terms 'folk' and 'popular' as they are presented in a range of texts and seeing where they lead, but also interrogating the adequacy of these terms to the historical and cultural relations they aim to describe.

It is important to acknowledge the dangers of concentrating on 'mediations' in the field of popular culture. It is easy to be led into reproducing a notion of 'the people' as passive consumers of texts and meanings. Insisting on the effect of the dominant culture on the subordinate, the effect of printed texts on folk songs, can lead to a writing out of the creativity and power of subordinate forms of culture. In the field of folk scholarship, however, the role of mediation, by collectors and by other texts, has been so consistently underestimated until recently that the danger is perhaps slight. Cecil Sharp's equation of folk song with social groups entirely removed from education and industrial social relations has a very strong hold.

Finally, I will also discuss certain individuals who have already appeared in this book, such as John Clare and Mary Howitt. This is part of the attempt to synthesize the various case studies into some more general account of the process of legitimizing certain popular cultural forms. It is hoped that the resonances between John Clare the poet and John Clare the folk song collector, or between Mary Howitt the progressive journalist and Mary Howitt the translator of German folk songs, will prove productive. They can perhaps suggest, at a more individual level, the necessary connections between the various analyses of popular culture discussed in this book.

OSSIAN

The Ossian controversy began in the 1760s with the publication by James Macpherson of three volumes of translations of the work of Ossian, a Gaelic poet of the late third century. The first volume contained mere *Fragments*, a series of disconnected short poems.[4] The impact of these, though limited, was immediate. Hugh Blair, who wrote a preface to the volume, and Home, the author of *Douglas*, provided the financial means for Macpherson to travel through the Highlands, in search of the complete epic poem which he believed to exist there. The result of these travels was the publication first of *Fingal* in 1762 and then of *Temora* in 1763.[5]

Suddenly, a body of texts which had been completely marginal, existing only in Gaelic, little recorded in written form, became a major international focus for debates on history, nationalism and poetic language. The controversy, begun in 1760, involving Hugh Blair, James Macpherson, Malcolm Laing, Herder, Diderot and a special committee of the Highland Society, continued well into the nineteenth century.

Macpherson and Blair claimed that the texts of *Fingal* and *Temora* dated back to the third century, and that they were the work of one man: Ossian, the son of Fingal. Both made this claim on the basis of particular accounts of the origins of Scottish society, and of its cultural history. The 1819 edition of *The Poems of Ossian* included a dissertation by Macpherson on the 'Aera of Ossian'. Macpherson produced a history of the Celts, some of it based on Roman historians' accounts of the Celts in France. He claimed that the Scottish Celts lived in stable, settled communities, governed by a mixture of monarchy and aristocracy, that is to say by a system of clans. Macpherson claimed that the religious and legislative powers in this system until the second century AD were the Druids. Their disappearance led to the increasing power of the Bards, individuals dedicated to the preservation and telling of epic tales, and thus to the survival of Celtic culture.

There was an important nationalist element behind this historical claim. The idea that Scotland had produced

> a bard living fourteen hundred years back, among a barbarous, unlettered people, was a phenomenon which struck with surprise the minds of men eminently enlightened by science and philosophy.[6]

The publication of the Ossian poems supported the claim that Scotland had an ancient and powerful literary tradition. In the eighteenth century, as the Scottish middle classes became increasingly Anglicized and political power became increasingly concentrated in London, the appeal of such a claim was considerable. It is notable that most of Ossian's, and Macpherson's, defenders were Scottish.

Macpherson was not constructing his theories of Scottish history in a vacuum. Interest in the poetic writings of Ossian was enhanced by their potential contribution to debates about the history of civil society. As examples of the cultural production of 'rude nations', they could be used to assess the tenability of theories of social and cultural progress.

The cultural, social and political implications of the increasing division of labour, which produced commercial society, were widely debated in the mid-eighteenth century. David Hume, in his essays on 'Commerce' and on 'Refinement in the Arts', was quite clear that the subdivision of mechanical arts was the necessary condition for commercial expansion, for industriousness, for the stimulation of production of a range of commodities, and thus, he argued, for political stability.[7] He also insisted that social and economic progress, through refinement in the skills and techniques of labour, implied an expansion and improvement in the sphere of culture.

By the time that Ossian's texts appeared in the 1760s, however, this confidence in the necessary superiority of commercial society, in economic, political and cultural spheres, was undermined by the perception of the weakening effects of social fragmentation, and the alienation and degradation of the labouring classes. Adam Ferguson's *Essay on the History of Civil Society* addressed the partial nature of the 'progress' represented by the social relations of commercial society. Ferguson analysed the beliefs and behaviour of 'rude nations'. He did this, to some extent, through a consideration of the fictional productions of rude societies, which revealed their 'conceptions' and 'sentiments', and also through a consideration of 'savage' communities existing in the eighteenth century, such as the American Indians. He rejected historians' accounts of rude society as too mediated, and too keen to exhibit the superiority of civilized society. Ferguson accepted the universal applicability of a model of historical progress which moved from 'the savage' to 'the barbarian' to 'civilization', but he did challenge the understanding and implications of these terms.

'Savage' communities, Ferguson argues, are characterized by an absence of property, by democracy, and by a complete absence of social hierarchy. He does admit that the domestic oppression of women in affectionate relations is the only thing which stops such social organizations from sliding towards slavery, and consequently tyranny, but this fact is repressed in the general model of savage communities as the realization of social equality.[8] Barbarous societies are characterized by the existence of property, but the absence of law. They are thus engaged in numerous battles and struggles, and are basically anarchic. Politically, they tend towards tyranny.

It is, Ferguson argued, the separation of the arts and professions, and their consequent rapid development, which turned the hunter and warrior into the tradesman and merchant, and thus established the basis of commercial society. This separation, however, produces many mechanical arts which require neither reason nor sentiment. It thus tends to brutalize large sections of the labouring populace, and to dissolve the social ties which produce coherence and stability. Adam Smith was to draw the same sorts of conclusions about the effects of the division of labour in *The Wealth of Nations*, and to recommend a programme of national education to lessen the worst consequences, but he was at least sure that the refinement in mechanical arts produced positive benefits for the leisured classes, allowing for the further advance of science and culture. Ferguson does not seem entirely confident, even on this front: his admission that the genius of the master of the workshop, who is granted leisure as a result of the division of labour, is 'perhaps' cultivated seems a little grudging.

The contrast with savage societies is quite clear, for Ferguson, and does not vindicate claims of social progress. He argued that the savage escaped the vices of the eighteenth-century lower classes by never learning dependency. He insisted that honour and generosity were equally present in rude societies as in civilized. His claim that civilized nations 'appear' to have gained the knowledge, order and wealth sought by savage communities is, at best, unconvincing.

Ferguson's interrogation of the contradictions and limitations of theories of the progress of civil society led him to valorize the social relations and cultural production of primitive societies. This was the theoretical development that led to a massive interest in the writings of Homer in the late eighteenth century.[9] Ossian's poetry, too, could be understood as valuable, because it came from a period when all members of society were capable of noble thoughts and deeds, were incapable of subservience, and were aware of their part in the fabric of society. Ferguson argued quite explicitly that poetry was a natural form, and that the strength and vitality of sentiments and impressions in savage society tended to produce powerful poetic writing. He celebrated the freedom of savage poets from rules of poetic composition and linguistic decorum.

Ferguson thus used the social relations and cultural production of savage communities to attack the distortions and pretensions of eighteenth-century society. It is important, however, in terms of a consideration of arguments about popular culture, to stress the distinction he made between savage communities and the eighteenth-century lower classes. If the general claim to progress of civil society was in some doubt, the decline of the lower classes was certain. Ossian would have had no place among the alienated and brutalized operatives of the eighteenth century. The ruling class and the dominant culture, on the other hand, at least as represented by the person of Ferguson, had at least developed to the stage that they were capable of appreciating the power of primitive poetry.

It is perhaps worth mentioning here that the subject of these histories, the 'he', is just what he appears to be: masculine. This much is clear in the ease with which Ferguson represses the structural role of the oppression of women in savage society. Also, Macpherson's history deals almost entirely with kings, chieftains and bards. The heroes of *Fingal* are soldiers: brave fighting men. The gender bias of the poems of Ossian is, indeed, so marked that even where there is need to refer to events or emotions that might be deemed indelicate, Ossian 'speaks in Terms utterly unintelligible to any Female that has been modestly brought up'.[10]

The ideological and practical importance of these historical claims is so marked that it is with the account of history, both political and cultural, rather than with the account of poetry, that Malcolm Laing began his attack on the authenticity of the poems of Ossian. Laing contrasted descriptions by Roman historians of the Celts, as hunters, living communally, with few clothes, and a bloodthirsty and violent culture, with the generous heroes, the chaste maids, and the lavish feasts of *Fingal*. The Romans were, of course, invaders, so their evidence might not be entirely disinterested, but Laing's sources are certainly more concrete than anything Macpherson could refer to. As Laing's argument progresses, however, it becomes clear that he too is arguing about more than historical facts. He asserts, 'That the poems were preserved by oral tradition, in an obsolete diction, or, in other words, a dialect already disused by the people, is alone sufficient to confute their authenticity'.[11] This is true only if it is assumed that an illiterate people is incapable of appreciating the conventionality and specificity of poetic language. This is, clearly, precisely what Laing does believe. He develops this position by claiming that 'the refined poetry which they admire so much was more likely to be produced by a cultivated genius of the present century than by an illiterate bard of the third century'.[12] Like the counter-claim by Macpherson, this claim seems to have much more to do with alignments within the dominant culture of the eighteenth century than with the texts of Ossian. Laing announced his project as being to disabuse his fellow Scots. His weapons included the fact that 'When Johnson visited the Western Isles, the natives had nothing to communicate that deserved attention'.[13] Johnson did not speak Gaelic.

Those who wrote approvingly of Ossian's poems focused mainly on their language and imagery, and the significance of these for a general theory of poetic language, even though the available translations were actually in prose. For Blair, the poems abound with 'that enthusiasm, that vehemence and fire, which are the soul of poetry' and Ossian's imagery is 'without exception copied from that face of nature which he saw before his eyes'. Blair insists that Ossian 'wrote from the immediate impulse of poetic enthusiasm'.[14] For Donald Macdonald, *Fingal* is simply 'the most stupendous Epic Poem that mortal wit ever produced'.[15]

Perhaps the best-known response to Ossian was that of Herder, who developed his theory of *Volkslied* in the context of a discussion of Ossian's poems. Herder saw the poems as exemplary in their proximity to nature, their simplicity and their spontaneity. They provided a model for poetic forms that could be both universal, in their simplicity, power and naturalness, and national in their mobilization of national character and history.[16] Herder insisted that Ossian's poetry was lyric rather than epic. The importance of Herder's work for the definition of folk song in the nineteenth century demonstrates the complex relations between different moments in the construction and recovery of popular cultural forms. When Mary Howitt uses the term 'Folk's song' in 1847, she is clearly referring to Herder.[17] Indeed, the fact that she uses '*Volkslieder*', 'people's songs' and 'Folk's songs' interchangeably shows that she is still writing at a period of transformation, before the development of a hegemonic set of meanings of the term 'folk song'.

Laing argued that the appeal of the language of *Fingal* and *Temora* for eighteenth-century critics was not accidental. Looking at Macpherson's own earlier poem, *The Highlander*, Laing finds a significant continuity between its narrative structure and imagery and those of *Fingal* and *Temora*. He points to specific images, as well as to general atmospheric phenomena such as towering mountains, howling storms and ghosts. For Laing, then, the position is quite simple: Ossian seems like a powerful, unique, poetic force, because his poems were actually written by Macpherson in accordance with specific ideas about the relationship between nature and poetic language.

So far, I have avoided making any claims about the authenticity of Ossian's translations. It seemed important to reproduce the debate in its own terms: to show the priorities and assumptions that were brought to the texts in the eighteenth century. In addressing 'the truth' of the Ossian poems, I am not pretending to an objective position, devoid of any cultural, national or political presuppositions. Nonetheless, recent research does allow a tentative restatement of the history of Ossian's texts.

The Highland Society Committee set up in 1805 to investigate the authenticity of Macpherson's translations interviewed and received correspondence from large numbers of individuals claiming acquaintance with Gaelic versions of Ossianic texts, some of whom had been visited by Macpherson in his travels. The Highland Society argued that the existence of a body of texts popularly attributed to Ossian, and preserved and transmitted orally, was indisputable. The committee also concluded that Macpherson had had access to these texts and had translated some of them with reasonable accuracy. They were, however, unwilling to support Macpherson's claim that the texts he produced had existed in the same form since the third century, or that they were all written by one particular individual. Indeed, though they rejected the charge of 'forgery' against Macpherson, they attacked his rewriting of the culture and the texts he discovered:

> He was in use to supply chasms, and to give connection, by inserting passages which he did not find, and to add what he conceived to be dignity and delicacy to the original composition, by striking out passages, by softening incidents, by refining the language, in short by changing what he considered as too simple, or too rude for a modern ear.[18]

In particular, the Report criticized the translation of *Temora*, suggesting that fame made Macpherson increasingly careless of the integrity of the texts he was dealing with.

Derick Thomson, writing 150 years later, comes to much the same conclusions as the Highland Society. There was a body of Gaelic songs and ballads existing in the Highlands when Macpherson undertook his research. Several individuals are known to have possessed manuscript collections, some of which Macpherson consulted. However, Macpherson travelled for a relatively short time: a period of six weeks, followed by a period of up to two months. This left little time for comparative studies of versions of texts, or an assessment of their strength within the culture. It certainly did not give him time to establish the existence of the coherent epic text he had set off to find. In the end, Thomson argues, Macpherson simply combined a number of more or less fragmentary texts into something approximating a coherent narrative.

In the case of *Fingal*, Thomson locates twelve passages which can be found in other collections of Gaelic songs. In the case of *Temora*, however, he finds only one, thus confirming the Highland Society's unease over this text. As Thomson admits, this argument depends on passages existing in other printed collections. It is clearly possible that Macpherson could have collected passages orally.

The reliability of oral culture was very much a stake in the Ossian debate. Malcolm Laing demanded the production of ancient manuscripts as proof of the existence of ancient songs.[19] Yet, as the Highland Society pointed out, the Church, which was the major literate institution in the Highlands, actively discouraged the recitation and preservation of Ossianic literature. The absence of manuscripts might not, in itself, prove anything about the authenticity of Macpherson's translations. Yet Macpherson clearly felt the force of Laing, and indeed David Hume's prioritization of printed texts. He suggested that complete manuscripts of Ossian's works existed, and were in his posssession. But such manuscripts never appeared. Finally, after Macpherson's death, the 'original Gaelic' version of Ossian's poems appeared. This was clearly a forgery: a translation of the English texts, and a very bad one.[20]

The use of oral sources by Macpherson is very significant, particularly when compared with Thomas Percy's method of collecting his *Reliques of Ancient English Poetry*. Percy relied on one particular manuscript collection supplemented by available collections in libraries in Oxford, Cambridge and London. This reflects Percy's conviction that he was dealing with cultural forms which had decayed, disintegrated and disappeared. He argued that the process of decay began with the final disappearance of a tradition of Minstrelsy at the end of the Elizabethan period. He contrasted the vitality and power of pre-Elizabethan balladry with the debased forms of the seventeenth and eighteenth centuries. The old ballads:

> abound with antique words and phrases, are extremely incorrect, and run into the utmost licence of metre; they have also a romantic wildness, and are in the true spirit of chivalry – The other sort are written in exacter measure, have a low or subordinate correctness, sometimes bordering on the insipid.[21]

Given this position it would have been quite incoherent for Percy to have undertaken a search for ballads surviving orally in his own time. They would simply have been even more debased and inauthentic.

Macpherson was also working with a model of cultural decline. In his case, however, it was a decline into civilization. He contrasted the naturalness and poetic power of Ossian's poetry with the artificiality and tedium of eighteenth-century poetic writing. Macpherson posed the Highlands precisely as a cultural enclave, whose geographical isolation and high levels of illiteracy had preserved it from the debilitating effects of refinement in the arts. Macpherson effectively wrote out 1,400 years of history as he constructed his history of Highland society in the third century on the basis of his fascination with Highland society in the eighteenth. His 'history' was less careful research than imaginary projection. If the Highlands had escaped the effects of history, of the progressive separation of the arts and professions, of urbanization, of capitalism, then the bards could still exist there, as they had done since the third century. The project of oral collection was, therefore, quite coherent, although Macpherson could not find the vocabulary to defend the practice against charges of 'forgery' and 'corruption'.

The 'Ossian controversy' thus served to concentrate a number of questions, about history, national identity, and poetic language onto one text. It did little, however, to provide information about the existing culture of the eighteenth-century Highlands. Macpherson plucked a few texts out of context, and published them as illustrative of a culture. He knew very little about the place and meaning of those texts. Although it did involve the collection, translation and publication of texts which had been little known outside the Highlands, the Ossian debate did little to empower, or legitimate, the bearers of these texts. Macpherson's sources were not acknowledged. His identification with the texts became sufficiently strong for him to encourage suggestions that he had written them. If the Ossian debate did disturb perceptions of English cultural superiority, it did so at the cost of constructing an imaginary political and cultural history of the Highlands which could only serve, finally, to confirm their marginality.

FOLK SONG

It is this dichotomy between a language of revival and reassessment and a practice of marginalization and appropriation which provides the focus for Dave Harker's study of folk song in his *Fakesong: The Manufacture of British 'Folksong' 1700 to the Present Day*. This book provides the framework for the discussion of folk song in this chapter. Harker writes a history of the mediations, and mediators, involved in the collection and publication of folk songs. He 'aims to show why these people mediated songs, who they did it for, and how their practices and the results of their mediations related to more general cultural and historical tendencies and developments'.[22]

Harker argues that the collection of folk songs, and the discussion of folk culture, shows a constant, indeed even a necessary, tendency towards the construction of imaginary and reactionary categories of cultural analysis. He insists that the concept of 'folk' empties social and cultural relations of their class dimension, eliding historical antagonism in the interests of continuity. Harker supports this argument with an impressive analysis of the personal histories, class positions, ideological investments and editing techniques of folk song and ballad collectors from 1700 to the late 1960s.

In fact, Harker's alternative category of 'workers'' culture seems equally, though differently, problematic. It, too, is premised on a partial, and a gendered, cultural history. At this point, however, I want to concentrate on Harker's analysis of the work of individual mediators, and to develop it by attention to some of the categories and questions that have already come up both in this chapter and in the book as a whole: the notion of cultural decay, the positing of authenticity, the disappearance, or repression, of history, the relationship between national identity and culture, and the troubled place of women, both real and represented, in the practice of cultural analysis.

The history of folk song collecting presents some difficult

problems of writing. 'Folk song' seems to point to an ancient historical phenomenon: a category that precedes industrialization and the commercialization of culture. Harker, indeed, begins his history of folk song collecting in the early eighteenth century, with Allan Ramsay and James Watson. Yet the term 'folk song' does not really enter the English language until the 1870s.[23]

It is neither uncommon, nor incoherent, to analyse historical phenomena with categories developed at a later historical moment: thus we can look at sixteenth-century culture, or at the class structure of Ancient Rome, although neither 'class' nor 'culture' were concepts current during those periods. When the object of historical study is the language of mediation and analysis itself, however, there do seem to be more difficult problems. The interest in this chapter is in tracing the development of the concept of 'folk culture', and I have thus elected not to look at the song collectors of the seventeenth and eighteenth centuries, who did not consider their work in relation to the cultural and social identity of the 'folk'. I will therefore, begin my analysis of folk song collecting with Sir Walter Scott and William Motherwell, in the early nineteenth century. Thus I will not deal with the folk song collecting of Thomas Percy or of Joseph Ritson, although both appear in Harker's history. I have also decided to exclude the study of balladry, in its later and more literary manifestations, from this analysis, as it does seem to have a specificity which would be lost by such treatment.

Even within these limitations, the problems remain formidable. The attempt at synthesis will, almost necessarily, do damage both to the historical specificity of each collector, and to the sense of a coherent, historical narrative, which is so clear, for example, in Harker's work. The refusal of a chronological account is part of the attempt to represent and analyse a process, rather that a set of events. The risk that denseness will become impenetrability, however, convinces me that a brief sketch of the development of folk song collecting from the early nineteenth century to the present day would be useful at this point.

Sir Walter Scott and William Motherwell were both collecting and publishing songs and ballads at the beginning of the nineteenth century. Scott concentrated on *The Minstrelsy of the Scottish Border* and Motherwell on the romantic and historical ballads of Scotland.[24] Scott used oral as well as manuscript sources, as did John Harland and Robert Bell later in the century. They were interested in folk song as part of a more general category of folklore. Their interest was in the texts rather than the tunes of folk songs. This interest was developed by Francis James Child, whose collection of ballad texts was based entirely on manuscript sources.

In the second half of the nineteenth century a number of folk song collectors, influenced by Carl Engel's theories of 'national music', set out to preserve the folk music of England.[25] Lucy Broadwood, Charlotte Burne, Kate Lee and Sabine Baring-Gould were all part of this group. Their work culminated in the formation of the Folk Song Society in 1898.

Cecil Sharp's collections date from the early part of the twentieth century. His work is significant, not just because of the material he collected, but because of the continuing power of the definitions he produced in *English Folk Song: Some Conclusions* which was published in 1907. Alfred Williams's collection of *Folk Songs of the Upper Thames*, which appeared in 1923, was concerned with words rather than music, and with the extent to which these could be used as historical documents.

A. L. Lloyd's is the name most commonly associated with the folk song revival which began in the 1950s. He argued for the importance of seeing folk music as part of a history of resistance and struggle. He developed this position in terms of a consideration of 'industrial folk song', the song culture of the nineteenth- and twentieth-century working classes.

Finally, this chapter will also consider more recent work of people like Michael Pickering and David Buchan, who have tried to rewrite the history of folk song collecting and of folk song. Pickering challenges some of the assumptions of folk scholars about history, and about cultural transmission, in giving his own account of *Village Song and Culture*. David Buchan has tried to write an account of folk culture on the basis of a theory of history, rather than the other way around.

FOLK SONG AND HISTORY

Since the account of history turned out to be so crucial to the analysis and evaluation of the poems of Ossian, it is perhaps reasonable to begin by looking at the accounts of history produced by the collectors and theorizers of folk song. Sir Walter Scott's introduction to his collection of the ballads of the Scottish borders contains an account of the history of this geographical region in the Middle Ages. He describes a society of heroic chieftains engaged in more or less perpetual battles. The Borders are seen as tough and uncivilized. Scott insists that the rudeness of the society is in direct relation to the power and emotion of its poetry and music. He sees the Borders as wild and savage, but also as rich in legend: 'no part of Scotland teemed with superstitious fears and observances more than they did'.[26] Writing at the beginning of the nineteenth century, when Scotland was becoming an increasingly industrialized, economic and political satellite of England, Scott looked back to a 'pre-working class mythified history': a time of superstition rather than sedition.[27]

Accounts of history are frequently condensed into descriptions of 'the people', of their characteristics and their social role. Thus Parry, in the inaugural volume of the *Journal of the Folk Song Society*, in 1899, spoke of: 'the quiet reticence of our country folk, courageous and content, ready to meet what chance shall bring with a cheery heart'.[28] These are the people he sees as the (unknowing) bearers of a folk tradition. Similarly, Motherwell argued, in 1827, that ballads were the property of 'the patriotick children of an ancient and heroick race', who were to be distinguished from the contemporary working class.[29] Sharp saw the peasants who preserved and transmitted folk songs as 'simple people'.[30] Williams described the singers from whom he collected songs as 'all very primitive. They are fresh and unspoiled, born of the earth, beautiful children of nature, young all their lives, changeless under hardships, afflictions and other adversities.'[31]

All this amounts to an imaginary representation of the rural past, as unified and organic. It neglects the transformations in class relations between the Middle Ages and the nineteenth century, and presents instead a model of a coherent and integrated culture, supported by simple, earthy, illiterate peasants, which is suddenly under siege.

If A. L. Lloyd sees a continuity in the history of folk song, it is not in terms of stability, but of struggle. Lloyd sees folk music as the property and the expression of the lower classes. He says it was 'born of revolutionary struggle'.[32] The history he points to is one of oppression, of the peasantry and of the English language. He traces the emergence of songs attacking tyrannous barons, lecherous monks and dishonest millers in the fifteenth and sixteenth centuries. From this point on, his history changes between the publication of *The Singing Englishman* in 1945 and *Folk Song in England* in 1967. Initially, Lloyd argued that folk song disappeared with the disappearance of the peasantry, the class that produced it. He thus echoed earlier, nineteenth-century versions of a culture under seige. He later argued, however, that the working class could be seen, structurally, as occupying the same place within capitalism as the peasantry had within earlier social formations. Thus folk song did not disappear, it merely got displaced. The unity of pre-industrial culture is displaced onto the unity of the male, industrial, working class.

AUTHORSHIP AND TRANSMISSION

The assumption of a stable rural community, unaffected by social transformations, by industrialization, or by literacy, clearly had implications for the ways in which folk song collectors perceived and theorized cultural history. Questions of authorship and transmission became central to the project of defining and evaluating folk culture: who wrote the songs, how were they preserved, what was the role of printed texts?

Motherwell's answers to these questions were quite clear. Folk songs and ballads were originally written by professional musicians and Minstrels. The Minstrels' romances were broken down into shorter songs, which were then preserved orally, and with remarkable fidelity, over hundreds of years.

Cecil Sharp shares Motherwell's conviction about the centrality of oral transmission, but rejects the notion of professional authorship. Sharp argues that folk songs are created by the unlettered classes, they are 'traceable to no other sources than the minds of unlettered men'.[33] Sharp is clear that the unlettered are to be distinguished from the 'merely illiterate'. The unlettered are those who have never been compromised by acquaintance with a literate culture. The illiterate are the urban dwellers who live in ignorance of any culture.

Folk songs, according to Sharp, originate in remote country districts which 'have escaped the infection of modern ideas'.[34] He sees the process of authorship and transmission as essentially communal. Songs are written by one individual, but are so transformed by tradition, via the principles of continuity, variation and selection, that they become communal creations. The music thus created is the product of a 'natural instinct' to self-expression among the folk. There are values attached to this communal process for Sharp. It seems to be some sort of guarantee of decorum and decency. Coarse and lewd ballads are singled out by Sharp as being individually, rather than communally produced.

Throughout the history of folk song collecting, the emphasis, and the interest, has been in an oral culture: songs passed from father to son. In the interests of discovering an authentically 'folk' culture, collectors have treated broadsides and chapbook versions of songs with suspicion and disdain. The communal, the anonymous and the illiterate were all seen as essential aspects of a continuous and coherent folk culture. The undermining of these aspects was thus seen as part of the process of decay into individually written, mass-produced, and mass-consumed popular music.

A. L. Lloyd argues that this set of emphases, on illiteracy, anonymity and orality, has led to a serious misrepresentation of the history of folk song. In fact, village singers, far from being illiterate peasants, were likely to be able to read both books and music. This point is developed in a detailed study of the broadside ballad trade by R. S. Thomson.[35] Thomson shows the importance of printed versions of ballad texts to singers and their audience from the sixteenth century. The very large sixteenth-century trade in 'stock ballads' was developed in the seventeenth century by the growth of ballads on topical subjects. By the eighteenth century, the growth of the provincial presses, and the development of their distribution networks, opened up an even greater market for ballad texts. For example, William Dicey, who published and sold large numbers of ballads, used the chapmen who delivered his *Northampton Mercury* to expand the market for balladry and songs. John Clare lived on the distribution route of the *Northampton Mercury*.[36] His early reading thus consisted of chapbooks and broadsides, but he also collected ballads and folk songs.

Most folk song collectors see broadsides as damaging to the authenticity of folk song. Thomson disagrees. He points out that since the disappearance of the ballad trade, folk collectors have been able to find only fragments of songs. Perhaps the folk culture, far from being destroyed by print, was reinforced by it.

Michael Pickering, in his study of village song in the nineteenth century, is equally critical of the emphasis on one coherent, unmediated, oral culture.[37] Rather than separate cultural enclaves: 'folk' versus 'commercial', Pickering sees cultural complexity. Looking at the village of Adderbury, where Janet Blunt collected in the first two decades of the twentieth century, Pickering finds evidence that village singers had a varied repertoire of songs. Some songs existed in printed form, some were preserved orally. Certain singers concentrated on songs recognized as traditional, though they would certainly know others. Generally, people listened to or sang a range of songs that folk collectors would see as completely incompatible. Different groups within the village would claim different parts of a developing song culture: women, children, artisans, the poor, would all tend to perform different types of music in different places. Yet Janet Blunt, in the search for the essential defining features of a folk culture, ignored this complexity, this history of mediation and fragmentation, and concentrated solely on traditional songs.

The search for one form of creation and transmission which would cover, and indeed define, all folk songs had a very strong pull for all the collectors. Even A. L. Lloyd, who argued for the variability and mediation of folk culture, reverts to a familiar set of preoccupations in describing the moment of creation of a folk song: 'We will suppose a man is ploughing a field. The work is dull, and he is upset over his girl's behaviour.'[38] Despite his rethinking of the category of 'folk song', as industrial as well as rural, Lloyd's description of the moment of creation is resolutely rural, and gendered.

There is, of course, a danger in stressing the mediations involved in the transmission of folk songs. It can lead straight back to the convictions of Motherwell, or earlier of Percy, that all cultural texts consumed by the people were originally created by professionals and handed down to them. This amounts, in effect, to denying the creativity of working men and women, repressing their involvement in and contributions to one of the few cultural forms to which they have had access continuously since the Middle Ages. It is, however, important to analyse the terms of this access, and the uses and significance of song cultures for particular social groups, rather than merely to celebrate the discovery of tradition and continuity.

CONTINUITY

This very continuity became an important stake in discussions of folk song. The search for authenticity was often supported by an assertion of continuity. Sharp's preference for tune collecting lay in his belief that music was less likely than text to be corrupted, because it was less likely to pass through the mediations of print, and because singers were often found to be more or less unconscious of the tunes they sang, although they were quite conscious of having learnt the words. Just as in the case of the peasant poets, lack of consciousness was thus equated with cultural authenticity. Sharp eventually concedes that this claim to continuity of folk music is quite unverifiable, as we have no records of earlier versions of most tunes, and settles instead for the assertion that: 'however corrupt they may be, they are, nevertheless, indisputably very fine melodies'.[39]

The desire for continuity is, however, significant. It reflects the emphasis in Carl Engel's *National Music* on the absence of external musical influences on folk tunes. Engel saw this absence, and the resultant continuity and naturalness of folk tunes, as the basis of a national identity in music. Sharp also sees continuity as the fundamental basis of a national musical tradition: it is the force that restrains the opposing active principles of selection and variation.

This assertion of continuity is always in tension with the evidence of changing social and cultural relations. This is, of course, precisely the tension that produces a fascination with folk culture. Sharp sets up the process of development and preservation of folk songs as autonomous, unaffected by social transformations or upheavals, until folk song's demise. The history of folk song becomes an enclave with its own causal processes and forms of inertia.

In fact, as Pickering argues, the history of folk song can never be understood outside the history of the social relations in which it participates. Alfred Williams acknowledged as much in his conclusion that folk song could never be revived, except as a curiosity, after the disruption to village life caused by improved education and communications. John Harland and T. T. Wilkinson made the same point in 1867, in relation to the disappearance of folklore and superstitions: 'an improved education has driven them from more intelligent communities'.[40] The 'improvement' is here both curiously violent in its driving force, and interestingly selective in its concentration on the more 'intelligent' communities.

Still, the conviction that continuity is an essential element of an authentic folk culture remains. R. S. Thomson distinguishes folk culture from popular culture, in terms of its preference for continuity over topicality, although he also argues that ballads frequently dealt with topical issues as early as the seventeenth century. A. L. Lloyd's project of inserting working-class culture within a history of folk culture depends crucially on the concept of the structural continuity of the lower classes from the Middle Ages to the present day.

FOLK SONG COLLECTING

Thus far we have concentrated more on the context than the practice of folk song collecting. It is in the actual practice of collectors, and their relations to their sources, however, that we can perhaps best observe the contradictory attitudes surrounding the recovery, or construction, of a folk culture.

Generally, we know very little of the people who provided the collectors with their material. It is clear, however, that there is often a dichotomy between the putative bearers of a folk culture and those to whom the collectors turned in search of it. Scott's sources for his ballads were farmers, professional people, pipers, and occasionally singers. Charlotte Burne, in 1890, was to encourage those in search of folklore to turn to the parish clerk, or to small employers, rather than to working people, with whom it was particularly difficult to communicate.[41]

When collectors did turn to men and women of the lower classes for material, they had very clear ideas of what they were looking for, and of how to get it. Sharp talks of having singers 'at his mercy'.[42] Kate Lee describes, in 1899, how singers who had come to sing to her 'positively shivered with fright'.[43] In a very powerful image of the terror, and the self-esteem, that were associated for the singers with this unexpected interest in their traditional repertoire, Kate Lee also tells of a singer who visited her in Norfolk, 'dressed up in his best, and shaking with fright'.[44]

The collectors were only interested in the singers' repertoire of traditional songs. Lucy Broadwood, for example, published many more songs from a singer who sang to her than from one who wrote his songs down. Indeed, the latter, Samuel Willett, wrote to her in some desperation:

> I do not know if there is sufficient rusticity in the above song to answer your purpose; if not my powers of discrimination are too limited to work out the process of winnowing you suggest in your letter.[45]

Likewise, Thomson argues that singers hid their collection of broadside ballads from collectors, who, anyway, did not suspect their existence.[46] The singers knew that collectors preferred the songs they could perform from memory.

Collectors also preferred modal tunes, those written in scales which predated the universal acceptance of major and minor scales in Western music. Modality was held to be a mark of authenticity, and Vic Gammon argues that collectors all tended to overemphasize the number of modal tunes collected in their eventual publications, and consequently to treat with suspicion tunes written in accordance with the major scale.[47]

Focusing on folk songs collected in Sussex and Surrey in the late nineteenth century, Vic Gammon points out the relatively narrow base from which they were gathered. Large numbers of the singers visited provided very few songs, whereas a small number of the singers provide a large percentage of the songs collected. Similarly, in Cecil Sharp's collection of *English Folk Songs*, most of the tunes were collected in Somerset, and of those 82 per cent came from only 10 per cent of the county.[48]

Again, the implication is that rather than trying to record an existing culture, the folk song collectors were looking for something particular. William Motherwell was quite confident that he would recognize it when he found it, by means of 'a kind of intuitive perception [which] cannot be communicated by words to another'.[49]

This sort of mystification was relatively common, for example in the claims that Child could never be fooled by a forgery, and had an instinct for the authentic ballad.[50] It is not, however, a strategy that John Clare was forced to resort to. His own class position, and his status as a 'peasant poet' gave him a confidence in dealing with folk songs: sufficient confidence to correct, and even rewrite, many of the texts that came into his hands. Clare's collecting does show up a more general dimension of the whole business of folk song collecting, however: it is crucially affected by the gender of both collector and source. Clare collected many of his songs in the Blue Bell pub, but this was not a place which women collectors could readily enter, hence Lucy Broadwood's strategy of inviting singers to her house. Likewise, relatively few songs are collected from women, as they are unlikely to have the status of 'village singer' or to be willing to sing in public.

Alfred Williams, writing in 1923, gives the relationship between collector and source a further twist. As we have seen, the differential power relationship was generally fraught, and determining, but unacknowledged, throughout the nineteenth century. Williams, however, makes his differences from his sources quite clear. The complexity of his own class position perhaps makes this essential. Thus Williams generalizes about the rustic population, that they prefer the old to the new, are suspicious of change: 'they dislike photographs. That fact alone is significant.'[51] Yet, Williams compares the moment of expectation, waiting to hear which song a singer will produce, with the excitement of waiting in a darkroom for a photographic plate to develop. The language makes Williams's investment in this process clear: he, for one, does not dislike photographs.

If Williams signals his difference from his sources, A. L. Lloyd indicates his difference from other collectors, and his identification with his sources. He attacks 'the ideas of scholars who at heart dislike the materials they are working with almost as much as they dislike the bearers of that material'.[52] He excludes himself from this category of the 'conventional folklorist', gaining his right to speak from his ability to recognize the silences of earlier folk scholars. 'Romantic ballad scholarship' and 'dry-stick minds' are also criticized as being unequal to the task of imaginatively reconstructing the history of a culture that is always in struggle, and still very much alive.[53] As we shall see, however, Lloyd's assertiveness, and his identifications, also leave some important gaps and silences.

The mediations involved in the act of collecting are necessarily multiplied by the practice of editing. As William Motherwell said:

> The tear and wear of three centuries will do less mischief to an old ballad, among the vulgar, than one short hour will effect, if in the possession of some sprightly and accomplished editor of the present day.[54]

There are numerous examples of the ways in which editors intervened to make their texts more interesting, more coherent or more acceptable. Vic Gammon points out how Lucy Broadwood changed the words of songs in her collections, making it very clear which she found 'objectionable'.[55] Dave Harker argues that nineteenth-century collectors generally removed erotic references, excluded songs dealing with drink, and minimized those dealing with struggle.[56] It is impossible to discuss each of these charges in detail within the confines of this chapter. It is important to note, however, that later editors returning to folk song collections or ballads always find evidence for such mediations. The history of folk song collecting is punctuated by examples of editorial creativity, in the construction of coherent and acceptable cultural texts.

FOLK SONG IN DECLINE?

The need for such revision came from the strength of the collectors conviction that folk song represented a bulwark of coherence and significance, against a culture of decay, triviality and commercialization. Folk song itself, however, was also seen as in decline, as becoming less authentic. This perception is true of virtually all the collectors, from the early nineteenth century to the present day, although the moment and nature of decline were differently perceived.

As we have noted, Sir Walter Scott's interest in ballads was as the remnants of a peasant culture. He argued that the ballads themselves were, necessarily, in decline, and that the authentically national Scottish ballads were those written two hundred years previously. This pushing back of the moment of significant creativity to a pre-industrial, and pre-capitalist past was echoed in Child's analysis of the development of balladry. Child saw the ballad as in decline since the seventeenth century, a decline accelerated by the corruptions of the vulgar.

George Deacon's book on the folk song collecting of John Clare points up the continuities in these sorts of assessments. Deacon himself states that the folk song tradition was in decline in the 1860s. He also draws attention to Clare's own suspicion of 'the trash of the Ballad Singers'.[57] Clare collected and admired songs he recognized as belonging to an older tradition, but condemned the contemporary manifestations of this same culture as debased.

Cecil Sharp begins his *English Folk Song: Some Conclusions* by describing folk song as constituting 'a great tradition that stretches back into the mists of the past in one long, unbroken chain, of which the last link is now, alas, being forged'.[58] This is a picture of a continuous and coherent tradition, stretching right up to the present day. The image of the chain suggests the possibility of revival, of forging new links, which fits in with Sharp's project of reintroducing folk song into the dominant culture through the schools. At other times, however, he says that the folk song collector of the early twentieth century is a hundred years too late. Elsewhere he asserts that, 'as recently as thirty of forty years ago, every country village in England was a nest of singing birds'.[59] He finally concludes that folk song will be extinct within a decade. In Sharp's defence, it must be said that he does distinguish words from music, and that his more pessimistic judgements are generally in relation to the survival of ballad texts, rather than their music. As we have seen, however, Sharp cannot really support his claim for the continuity of folk tunes, so, in the end, his cultural judgements and predictions seem to become largely imaginary, in relation both to the history of folk songs and the history of their bearers.

For Robert Bell, writing in 1877, the moment of decline was significantly earlier:

> The gradual decline of these compositions may be traced to the accession of James I, when the Border feuds ceased to supply the bold and picturesque sources of interest which fired the imagination of the ancient minstrel.[60]

Bell is here reproducing the idea that the culturally significant and powerful aspects of folk song derive from professional musicians.

The role of the folk is to behave in ways which suit the forms of representation of the ballad. When they cease to do so, their culture becomes debased.

We have seen that Robert S. Thomson avoids, and challenges, the stress by folk song collectors on oral transmission. He demonstrates the links between folk singing and broadside ballads from the sixteenth century, showing that the presence of a printed text sustains rather than undermines a folk culture. To this extent, he refuses the inherited emphases and presuppositions of folk song collectors. But Thomson, too, is in no doubt that folk song is under siege, and in decay.

Initially, he seems to locate this decline at the end of the nineteenth century. He describes the transition from ballads to popular songs as representing the 'breakdown of almost four hundred years of continuity'.[61] Yet, when he goes on to examine the various surviving forms of one particular ballad, far from finding continuity, he finds, 'a rather dismal picture of steady decay that does little to support the notion of a vital folksong culture'.[62] Perhaps this says more about the notion than it does about the culture. Thomson seems to acknowledge as much, when he observes that Lucy Broadwood and Frank Kidson felt, 'like all collectors before them . . . [that] they were in at the death of a traditional art'.[63]

In *The Singing Englishman*, A. L. Lloyd tells more or less the same story of decline. He attributes it to cultural fragmentation in the fifteenth century, and to the growth of the ballad trade in the sixteenth century, which produced a series of 'vulgarisers' and 'burlesquers'.[64] He sees a further decline in the late eighteenth century, when folk song became 'something empty, and vulgar and debased', and again in the 1820s, when folk song slipped 'more and more into burlesque'.[65]

In fact, the evidence he produces in the book contradicts this picture of steady decline, of the disappearance of a whole culture. Lloyd discusses sea shanties, and ploughboy's songs, which did not even begin to be produced until the nineteenth century. What he documents are cultural transformations, not the disappearance of a whole culture. Yet he perceives it as a steady, and inevitable, picture of decline.

Michael Pickering warns against a simple thesis of decline in his book on *Village Culture*. He insists that there are elements of growth as well as decay to be found in the history of folk song. He argues that the rejection of traditional songs does not necessarily mean that people are turning their backs on authenticity, and giving in to the trite and commercial. The rejection may quite simply amount to a recognition that the social relations which produced certain forms of song have changed. It need not be seen as false consciousness, but rather as a consciousness that certain inherited cultural forms are now false.

Lloyd seems to concede this in *Folk Song in England*. He revises his earlier conclusion that folk song has disappeared. Indeed, he points out that folk song is still being actively created, not in the countryside, but in mine and mill. Yet, despite Lloyd's attempt to formulate a living, contemporary folk culture, the strength of the traditional model of decline reasserts itself. He is arguing, basically, for a continuity between rural and urban cultural forms of the lower classes. But, as we have noted, the pull of the rural, historical model of folk song creation is very strong. It is not surprising that Lloyd concludes that the new songs do not have the 'star-reaching beauties' of the old folk songs.[66] His project involves an attempt to salvage certain elements of the musical culture of the 1960s, in order to reconstruct them as part of a tradition. His judgements of value are rooted firmly in the tradition of rural, orally transmitted folk song.

Although folk song is seen as being in decline, it is also consistently described as healthier, more coherent, and more worthwhile than the other forms of song culture surrounding it. Images of virility, power and masculinity recur in relation to folk music. In the early part of the nineteenth century, Motherwell asserted that no one 'who has an unsophisticated and manly taste' could neglect ballads.[67] Robert Bell saw himself as 'resisting everywhere the invasion of modern namby-pamby verse'.[68]

The first volume of the *Journal of the Folk Song Society* contained an Inaugural Address by Sir Hubert Parry. In it he described popular songs as the enemy of folk music, as repulsive, and as admired only by those 'who live in these unhealthy regions . . . people who, for the most, have the most false ideals'.[69] He also insisted on the need 'to distinguish what is genuine from what is emasculated'.[70] He made the point even more forcibly in 1924, describing 'modern tunes' as representing, 'all the brazen affrontery, the meanest grossness, and the most hideous and blatant repulsiveness'.[71] Cecil Sharp was equally confident of the role of folk tunes in relation to the growth of popular music. Once more he insists on the need for discrimination, the need, 'to distinguish between the instinctive music of the common people and the debased street music of the vulgar'.[72]

For the nineteenth-century folk song collectors, the main enemy was Music Hall. Music Hall represented, at least on its initial stages, a new cultural form which addressed itself quite consciously to the urban working classes. It could not be assimilated into a history of continuity, decorum and good taste. It was thus repeatedly stigmatized by the folk collectors. Alfred Williams compared the eroticism of folk songs, which he saw as 'morally immoral', with the 'cunningly suggestive and damnably hypocritical' songs of the Music Hall.[73]

A. L. Lloyd partly recuperates some of this condemned culture, showing how urban workers' songs can be seen as part of a folk tradition, even though they may eventually have been printed, recorded, and even sung professionally. About his own contemporary culture, however, Lloyd is just as scathing as his nineteenth-century predecessors. He talks of the 'mumbled withdrawals or frantic despair', and, later, of the 'dim cloud-cuckoo land' of pop music. He sees the pop music of the 1960s as 'up to the nostrils in a sea of inanity'.[74] Lloyd is as much out of sympathy with the producers and consumers of such music as the nineteenth-century collectors were with the performers and patrons of Music Hall.

WOMEN AND FOLK SONG

The metaphorical equation of folk song and masculinity sits uneasily with the fact that women were, from the mid-nineteenth century on, very active in the collecting of folk music, and that women have often played an important role in the transmission and preservation of popular songs. The relationship of women to the practice of folk song, and of collecting, was clearly limited to some extent by their gender. Women could not readily go into pubs, where folk songs were frequently sung. Indeed, Ginette Dunn's study of popular singing traditions in East Suffolk demonstrates that this difficulty of access has remained a problem for women singers.[75] Dunn demonstrates the ways in which economic, social and religious factors interact to keep women out of village pubs, thus ensuring that regular communal singing is dominated by men.

Women might have difficulty uncovering, or publishing, texts dealing with 'improper' topics.[76] Generally, however, in the mid-nineteenth century, gender is invisible in texts dealing with folk song. That is to say that it causes no disturbance. The role and practice of women folk song collectors is not perceived as threatening musical or cultural institutions. All the collectors are marginalized to some extent in relation to the dominant culture and gender is rendered invisible within the general project of revival. It is invisible in another sense too: there is little attempt to detail the different songs sung by women, the different contexts in which they were sung, or the different meanings that may have been attached to songs by women. The 'folk' is a resolutely masculine construction.

In later texts, however, the issue of gender becomes not just absent, or metaphorized, but positively fraught. When Vaughan Williams is discussing Sharp's intervention in folk song collecting, he talks disparagingly of those who 'discussed over a cup of tea in a dilettante spirit', songs that were 'sweetly pretty'.[77] He is thus contrasting Sharp's rigorous research and analysis with earlier forms of domestic and amateur collecting, which he dismisses as effeminate. Vaughan Williams sees Sharp's greatest achievement, however, as lying in his publishing of songs, 'which the average amateur could easily sing . . . with accompaniments which their sisters or girlfriends could easily play'.[78] Thus the role of preservers and transmitters of folk culture is handed over to men, that of accompanying it given to women.

A. L. Lloyd's project was to recover the history and culture of 'ordinary and obscure labouring men'.[79] This means precisely what it says. Lloyd brings labouring men, and organized male industrial workers, into the centre of his account of folk song. But, in replacing 'the folk', which was undifferentiated by gender, with the urban industrial worker, Lloyd actually writes women more definitively out of his account.

Lloyd also treats women collectors with an irony and resentment which surpasses the critique he launches on the basis of class assumptions. He scorns the 'maiden ladies on bicycles', as if absence of sexual experience, or at least of a husband, were uniquely debilitating for women collectors.[80] He talks scathingly of the 'indomitable Miss Broadwood'.[81] Michael Pickering's language is similar, as he describes Janet Blunt as 'a spinster' and as the 'Lady of the Manor'.[82] Her class culpability seems to be exacerbated by her gender.

Richard Dorson's position is very much the same when he undermines women collectors by attributing their enthusiasm to 'wifely devotion'.[83] Dorson does look at the work of some women collectors in detail, although he warns us that 'the modern reader will be repelled by the florid feminine style of Mrs Bray'.[84] Anna Eliza Bray was a folklorist, whose work was eventually published in the form of letters to Robert Southey. Dorson also details the career of Anne Grant, who published a work on the *Superstitions of the Highlands* in 1811. Dorson claims, 'Her fame rivalled that of

Ossian's Macpherson, and her visitors included Scott, Southey, James Hogg and Wordsworth.'[85] This claim cannot really be supported, in that, as we have seen, the 'Ossian' debate was both international and prolonged. Nonetheless, it is interesting that a women collector who was both famous and respected in the early nineteenth century should have so completely disappeared from most histories of folk collecting.

The vulnerability of women in cultural history is illustrated by David Buchan's account of the song collecting of Anna Gordon, generally referred to as Mrs Brown. Anna Gordon's collecting is very much part of a history of women's songs and singing. She collected songs from her mother's side of the family, from her aunt, via the nurses and other women in her aunt's employment. Yet the history of Anna Gordon which Buchan gives us is resolutely patriarchal. As explanations of her position are offered the fact that her father held the chair in Humanities at King's College, Aberdeen, that her husband was a minister, and that her mother was the daughter of a Baillie of Aberdeen.

The exclusions of such patriarchal histories are not always a matter of deliberate decision. In many ways, Dave Harker is careful to point to what women were doing within the folk song movement, or at least to why we don't know what they were doing. Yet, the very conception of his book ensures the absence of women. He says that, since he is going to look only at those who have both collected and published folk songs, women will, unfortunately, not be dealt with in any detail. Yet, the very fact that women collectors often had no access to publication is a product of their marginalization within nineteenth century culture. Thus the marginalization and exclusion reproduce themselves up to the present day.

FOLK SONG COLLECTING IN CONTEXT

Throughout this history of folk song collecting, certain continuities have emerged: an idealized concept of history and of the people, a cultural history based more on fantasy than on analysis, the positing of a coherent, organic culture suddenly under attack, the invisibility or active marginalization of women, and the conviction that folk song represents a culture in decline. There are clear parallels with the case of Ossian discussed above, and like the Ossian controversy, the practice of folk song collecting was part of a larger ideological and cultural project.

One aspect of this project was the supposed link between folk song and national culture. Carl Engel's argument that the music of working people, being the most free from external influences, was the clearest articulation of national identity, provided the impetus for collectors in the second half of the nineteenth century. Sharp tried to develop and support this idea in his collecting, asserting that since folk music was unwritten it must proceed 'from out the heart and soul of a nation'.[86] Sharp was involved in the construction of a national culture. As we have seen that a large percentage of his *Folk Songs of England* actually came from a small part of one particular county, namely Somerset, this project is not without its problems. Dave Harker puts the point more strongly, in claiming that Sharp, 'felt happy in passing off a selection of doctored texts and tunes, imbued with militaristic, patriotic, monarchistic and socially conservative values as "British"'.[87]

Sharp, and, later, A. L. Lloyd, argue that folk music also has an international dimension: 'minds of men, at equal levels of cultivation, are everywhere substantially the same'.[88] If folk music is about basic perceptions and feelings, and their national expression, then it must be basically international. For Sharp, this contradiction between nationalism and internationalism is insoluble, since he reduces both these terms to essences. He has no way of theorizing the material conditions of production of particular songs, and thus no way of linking the history, geography and cultural development of a country to its folk music. He cannot therefore explain the relationship between folk songs and national identity, except in ways that are entirely mystificatory. He merely asserts the relationship and uses it to argue for the appropriation of folk tunes by composers concerned to articulate English national identity. This strategy reminds us of the fate of Ossianic literature, which rose to fame while it supported or challenged particular theories of poetic language, but then returned to the obscurity of a culture which was largely misunderstood and mostly despised.

The importance of folk song collecting, its theorizations and its practices, in the late nineteenth century, can be seen in relation to the formation of the Folk Song Society in 1898. This society itself was preceded by the Folk Lore Society which was formed in 1878. The study of folklore was perceived as the science of primitive social relations, practices and beliefs, which focused both on the 'savage' peoples of India and Africa, and on the less developed peoples of Western Europe.[89] The word 'folklore' was coined in 1846. From this moment on, vast numbers of texts were produced to define and categorize 'the folk'.

The formation of the Folk Song Society represented the institutionalization of collecting, and the hegemonic victory of its conceptions of national popular music. Those actively involved in the Society included professional singers, musical journalists, the professors of music at Oxford and Cambridge, the Principal of the Royal Academy of Music, and the Director of the Royal College of Music. It was formed in order to facilitate the collection and preservation of folk songs, ballads and tunes. All prospective members had to be approved by the committee, and, with subscriptions at 10s. 6d., the Society was scarcely likely to attract those from whom had collected, whose culture they aspired to record, into their ranks.

The investment in folk song, then, was closely related to evaluations and assessments of the national culture. Vic Gammon relates this very convincingly to struggles within the musical profession, over the status of German music. The Academies and Schools of music were producing increasing numbers of professional musicians, who had to challenge the dominance of German music and musicians if they were to have any hope of employment and of participating in a creative musical culture.

This theorization of national identity exceeded the confines of musical transformations, however. It participated in a series of assumptions about cultural authenticity and value in pre-industrial England. The health and vigour of the folk song thus represented a continual challenge to, and critique of, industrial society. If the worth of a society could be measured by the strength of its cultural products, then British society in the late nineteenth century, for the folk song collectors, was clearly in decline.

A. L. Lloyd also saw the analysis of folk song as part of a larger political project. He criticized the legacy of the nineteenth-century collectors, their appropriation and depoliticization of folk-song texts. He ridiculed the reduction of folk dances to 'a prancing curate in cricket flannels'.[90] He asserted that the folk song revival of the 1960s was significantly different from earlier attempts to preserve or celebrate the tradition of folk singing, in that it came 'from below'.

The very fragmentation of folk song, however, and the proliferation of commercialized and superficial song was, for Lloyd, an indictment of capitalist social and cultural relations. The ghetto of 'folk' or 'workers'' culture is produced by a dominant culture which is obsessed with both the practice, and the repression, of class politics. Lloyd argued that a socialist society would have no need of the distinction between 'folk' and 'cultured' music.

The debate about the nature and potential of folk music did not end with A. L. Lloyd. *Marxism Today* contained a series of articles in 1966 which variously argued for folk song as a bastion of health against the inanities of pop music, for the inevitability of the decline and debasement of folk music after the introduction of printing, and for the need to rethink the cultural elitism and reaction which led Left-theorists to condemn pop music.[91]

A final piece of absurdity, but one which is arguably overdetermined by the history of folk song collecting, is to be found in *Scottish Folk Notes*, of 1967. As well as reproducing music, and explaining lyrics, the first volume dedicates three pages of pictures and text to an explanation of the process of making a crook from a ram's horn. This is not done as part of social history, but as part of the construction of an imaginary continuity between the readers and the shepherd, which will be mediated by folk song. The same volume contains a 'Folk Recipe' for Potted Hough, which, we are told, is part of, 'a recipe card pack from Johnston and Bacon. Each recipe is printed on a washable card backed with a genuine tartan.'[92]

Dave Harker's conclusions about the concept of 'folk song' seem fairly inescapable at this point. While the term had an important role to play in relation to the dominant culture, as an explanatory concept for the analysis of the cultural history of the lower classes it is 'simply a problem'.[93]

ARTS AND CRAFTS

The history of the Arts and Crafts Movement provides a useful, though difficult, end to this chapter. I will begin by looking briefly at the origins of the Arts and Crafts Movement, particularly at the work of William Morris, whose theoretical writings have provided the terms for many subsequent analyses of the social and cultural relations of popular art. The work of Bernard Leach in the 1930s and 1940s will also be examined, since it reintroduces the concept of 'folk' art, and, like many of the folk song collectors, relies on a contradictory, but powerful, notion of tradition.

The Arts and Crafts Movement presents some analytical problems: many of the participants are the subjects of extensive debates which, while pertinent to the topic of this book, cannot effectively be reproduced within it. Also, the cultural products of this movement are not textual. They are peculiarly fragmentary, potentially subject to the discourses of fine art, and of economics.

These facts are not debilitating in themselves; the same, after all, could be said of literature, but they do threaten to exceed the theoretical framework of the present work. The following analysis thus both recognizes the centrality of the *practices* of the Arts and Crafts Movement to any history of the appropriation of popular cultural forms, but also, necessarily, displaces attention on to the theoretical and political texts which surrounded, and to some extent constituted this movement.

The linking of pottery with the study of folk song is neither arbitrary nor simply strategic. If we look at *The Athenaeum* of 22 August 1846, we find William Thoms's coining of the term 'folklore' in a letter, in which he asks readers to participate in the collection of legends, traditions and ballads. This is the beginning of the science of folklore, of analysis of the significance of certain texts and practices in the lives of 'primitive' peoples. In the same journal, we can find a review of Alexandre Brongniart's *Historical Illustrations of the Art of Pottery*. The reviewer asserts that forms of pottery can be used as markers of different civilizations, that they show the development of technologies, taste and religious beliefs.

It is to precisely this relationship that William Morris addressed himself. He opened up the possibilities of cultural politics by insisting on the relationship between the organization of work, the class structure of nineteenth-century Britain, and the standards of craft and artistic production. Morris asserted that, 'the leading passion of my life has been and is hatred of modern civilization'.[94] He condemned it for its unnaturalness, its exploitations, and its relegation of human beings to the status of mechanical appendages. He argued that modern civilization merely organized towards and for misery, that it debased simple pleasures and destroyed art.

The Firm, which Morris established with, among others, Dante Gabriel Rossetti and Ford Madox Brown, was an attempt to challenge the social and cultural relations of industrialization. Starting as a small-scale cooperative, and growing into a large commercially successful business, The Firm trained people in the production of pottery, embroidery, furniture, wallpaper and household objects. These objects were initially produced individually: 'every real work of art is inimitable'.[95] Eventually, however, the production of The Firm was split between individual creations and more repetitive and routine work, such as wallpaper and fabrics.

The legitimating moment for Morris, and for The Firm's practice, was the Middle Ages. Following Carlyle and Ruskin, Morris argued that the Middle Ages represented a time of unsurpassed integration in terms of individual creative impulses and social need. The medieval artisan was the model of an independent labourer fulfilling a social need, and producing an aesthetically admirable object. J. Bruce Glasier used a similar argument in relation to minstrelsy and folk song in the *Labour Leader* in 1908.[96] Glasier insisted that the Middle Ages were characterized by social relations that could be considered socialist: a system of guilds and of common property. Oppression was external, and did not take hold of individual subjects or of their creativity. Thus medieval villages were 'oftimes vocal with minstrelsy and mirth'.[97]

This validation of the Middle Ages represented a critique of industrial society and its culture. As Morris said, science and commerce, 'cannot produce so much as the handicraft of an ignorant, superstitious Berkshire peasant of the fourteenth century'.[98] Such a formulation is not, however, unambiguous. Struggles over historical representations can often shift into romanticism, as we saw in relation to the folk song collectors above. Morris's medieval Britain seems very short of the disease, poverty and social dependence which were manifest in the fourteenth century. Also, the 'ignorant peasant' is worryingly reminiscent of the 'illiterate singers' whose existence was so important to the folk song collectors. The implications of Morris's rejection of his contemporary culture and civilization are not straightforward. For Morris, the validation of medieval social relations was always part of an attempt to transform nineteenth-century social relations. At the same time, however, in placing the illiterate peasant above the urban industrial worker, Morris does fail to engage with the complex transformations that had taken place within the working classes, who could never simply be turned back into medieval peasants.

Morris's analysis of craft production was resolutely social. He was concerned with the conditions both of production and of consumption of household goods. The Firm rejected the division of labour characteristic of industrial production. Work in itself was not seen as a necessarily fulfilling activity, indeed Morris described such an equation between earning a living and doing good as merely, 'a convenient belief to those who live on the labour of others'.[99] Work was useful only in so far as it produced something useful, and provided creative pleasure. It could not do this if it consisted merely in the mechanical repetition of a simple gesture.

Morris's history, although it tended towards romanticism, never tended towards idealism. He insisted that social relations must change in order for aesthetic innovations to be sustained. His emphasis was always on the type of production rendered possible by particular organizations of labour. In insisting on this connection, a very deep structural connection, while trying to produce useful, beautiful and popular art within a capitalist economy, Morris was obviously involved in a contradiction, a contradiction for which he is frequently attacked. However, Morris's attempt to produce popular forms of culture, while theorizing their impossibility was not simply a matter of bad faith or hypocrisy. There was, at the time, no significant working-class market for consumer goods. Most working-class homes had little furniture and almost no decoration. The customers of The Firm were in fact, 'the rich merchants and manufacturers who would not live with the things their factories turned out'.[100] They were the only people who had the financial means to reap the benefit of 'popular art'.

Thus, the cultural artefacts which had been validated because of their status as popular art were in reality quite actively divorced from the people. Potentially, those whose cultural forms were abstracted in order to produce certain standards of taste and judgement could then be condemned for their failure to reach, or aspire to, these standards. The importance and significance of popular art therefore becomes a matter of history, texts and practices handed down by tradition, and ceases to have any living relationship with the working classes of nineteenth-century Britain.

Morris's politicization of the domestic, his articulation of class struggle in the home as well as in the factory, represents a potentially exciting development of the set of ideas we have inherited as 'marxist'. It might perhaps seem that it would also represent an undermining of the assumptions about gender which characterize analyses of the people and their cultural forms. This, however, is not the case. Morris's metaphors should already alert us to the potential problems. After characterizing useful and useless toil, Morris says that 'it is manly to do one kind of work, and manly also to refuse to do the other'.[101]

Anthea Callen makes it clear that the Arts and Crafts Movement largely reproduced the gender and class structure of nineteenth-century Britain. Within The Firm, as in other craft organizations, women worked on traditionally female pursuits: Jane and Elizabeth Burden worked on embroidery, Georgina Burne-Jones worked on embroidery and woodcarving, and May Morris worked on embroidery, wallpaper and jewellery. Women's involvement in the Arts and Crafts Movement basically took two forms, depending on their class position. Working-class women were employed in the revival of traditional rural crafts, such as lace making, and mostly worked at home. Middle-class women who needed, or wanted, to earn their own livings trained at the recently formed Schools of Design and worked mainly in embroidery and pottery, particularly painting flowers on pottery. Their position within the movement was always precarious. The Art Workers' Guild, which was formed in 1884, was all-male. Its members went on to fill the powerful jobs within the developing institutions of craft and design. In 1908, Charles Ashbee, of the Guild of Handicraft, expressed his concern thus: 'our fellows are rightly nervous of the competition of the amateur, especially the lady amateur'.[102]

The idea that women were merely 'amusing themselves' or 'filling in time' proved very resilient, and made the entry of women into the Arts and Crafts Movement slow, uneven and difficult. In certain areas, such as gold working, furniture making and glass blowing, they were actually excluded from apprenticeships. It is not hard to understand Anthea Callen's assessment that the Arts and Crafts Movement, 'turned out to be reactionary in its reinforcement of the traditional patriarchal structure which dominated contemporary society'.[103]

Bernard Leach began working as a potter in England in the 1920s. His 'first endeavour was to search for what remained of the English tradition'.[104] In his pottery, and in his writing, he attempted to theorize the history of that tradition and to assess its relevance for contemporary craft production. In this he was very influential, not just in relation to other potters and artists working and living in the same community as himself, St Ives, but also in relation to the emergence of a hegemonic definition of traditional, authentic and popular pottery.

Unlike Morris, Leach's focus was not social. His early writings are concerned with the individual, with the possibilities of the materials and forms of pottery as media for complete unified human expression. He defined a pot as a 'projection of the mind of its creator'.[105] Certainly, Leach condemns the fact that 'factories have driven folk art practically out of England' but this does not move towards an analysis of the relationship between society and culture.

The dominant themes of Leach's earlier writings are the familiar modernist ones of discontinuity, disruption and alienation: these are resolved by appropriation and disavowal. Leach is concerned that the potter in England faces a 'broken tradition' and a culture in the act of changing.[106] The old peasant potteries are in decline, unlike in Japan, where Leach had 'met a living peasant school of country potters, continuing on from father to son'.[107] The element of appropriation comes in Leach's project of collecting elements and practices of folk culture, which will then be reinscribed in a different context, that of the 'artist-potter', and given new meanings. Leach is quite clear that a mere effort of will cannot make him into part of a living tradition. He is necessarily and consciously 'outside' such a tradition. He looks to folk art, not to duplicate it, but because he admires elements of design and decoration found in folk art, and nowhere else. Quoting Yanagi, his Japanese colleague, he argues that: 'what is so appealing in the art of the people is this very quality . . . beauty accompanied by the nobleness of poverty'.[108] The element of disavowal comes in Leach's reaction to the popular taste of his own time. He condemns the fussiness of industrially produced pots: 'an indictment of our own popular half-culture'.[109] Having aestheticized and valorized the 'art of the people', Leach seems to blame the people for its demise.

This move, of appropriating values and condemning their erstwhile bearers, is rendered almost inevitable by Leach's notion of creativity and of history. We have seen that he perceives creativity as fundamentally individualistic. He does, later, modify this position, arguing instead for the artist's need to repress individuality and to produce as part of a tradition. But since the emphasis remains on the adequacy of the will of the individual 'artist-potter' to the task of self-renunciation, the individualist focus remains. Leach's account of history is, likewise, individualist and idealist. He represents history as the history of consciousness. He sees history as a more or less random space, punctuated by particular manifestations of creativity and will. It seems to be impossible, on this model, to account for the transformation in the production and consumption of pottery which Leach describes, without seeing these simply as a matter of bad faith, or bad taste, on the part of the people.

Leach certainly acknowledges historical changes, in his insistence that folk art cannot simply be revived:

> the people who are attracted to-day by the hand crafts are no longer the simple-minded peasantry who from generation to generation worked on in the protective unconsciousness of tradition, but mainly art students.[110]

But this seems to amount simultaneously to recognition and misrecognition. The facts of shifting cultural hierarchies are clearly stated. The historical degree zero of the 'simple-minded peasantry', however, is becoming familiar to the point of banality in relation to the processes examined above. Leach is here involved in cultural polemic, not cultural history.

Leach's notion of history is linked to his concept of tradition. This term is actually both fragmentary and troubling in relation to Leach's work. He announced himself in search of a tradition, but also announced himself unable to find it. He argued that potters 'suffer inevitably from the almost entire loss of our own birthright of traditional craft lore', but often represents the value of his own practice as being in its authentic use of just such craft knowledges.[111] In fact, Leach's practice borrowed from a range of different national and historical styles in pottery. He studied Chinese, Japanese, Greek and English techniques at different historical periods. His work involved techniques and materials adapted from many different traditions. According to Oliver Watson, this intervention was so characteristic that it amounted to Leach's founding 'a new tradition of British pottery'.[112] Tradition thus seems to be dead, powerful, and recreated, all at the same time. This contradiction is paralleled in the representations of Japanese pottery which occur in discussions of Leach. Leach is described as having discovered an ancient and powerful tradition of pottery in Japan before 1920. Yet, Hamada, who worked with Leach, apparently returned to Japan 'where he became the leader of a . . . revival of craft pottery'.[113] Brian Moeran argues that this revival was itself profoundly influenced by cultural developments in nineteenth-century England.[114] Yanagi, who coined the term *mingei* (popular or folk art) in the 1920s, was influenced by the writings of William Morris.

'Tradition' has certainly remained a powerful term in relation to perceptions of Leach's work. The recognizable forms of cider flagon, jug and pot, and the distinctive decoration in browns, greens and greys have become accepted as the natural traditional forms of English pottery, what Peter Dormer calls 'a pottery version of the . . . ploughman's lunch'.[115] There are, in fact, other traditions of pottery manufacture in England, including those forms which derive more directly from the studio potteries of the Arts and Crafts movement of the nineteenth century. Yet the conjunction of rural, simple, self-effacing and apparently ahistorical qualities of the 'Leach tradition' are such as to render its hegemony within craft pottery entirely comprehensible.

The reference to cider jugs and flagons brings us, finally, to the contradiction between discourses of utility and aestheticism in relation to this form of popular art. Leach insisted that craftsmen must supply a need. Yet, he continued over a number of years producing items of pottery in stoneware, which he himself had said lacked the qualities of durablity and practicality of industrial pottery. Large pottery jugs and cider flagons inevitably change their significance in an era of cheap, lightweight pottery, and plastic bottles. They become markers of style, perhaps of resistance, but, surely, not of utility: 'few people have used their bottles and cider flagons and the plethora of jugs for anything other than putting flowers in'.[116] Here, then, is not a simple revival and valorization of popular cultural forms, but a complex process of transformation, appropriation, resistance and continuing struggle over history, significance and tradition.

5

Workers'/Popular Theatre
1919–1945

In this chapter, the argument about the construction of 'popular culture' takes a further twist. Rather than looking at the terms of, and motivations for, the appropriation by the dominant culture of forms deemed 'popular', this chapter will investigate attempts in the 1920s and 1930s to construct popular cultural forms from a position consciously outside, and indeed in opposition to, the dominant culture.

In doing so, as the title of this chapter suggests, we immediately come upon problems of terminology, which are in fact problems of politics and culture, and their mutual relation. The constant slippage in the texts examined in this chapter between 'workers'' and 'popular' as descriptions of the theatrical forms and practices under discussion is indicative of a real theoretical problem. Are the two terms synonymous, or oppositional, or merely subtly different?

In the last chapter, we saw that 'folk culture', although it was offered as something coherent, separate from, and even antithetical to, 'popular culture', in fact represented merely a concentration of certain familiar arguments about the culture of the people. It was one of the terms used to establish claims about cultural authenticity, historical continuity, and aesthetic value in relation to popular culture. A structurally similar argument will be made about 'workers' culture' in this chapter, and, indeed, about 'mass culture' in the next. Many of the texts examined in this chapter will not talk about 'popular theatre' but rather about 'workers' theatre' or 'proletarian theatre'. Yet, the concerns addressed, and the terms employed are largely those we have recognized in other sets of texts on popular culture. Once again, we find a constant confusion of terms, with 'popular' and 'workers'' being used in the same article, or by the same writer at different times. It was, after all, the Hackney People's Players who went on to found the Workers'

Theatre Movement (WTM), and one of their members, Tom Thomas, who was to describe the work of the WTM as 'popular theatre'.[1] Each of the terms examined below, 'workers' theatre', 'proletarian theatre', and 'labour theatre', in designating a certain set of cultural forms and practices, simultaneously engages with definitions of 'the popular'. So, the difficulty of terminology, far from being a distraction, is part of the problem addressed in this chapter.

The choice of the theatre as an example of the conscious construction of alternative cultural forms in the 1920s and 1930s perhaps needs some justification. First of all, the achievements of the workers' theatre movement, and especially of Unity Theatre, have long been perceived as important models for the reformulation of relationships between culture and politics. The large numbers of people involved in these movements, their theatrical innovation, and their long-term effects on definitions of 'popular culture' make them objects of great interest for contemporary cultural theorists. Also, the extent to which the Communist Party, as a revolutionary, national organization, was involved in these movements, at the levels of personnel, cultural theory and political organization, allows for an analysis of important problems in the relationship between 'the people' and 'the party': problems which are clearly part of any attempt to win 'the people' or 'the popular' to a revolutionary political vocabulary.

The choice of popular theatre as an object of study also has the virtue of topicality: Raphael Samuel, Ewan MacColl and Stuart Cosgrove's *Theatres of the Left 1880–1935*, has made material on the WTM much more generally available, and has generated substantial debate about the history, success and contemporary relevance of the WTM. Likewise, several texts on Unity, and of Unity plays, have been published in recent years, and clearly form part of a more general reassessment of the cultural and political history of the 1930s.[2] Again, the motivation is a search for examples, or warnings, in relation to the contemporary political situation, and the perceived crisis of Left political and cultural theory. The danger in all this lies in the temptation to mythification. Samuel, as we shall see, offers us a history of the WTM as a movement of authentic and powerful class struggle, wilfully neglected by historians. Accounts of Unity often grant it a power and appeal which is not only hard to believe, but also makes its demise incomprehensible: did every member of the audience really rise up, shouting 'Strike! Strike!' at the end of *Waiting for Lefty*?

There may seem something perverse about concentrating on

theatre in a period when film and broadcasting, which we now think of as archetypal twentieth-century forms of popular culture, were on the increase. However, the aim of this book is to understand the construction and importance of the concept of 'popular culture' in different historical moments, and not to speculate on what was 'truly popular culture' at any given period. It is quite clear that, in the 1920s and 1930s, it was precisely the exclusion of theatre from the structures of mass reproduction that made for its centrality to discussions of popular culture. According to writers in *Plebs* magazine, for example, film and radio were agents of capitalist propaganda, and sellers of fantasy and seduction, but the theatre could be won over and transformed into a cultural form representing the people and their interests.[3]

Further, the history of the theatre seemed to encourage this conviction. Writers pointed back to the medieval miracle plays, or to the Renaissance stage, as examples of theatre which was accessible, powerful and popular. The absence of women from these stages might have given them cause for concern, though in fact it didn't, but, generally, theatre was represented as an originally, and indeed essentially, popular form, which had been hijacked and trivialized over 300 years.

This confidence in a moment of organic, popular theatrical practice in the past was supported by arguments about the power of possible transformations in the future. Unlike film, which needed expensive equipment and technical skills, theatre seemed much more readily appropriated, more flexible, and accessible to large numbers of people with little, or no, previous experience. In purely financial terms, theatre seemed, to those involved with the development of oppositional and politicized forms of culture, the most promising site of intervention.

Finally, there is a particular interest, in terms of this book, in workers' theatre of the 1920s and 1930s as a site of debates about the nature of popular culture, because of the international dimension of these debates. Earlier discussions of popular culture have nearly always made some reference to national identity. That is certainly true of folk music, of peasant poetry and of the works of Ossian. But, the construction of alternative theatrical forms in the 1920s and 1930s went on, quite consciously, in an international context. Like much Left argument after the First World War, it was suspicious of any calls to national identity and patriotism. The construction of a workers' culture was felt to imply no national boundaries, and the influence of German, Russian and US theatrical practice on British theatre groups was, as we shall see, profound. Only in Scotland did the problem of national identity remain a crucial part of the project of creating a workers' theatre movement, since here the rhetoric of nationalism seemed less fatally compromised.

So, the 1920s and 1930s are interesting as a site of developing critiques of the dominant culture, and of attempts to construct politically progressive, and generally accessible forms of popular culture. The theatre is interesting because of the power and persistence of arguments about its essentially popular nature, and because of its potential as an accessible, flexible and powerful cultural medium. The aim of this chapter will be to see how these various factors interact: the historical context, the political theory, the plays, the players, the audience and the cultural critics.

Obviously, many of the debates about, and analyses of, culture which we will examine are, in the simplistic sense, debates about politics. It would be illusory to pretend that by 'solving' the cultural problems one could also arrive at conclusions about the correctness of particular political 'lines', and folly to pretend that the political positions do not overdetermine assessments of the cultural strategies. In other words, this is a political minefield, and, if it blows up, it is to be hoped that the observations about the importance in all this of the concept of 'popular culture' remain. Rather than solving the major problems about political strategy, the relation between class and party, or the success of the Popular Front which the chapter, necessarily, raises, I hope, rather, to show the extent to which inherited ways of theorizing popular culture remained dominant, and 'got in the way' of progressive debate. I aim to show how categories of 'the popular', such as 'continuity', 'tradition', 'authenticity' and 'autonomy' were used, abused, and insufficiently transformed.

As in earlier chapters, before examining the historical emergence of the workers' theatre movement, it is necessary to be conscious of the mediations through which these histories have passed in contemporary texts. *Theatres of the Left 1880–1935* is an important source of documentation and analysis of the workers' theatre movement, the more so in that Samuel's account of the history of this movement seems to offer a powerful and direct correlation between theoretical innovation and revolutionary politics.[4] The rest of this chapter will aim to disturb and undermine this easy correlation, to reintroduce the complexity, negotiation and confusion of cultural politics.

Samuel is harsh in his criticism of political theatre in the period of the Second International. Such theatre illustrated the tendency of nineteenth century socialists to 'worship at the shrine of art'.[5] It accepted conventional literary and theatrical values, but sought to make these more available to the working population. Socialism in this period, Samuel argues, borrowed its language and imagery of struggle from literature, and thus assured its own weakness and complicity with the dominant culture and social order.

Samuel goes on to charge political theatre in the early 1920s with hypocrisy: it avowed realism, but actually produced texts that were symbolic, melodramatic, or farcical. This charge amounts to a curious sort of double-think. Samuel is critical of the revolutionary potential of a realist aesthetic, and condemns as reactionary the early 1920s impulse to realism. He then further indicts the period for failing to live up to its own realist ideals. But, surely, this failure, on Samuel's own terms, should be its greatest strength.

In contrast to this period of collaboration and political confusion, Samuel praises the profound rupture in cultural theory and theatrical practice that is signalled by the emergence of the WTM, particularly in its second, and more revolutionary, form of 1928. He describes the WTM as 'a phenomenon of the general strike rather than the Popular Front', which produced Unity, and applauds the WTM's 'exuberant sectarianism'.[6] Rather than attempting to mediate high culture to the people, or escape from an inferior class position, Samuel argues that the WTM celebrated its exclusion from dominant culture, and struggled to produce a self-consciously proletarian aesthetic.

The WTM, Samuel argues, represented the alliance of communism and the avant-garde. It thus represented both a political and a theatrical rupture, from the reformist, enlightening and realist practice of earlier socialist movements. The WTM represented agitation and propaganda rather than moral uplift.

Samuel thus argues for a clear dichotomy between socialist theatre in the early 1920s and the work of the WTM. The transformation that is represented by the emergence of Unity was, it seems, equally abrupt. In the mid-1930s, the vigorous, innovative theatre of the WTM gave way to the 'fairly simple naturalism' of Unity.[7] The difficulty caused for this model by Unity productions such as *Busmen*, *Babes in the Wood*, or *Waiting for Lefty* is clear. This difficulty perhaps explains the claim in *Theatres of the Left* that Manchester Theatre of Action, which Samuel sees as part of the WTM, did a production of *Waiting for Lefty* before Odets even wrote it.[8] The first British theatre group to perform *Waiting for Lefty* was, in fact, The Rebel Players, who went on to form Unity Theatre. The play may not represent a consistently working-class analysis, but it is certainly vigorous, and scarcely naturalistic.

My aim in all this is not to dispute that the sort of theatre produced by the WTM was different from much that preceded it, or that Unity Theatre made many different sorts of decisions about plays and production from the WTM. Indeed, it is precisely the history of these differences, and the terms in which they were theorized, that interests me. The point is, rather, that Samuel's claim for sudden rupture, and the theoretical and political primacy and purity of the WTM, cannot be maintained, even in terms of the evidence he himself produces in *Theatres of the Left*.

The WTM is at one moment celebrated as something quite unique, but then Samuel admits that important initiatives preceded it, such as the plays of Joe Corrie, and the cultural theory of *Plebs* magazine. Also, Samuel admits that the early WTM was staffed by 'middle-class Bohemians', and that, even after 1928, it was run by individuals who were more plebeian than working-class: so where are we to locate the proletarian purity of the WTM? Samuel offers the possibility that the WTM was 'an aspiration rather than an achievement', which is helpful, but seems to undermine most of his celebratory rhetoric.[9] Finally, Samuel offers the fact that 'street theatre dominated the WTM's self-conception'.[10] This, for Samuel, seems to be an important part of the specificity of the WTM, its determination to bring theatre to the factory, the rally, and the streets, in contrast to Unity's retreat into established theatrical surroundings. But, Samuel also admits that 'most WTM performances were indoors'.[11] So, why does he offer the 'self-conception' as fact, and thus reproduce a mythology about the inescapable link between theatre in the streets and revolutionary cultural politics?

At this point, we must clearly move beyond Samuel's account, although still accepting the usefulness of the theoretical and dramatic texts he has made available. The rest of this chapter will be an attempt to clarify the history of workers'/popular theatre from 1919 to 1945. It will begin by analysing the positions held by Left theorists on culture, specifically theatre, politics and their relation. It will then look at the work of the WTM, the styles of performance, types of play, and the theoretical justifications that underpinned them. It will conclude with an analysis of the practice of Unity Theatre, and its relation to attempts to clarify the politics of the popular.

Socialist theatre did not, of course, begin in 1919. Plays of social protest, and a theatre of seriousness and social conscience were developing at the beginning of the nineteenth century. In the early part of this century, Clarion Dramatic Clubs and Co-operative

Society drama groups performed in small halls and at political meetings, in an effort to expand the context of socialist culture and education. They were heavily reliant on short sketches, and on the plays of George Bernard Shaw, which attracted interest because of their handling of social issues, their wit, and their abundance of fine speeches. Shaw's plays continued to play a central role in efforts to construct a 'popular theatre' throughout the 1920s and 1930s, and were the staple texts of many amateur socialist groups.[12]

The reason for starting this analysis in 1919, however, lies in a conviction that the experience of the First World War is crucial to the discussions of culture, human values and social ills which will be examined below. Writers constantly refer to their perception that society is fundamentally transformed, qualitatively different and therefore needs, and can only support, qualitatively different forms and practices of culture. In place of the repression of history, then, we find the claim that it has entered a fundamentally different stage. Ness Edwards, in 1926, located this perception in terms of economic relations: 'The development of a new economic order of society also requires the assistance of a new cultural order.'[13] This observation is, of course, both descriptive and predictive. But, the themes of crisis, transformation and radical difference are repeated throughout discussions of workers' theatre. Tentatively at first, and increasingly and more powerfully throughout the 1920s, the assertion is of decline, decadence and sterility in capitalist theatre, and virility, strength and innovation in workers' theatre.

The year 1919 also signals the beginning of an initiative that is important in any analysis of popular theatre: the publication of a series of 'Plays for a People's Theatre'. These plays were part of a project to provide the necessary materials for the construction of a people's theatre. The authors in the series included D. H. Lawrence, whose considerations on the nature of 'people's theatre' demonstrate the lack of any broad debate or analytical refinement in relation to this topic at the period. Lawrence struggles over his definitions, in a way that has become familiar, asserting that 'the people' is neither everybody, nor the working class, but rather decent, ordinary men who inhabit the spaces between 'the millstones of capital and labour'. 'If there are men,' he concludes, 'there is a people's theatre.'[14] Such a theatre, Lawrence argues, is crucial 'in this hour of confusion'. It can produce plays that show the complexity of social and sexual relations, rather than merely reproducing mechanical plots and stereotypical characters.

This hostility to what passed for theatre in the West End is widespread in Left and radical publications in the early 1920s, and is frequently contrasted with the human and cultural potential of popular theatre. The *Labour Magazine* in 1922 attacked the degradation brought to theatre by a spirit of commercialism. It wrote in praise of the policy of the Old Vic: the provision of good plays at cheap prices. Similarly, the journal of the Independent Labour Party (ILP), the *New Leader*, asserted that: 'The stage is the people's, its appeal is to no separated class, but to the vast general mass of the democratic world.'[15] This basically amounts to a defence of the seriousness and significance of theatre, against the perceived forces of trivialization. The *Labour Magazine* sees the arts as essential to a balanced and critical state of mind. It thus supports the cause of workers' theatre as a means to 'awaken the dormant artistic instincts of the people'.[16] Likewise, the ILP equates socialism with the desire for a fuller and better life, and asserts the central role of theatre, and the arts, within this project. This key role accorded to theatre echoes the insistence by the *Clarion* that theatre represents 'a higher and more beautiful' cultural form than film or radio, and is part of the same political and cultural project as Amabel Williams-Ellis's 'winning beauty for the masses' in 1925.[17] The early 1920s, then, produced arguments about the corruption and degradation of post-war capitalist culture, and an insistence on the importance of constructing theatrical forms that would enhance the lives of working people. Theatre was to be serious, significant, and relatively cheap.

There was little criticism of the forms of theatrical production available, or of the limitations of the stage and the proscenium arch. Although Left papers did consider the possibility, and necessity, of workers' theatre, they continued to give quite significant critical attention to the West End stage. Articles and reviews still focused on quality of performance, or on the soundness of casting. There was no attempt to develop alternative criteria for the assessment, or production, of workers' theatre.

By 1926, however, with the appearance of a series of 'Plays for the People', edited by Monica Ewer of the *Daily Herald*, attention began to shift from the necessity for fine-quality, generally accessible theatrical performances, to the importance of a socialist content within individual plays. These 'Plays for the People' were basically naturalistic plays, dealing with industrial militancy, working-class oppression and unemployment. *The Forge*, by Edwin Lewis, is fairly typical of the plays in the series. It represents a working-class household, and its domination by the shattering noise of the heavy hammer from the neighbouring factory. The noise of the hammer continues throughout the play, thus producing in spectators the frustration and exhaustion of the working-class family. The young male hero, Tom, struggles to reject the limitations of his monotonous, constrained existence, and strives to find ways to fulfil his 'inner spiritual needs', or even to find ways to express their existence. His fiancée, Amy, is completely incapable of seeing beyond the expectations of her current existence: marriage and a constant struggle against poverty, mitigated by trips to the cinema. The play ends in destruction of the hero and defeat of his values. The noise of the hammer stops, but only because it has broken down, killing both Tom and the possibility of emancipation. It is, as later critics were to point out, a fairly depressing narrative, but it does also provide a powerful symbolism, in the noise of the hammer, for the suffering and constriction of working-class life.[18]

Such plays were being written in the context of an expansion in the numbers of socialist amateur theatre groups. In 1925, Miles Malleson was arguing the need for the ILP to organize its drama groups and to expand their repertoire. He claimed that the way in which individuals spent their leisure was what determined their worth as human beings.[19] Thus, socialism's claim to provide a better and fuller life depended mainly on its cultural intervention. This seems a curiously idealist position on the nature of social and cultural relations, but it is not untypical of the arguments deployed in favour of popular theatre at the time.

The standard argument by those who defended West End theatre, on the other hand, was that, since it survived in a market economy, it must be providing what people actually want. Socialist critics were clear in their rejection of Box Office as a reflection of public taste and needs. An article written in 1925 pointed out the disproportionate power held by the purchasers of expensive tickets to determine what was performed in commercial theatres.[20] It also criticized the acting profession as essentially reactionary: a testament to their historical position as 'hangers-on' of the aristocracy. In this sphere, too, things were changing. The formation of an actors' trade union in 1924 led to attempts to organize the acting profession, to assert the seriousness and importance of acting skills, and to insist on the necessity of guaranteed levels of remuneration.

By the second half of the 1920s, these sets of interventions – making drama more affordable; taking acting seriously, and producing representations of working-class life – no longer seemed adequate to several writers. Ness Edwards, who was himself a member of the Plebs League, the revolutionary, syndicalist organization based in the National Council of Labour Colleges, turned to the topic of workers' theatre. He was profoundly suspicious of 'people's theatre': 'the middle class societies with the capitalist dramas desire to rebaptise the bourgeois theatre as the People's Theatre'.[21] He insisted on the class basis of all art. The history of drama, Edwards argued, is of sets of representations advancing the interests of the ruling class. Since history was now moving towards socialism, however, workers' theatre must develop to produce new forms of drama, representing the interests of the working class. Edwards argued that: 'Class art exists as the organisation and sublimation of the feelings and consciousness of a class.'[22] Since all art is class art, this can be taken as a statement of his position on the nature of workers' theatre.

Edwards insisted that workers' theatre must be left to the workers, and not to middle-class aesthetes and reformers. He saw it as the possible site of working-class confidence and creativity, and of fruitful representations of working-class life. The texts he suggests for such a theatre include the 'Plays for the People' and the works of Toller, Upton Sinclair and Karel Čapek. Clearly this list, for him, is unsatisfactory, containing defeatist and idealist texts, but Edwards sees them as a basis for the formation of a workers' theatre.

The *Labour Monthly* in 1926 echoes this perception of the class polarization of art, in its insistence that only the working class can create new and vibrant forms of theatre.[23] This confidence in the cultural and political potential of the working class is something that is manifested in a range of texts of the mid-1920s. This is related to the organizational and ideological effects of the General Strike, whose defeat merely clarified the necessity for autonomous working-class organization.

Stuart Macintyre, in *A Proletarian Science*, demonstrates the strength of working class auto-didact culture in relation to the membership and theoretical positions of revolutionary political parties and groups in this period.[24] This strength produced a conviction that the working class represented a distillation of progressive political and cultural values. This conviction was very different from earlier attempts to insist on the rights of working people to gain access to fuller and more creative lives, such as we examined in the case of the Chartist press. It was premised, rather, on the belief that capitalist social relations were inimical to art, and that the cultural forms it produced were necessarily corrupt. This case was argued quite explicitly in the *Labour Monthly*: capitalism is the enemy of collective life, and therefore of drama. All that is possible in capitalist theatre is sterile propaganda.[25]

This is a statement of the classic marxist position that 'capitalist production is inimical to some fields of spiritual production, like art and poetry'.[26] The position might be refined by the observation that it is capitalism in decline that produces particularly decadent and meaningless texts. It is a position that is widely accepted by socialist cultural theorists of the period.

The quotation from Marx, however, is not intended to provide the unimpeachable authority for this perception, and in fact it raises particular problems for the writing of a history of socialist analysis of culture in Britain. It would be relatively easy to assemble the writings of Marx and Engels, or Lenin and Trotsky, on culture, or on theatre, and then measure the writings of British theorists in relation to these. The difficulty, however, lies in knowing which texts would actually have been available to political activists, or theatre workers, at the time. Stuart Macintyre has shown that many of the writings of Marx and Engels were unavailable, except in expensive foreign editions, in the 1920s.[27] Marx's early writings were particularly badly represented. The works of other European Marxists, such as Gramsci or Rosa Luxemburg, were not available in English at all. Of course, a certain number of texts and arguments about culture got through to activists in Britain. The British Communist Party had extensive international links, at both personal and institutional levels. By the 1930s, these international links can be clearly seen in the appearance of journals such as *International Literature* and *International Theatre* which published Marx's and Engels's writings on literature and culture, and described the work of socialist theatre groups throughout Europe, and in the United States. In the 1920s, however, the origins of particular arguments about culture are much harder to perceive.

As I have said, the claim that capitalist social relations are inimical to art is a standard marxist argument. The insistence on the power and specificity of working-class or proletarian culture is, however, less well supported by texts of the marxist/leninist orthodoxy. Lenin, in his 'Draft Resolution on Proletarian Culture' insisted on the need to appropriate and transform aspects of bourgeois culture, rather than simply creating autonomous forms of 'Proletarian Culture'. Likewise, Trotsky, in *Literature and Revolution*, which was available in English in 1925, challenged the relevance of the concept of 'proletarian culture' which was only conceivable post-revolution, at which point there would no longer be a proletariat. He, too, warned of the danger of ignoring or dismissing the historical accumulation of cultural texts. He remarked that: 'To say that Futurism has freed art of its thousand-year-old bonds of bourgeoisdom is to estimate thousands of years very cheaply.'[28]

The texts of Marx, Engels, Lenin and Trotsky on culture, then, are not necessarily very revealing in relation to attempts at theorization of workers'/popular culture in the 1920s. Many of the positions adopted in Britain represented an extrapolation of political arguments about the primacy and progressiveness of the working class and the imminent decline of the capitalist system. The enthusiastic adoption of 'agit-prop' as the appropriate form for working-class theatre is perhaps a reflection of this fact: 'agit-prop' was, after all, a political term before it was a theatrical one.

So, the *Labour Monthly*'s assertion that capitalism destroys the possibility of theatre is by no means idiosyncratic. The conclusion drawn from this, however, would certainly not command general assent: the *Labour Monthly* argued that the result of the spiritual poverty of capitalism was the reduction of theatre to propaganda. This was condemned as a perversion of the true nature of theatre.

Writers in the *Sunday Worker*, however, celebrated the power of theatre as propaganda. They attacked the dominant culture as the site of 'anti-working class dope'.[29] This imagery is picked up repeatedly: the *Red Stage* in 1931 described bourgeois theatre as 'the opiate of the people', and compared its effects to 'chloroform'.[30] *Plebs* ran a series of articles on culture in 1929 under the heading of 'Dope Distributors'.[31]

In contrast to the stupefying, trivial, cultural forms of capitalism, the *Sunday Worker* supported initiatives towards a workers' theatre. It argued that workers' theatre must represent a complete break with the past, politically and theatrically. Many of the *Sunday Worker* articles were written by Huntly Carter, who published widely on theatre and cinema in the Soviet Union. In *The New Theatre and Cinema of Soviet Russia* he described the theatrical innovation of directors like Mayakovsky and Meyerhold, and produced a categorization of Soviet theatre which saw Stanislavsky as on 'the right', catering to the new bourgeoisie created by the New Economic Policy, and placed Constructivism, Futurism and Bio-mechanics on the 'left'. Carter described the success of the Blue Blouse movement in the Soviet Union: 484 professional and 8,000 amateur theatre groups by 1928, performing sketches, revues, acrobatics, mass recitations and mimes.[32] Such a massive cultural and political initiative, he argued, was urgently needed in Britain.

Workers' theatre was to be something quite different from anything that had preceded it. It was to consist of material written by working-class playwrights, and performed by working-class actors. It was to concern itself directly with class struggle: 'the fighting theatre of the working class influencing the masses'.[33] Its aim was the 'revolutionary militant education of the toiling masses', and the organization of working-class victory in the class struggle.[34] This project had nothing to do with bourgeois theatre, except to attack it. The *Sunday Worker* insisted that to do anything in the workers' theatre that could be done in the capitalist theatre amounted to a betrayal.

The *Red Stage* was equally clear about the specificity of workers' theatre. The capitalist theatre repressed class struggle, workers' theatre would celebrate it; capitalist theatre depended on naturalistic plays, workers' theatre on agitational sketches; capitalist theatre was produced by an individual writer, workers' theatre was created collectively. It must be said, at this point, however, that these positions represent theoretical convictions about the necessary role of workers' theatre, rather than descriptions of workers' theatre as it existed at the time. Indeed, Tom Thomas, who was crucially involved in the formation of the WTM, was to argue that proletarian drama, as the drama of a whole class, was inconceivable before the revolution.[35]

In contrast to this 'class enthusiasm', however, the People's Theatre in Newcastle had changed its name from 'socialist' to 'people's' in 1921, feeling that this label was more 'all-embracing' and thus more 'democratic'.[36] The basic argument seems to have been that, since the business of theatre was to represent, rather than to transform, the broader the field of representation the more democratic the practice. Clearly, this is quite different from perceptions of theatre as agitation and propaganda in the interests of the emergent working class. The People's Theatre, in fact, felt such a conception to be contrary to the nature of theatre, which was concerned with the representation of conflict and contradiction: to be, in fact, a denial of theatricality.

Again, we see the terminological confusion that goes with theoretical and political problems. We have, over the last few pages, encountered 'the masses', 'the workers', 'the proletariat', 'the people' and 'labour'. Each term is used to refer, more or less, to the same group, but attempts to ally it to a particular political discourse: 'the masses' are the victims of false consciousness, while 'the proletariat' are the agents of historical progress. All these terms are concerned to denote a group which stands outside the cultural sphere and interests of capitalism, whose interests are inimical and perceptions fundamentally different. This search for an enclave of class and ideological purity, absolutely uncompromised by the dominant culture, is fundamental to analyses of the possibility of workers' theatre in the late 1920s. Structurally, this search is very similar to that of the folk song collectors, who tried to find cultural enclaves undisturbed by the social relations of capitalism. Both imply the construction of an imaginary unity, in order to deny the implications of negotiation and complexity.

The *Plebs'* interest in culture lay in its importance as a site of ideological intervention. It ran a series of articles in 1929 on cinema, wireless, theatre and the press attacking their role as agents of propaganda. It attacked capitalism for 'castrating the emotional life of the workers', and also for feeding them 'seductive dope'.[37] 'Castration' and 'seduction' may seem unlikely allies, but both point to the concern of *Plebs* writers with the power of capitalist culture to appeal to the irrational and unconscious desires of its consumers. This complaint was amplified by Charles Mann in 1932, who complained that capitalist culture gained power by offering women sexuality and men sport.[38] This concern echoes, interestingly, Fanny Mayne's concern about the excessive effects of reading penny fiction. Fanny Mayne also expressed concern about the seductive effects of reading cheap fiction, although her concern was with these texts as leading to possible revolution.

Maurice Dobb wrote about the theatre in *Plebs* in 1929. The specificity of the stage, for Dobb, lay in its ability to arouse emotion. The more successfully it offered a new direction to the emotions, the higher its status as art. The immediacy and power of its emotional effects, however, also explained its power as ideology: naturalizing its representations through the power of authentic emotion. This ideological power was diminished by the fact that theatre had become the property of a small leisured class, who could provide it with neither vitality nor conviction. 'Art theatre', which was set up to challenge the debasement and vulgarity of bourgeois theatre, could offer nothing but individualistic mystification. 'Popular theatre' could offer nothing more than the advanced products of the bourgeois theatre, and was, dangerously, 'often dominated by middle-aged spinsters'.[39] The hope for a vibrant and powerful theatre must, therefore, lie with the workers' theatre. Dobb conceded that workers' theatre could produce nothing substantial until after the revolution but, in the meantime, it could abandon the sterility of bourgeois or popular theatre, and turn to burlesque, satire and propaganda.

Throughout the 1920s, then, there was a move towards the theorization of theatre as an important site of ideological struggle.

This went along with a conviction that the working class represented the site of culturally and politically progressive values. This move is interestingly mirrored in the terminology of popular theatre. In 1919, the series of 'Plays for a People's Theatre' addressed the need for changes within the theatrical institution to allow for the production of more serious and significant plays. 'Plays for the People', a series begun in 1926, addressed more directly the facts of working-class oppression and the need for political change. 'Plays of the People', published in 1929, represented a further development: the emergence of working-class playwrights, producing their own representations of working-class life.

In the early 1930s, there is a certain amount of tension in accounts of the possibility of, and the role of, workers' theatre. Reports of the Workers' Theatrical Olympiad, held in Moscow, and attended by British actors, talked of the power of mass amateur theatre, and its role in education, political organization, and the mobilization of support for the Soviet Union. *International Theatre* asserted that the working class was ready to master art. It also warned, however, of the theoretical and theatrical inadequacy of simple 'class enthusiasm', and the limitations of actors simply 'acting themselves' on the stage. At the same time, the *Daily Worker*, unlike the *Sunday Worker* of the 1920s, was paying very little attention to theatre. It was far more concerned with film, particularly with organizing the distribution through film clubs of revolutionary Soviet cinema. This change of focus is perhaps reflected in the worried observation of 1935 that 'the working class don't take theatre seriously enough'.[40]

The changing languages brought to the problem of popular theatre can be observed in the writings of Joe Corrie. His early plays, such as *In Time of Strife*, which dealt with the difficulties of maintaining solidarity throughout a long strike, were performed by the WTM. In his theorization of the nature of popular theatre, however, he rejected the concepts of 'rupture' and 'revolution' outlined above, and turned instead to 'tradition'. He criticized the growth of cinema as providing entertainment that was consumed passively, and argued for the necessity of creating cultural forms which demanded active participation, as the old storytelling tradition had done. He argued for the centrality of culture, and insisted on 'art for humanity's sake'. He talked, not of the 'working class' but of 'the common people'.[41] He thus, to some extent, spoke the language of peasant poetry, or of the folk revival, rather than that of the WTM. It must be admitted that, by the late 1940s,

Corrie was despairing of the same 'common people' as interested in nothing but trivia, but still, the force of his commitment to extending the definition of culture, and to writing plays that reflected the lives of Scottish working people, remains.

The rigid autonomy of 'workers' theatre' was, then, already being challenged in the early 1930s. Workers' theatre groups began to work with professional directors and actors. André Van Gyseghem, who went on to become President of Unity Theatre, worked with the the Rebel Players in 1933. The idea that training in voice, movement and lighting would facilitate, rather than compromise, political theatre was being widely advanced, in contrast to the earlier insistence on autonomy and amateurness.

The development of Left cultural theories in the 1930s can best be traced in the pages of the *Left Review*, which began publication in 1934. The greatest perceived difference in the political climate at this time lay in the emergence of fascism, and it is to the dangers that fascism represented that the *Left Review* addressed itself. This development was also reflected in the Communist Party's change of tactics from 'class against class ' to 'Popular Front': an alliance of different social classes and groups who had a common interest in the defeat of fascism.

The *Left Review* argued for the importance of culture as 'the inherited solution' of political and personal problems, and thus as the property of all. It also insisted on the position that all art was, in some sense, class art, and, historically, represented the interests of the ruling classes. This seeming contradiction was dealt with by a policy of selective appropriation and critical transformation of existing cultural texts.

The *Left Review* also argued for a basic incompatibility between capitalism, certainly in its most extreme form as fascism, and cultural values. Literature, it claimed, concerns human values, whereas capitalism interests itself only in commodity relations. The struggle for socialism, as a struggle for fuller and more equal social relations, was thus a struggle for a more viable culture. Political activism was thus, directly, a form of cultural intervention.

This argument led to further arguments about the relationship between social values and aesthetic values: the best art was that which most truly represented human relations, and was thus on the side of progressive forces. This argument represents an important departure for accounts of the relation between culture and politics. We noted that nineteenth-century socialist thinkers were trapped into reproducing aesthetic judgements which they would have liked to refute, because of the lack of any developed vocabulary for the theorization of the relation between social and aesthetic values. They thus could not avoid representing the democratization of culture as its decline. The *Left Review* represents a significant development in seeing greater accessibility, and broader partici- pation, in culture as aesthetically beneficial. This position led to a predisposition towards realist texts, as those most accessible, and most able to represent social relations and human values.

The *Left Review* also argued that the dominant culture was doomed. The past twenty years had shown the inevitable collapse of culture into trivialization and decadence in the face of a capitalist system driven to war, fascism and mass unemployment. This was, however, an observation about culture under capitalism, and not an assessment of the real nature of culture. Culture, basically, represented an aspiration towards freedom. As such, it was indispensable, and had to be won over to the forces of progress and equality. Literature may have been used as propaganda, but *Left Review* was clear that culture was not just a form of propaganda. It represented the repository of human history and values.

In relation to theatre, these arguments manifested themselves in the claim that 'theatre is, essentially, a popular art'.[42] It exists in order to provide creative forms for the representation of human needs and problems and is thus, properly, the property of the people. John Allen extended this argument by claiming that, as an essentially popular form, theatre is also an essentially socialist form.[43] It is concerned with the representation of all facets of human life, and has striven to offer such representations to all. Once again, the Renaissance and medieval stages are cited as examples of theatre fulfilling its proper social role:

> Unity was trying to carry on that tradition dating back to the earliest times, when theatre was an important part of the life of the community, when it was part of, and not separated from the life and ideals of the people.[44]

The difficulty with such arguments lies in the extent to which they have to ignore vast segments of theatrical history: the Restoration theatre had little enough to do with the people. There is a difference between analysing and challenging the dominant culture and simply wishing it away. Simply saying, 'the theatre always has been popular, really' does not make it true. The desire for a continuous, popular tradition is not sufficient to constitute such a tradition, in folk song or in theatre.

There were, however, important initiatives throughout the thirties to make cultural forms more accessible, to reappropriate texts of the past and offer them in new contexts, to construct cultural forms that would represent the lives and interests of the working class, and to involve large sections of the labour movement in their production and consumption. Unity Theatre, and the Left Book Club Theatre Guild, represented such initiatives, and will be discussed in more detail below.

John Allen was committed to the development of popular theatre. He expressed concern that, in 1936, there was practically no theatrical activity among the working class.[45] This was an over-statement, since many of the amateur theatre groups established in earlier parts of the century continued to be active, but these were mostly local initiatives, easily marginalized, and poorly financed. Allen was convinced that socialist theatre, in order to have any power, must be aesthetically, as well as politically, convincing. Indeed, echoing earlier statements, he argued that socialist theatre, because of its commitment to progressive social forces, its youth and its vitality, would certainly surpass bourgeois theatre. Popular theatre could not, however, according to Allen, rely on tapping an existing working-class subculture. There was no such enclave of class and theatrical purity. Rather, it must turn to the existing theatre, borrowing as it needed, changing as it needed, and offering the results to a working-class audience.

Cultural theorists in the mid-1930s do demonstrate a certain unease about their own relationship to the project of popular theatre. Unity argued that 'A People's Theatre must dramatise their struggles'. They also talked of 'our own theatre' which later became 'a theatre of the people'.[46] There is a hesitancy in identifying the writing subject with 'the people'. This is even clearer in an article in *New Theatre*, published in 1945, which talks of people's theatre as 'dissemination of popular culture to the mass'.[47] So, whose theatre: 'ours', 'theirs', 'the people's' or 'the mass's'?

As well as initiatives to construct popular theatre, attacks on established West End theatre continued. It was seen as trivial, sterile, and blatantly ideological. The same sorts of arguments were made about film and radio. Ralph Bond, for example, argues that Hollywood cinema in the thirties merely produced trashy romances, which induced 'a state of stupor'.[48] Such cultural forms were unworthy of serious attention.

What is clear, throughout the 1930s, is both a commitment to, and the difficulty of, rethinking the relation between culture and politics. For Julian Symons, the project was bound to fail, and he condemns *Left Review* for publishing bad prose in the interests of political correctness.[49] This, however, is to travesty the project, and to ignore the very real advances in cultural and political theory produced within the *Left Review*. The difficulties are clear, however, in other writers of the period. Norman Veitch, for example, writing of the history of the Newcastle People's Theatre, and his own involvement in it, is unable to find any theoretical discourse that could unite aesthetic and political demands. He sees the spheres of performance and politics as quite separate, even within the individual actor. Joan Littlewood and Ewan MacColl, in Manchester, attempted to reconcile these two areas in the 1930s and 1940s. They instituted a systematic study of previous moments of popular drama and their dramaturgies, looking for techniques of popular drama, in a systematic way that went beyond wishful thinking. Yet, many within the Communist Party criticized their efforts and accused them of being 'too arty' and of ignoring the imperatives of political action.[50]

Having looked at the terms in which various theorists attempted to make sense of the concept of 'popular theatre', it might now be useful to look in more detail at the practice implied by, and supported by, these theories. Between 1919 and 1926, popular theatre was basically represented by the work of amateur groups associated with the ILP, the Labour Party, the Communist Party, the Co-operative Movement, or the Clarion League. They performed in small halls, with very basic lighting and production materials. The favoured texts of the period included the 'Plays for a People's Theatre' mentioned above. As well as *Touch and Go*, a drama of sexual and social relations by D. H. Lawrence, the series included *The Fight for Freedom* by Douglas Goldring. This play examined the oppression of men by the ideology of war, and the oppression of women by the ideology of domesticity. It ended on a fairly hopeless note, with the older woman character singing 'The Red Flag', while the younger one settled for familiarity, conformity and safety. Other frequently performed plays included *Hindle Wakes*, by Stanley Boughton, which examined the complexity of class relations precipitated by a sexual affair between the son of a mill owner and a working class woman; *'D' Company* and *Black 'Ell*, by Miles Malleson: plays about the pettiness, and ultimately the horror of war; and Hamilton Fyfe's *The Kingdom, the Power and the Glory*, whose imaginary, historic setting provided the terms for an examination of power, and the conclusion that 'there is no kingdom but the kingdom of love'.

The general tone of British socialist plays of the early 1920s was apocalyptic. They were anti-war, and therefore also about war.

They presented the sickness of society, its barbarism, hypocrisy and decline, but offered no solutions. They were powerful, but also despairing, and very often confused. Theatrically, their only innovation was a sense of social responsibility.

British workers' theatre groups also performed foreign plays. Those of Karel Čapek were particularly favoured. *Rossum's Universal Robots* (*RUR*) represents a society in which labour is undertaken by robots, who, because they have no souls, waste no time. Clearly, this was an exploration of the dehumanization implicit in capitalist social relations. The robots eventually revolt, however, having been given souls by a well-meaning scientist. By the end of the play the human race has completely disappeared, and only the newly humanized robots, now capable of love, survive to begin a new civilization. Again, the themes of capitalist decay and of redemption through human values and love are prominent. *The Insect Play*, by Josef and Karel Čapek, was a more sustained satire, which was frequently performed by workers' theatre groups throughout the 1920s and 1930s. Here, various insects represent the different facets of capitalist society: butterflies, the nastiness and superficiality of drawing-room society; beetles, the capitalist tendency to senseless and ceaseless acquisition; and ants, the mindless regimentation of war. The play ends with the death of the moth, the figure representing the life force. It is thus, though suggestive and humorous in its satire, despairing in its conclusion.

As well as this apocalyptic, and satirical theatre, there was also a developing strand of socialist realist theatre. Ruth Dodd's *The Pitman's Play*, first performed at the People's Theatre, Newcastle, in 1922, was about class politics, and the formation of trade unions in mining communities. The play represented the organization, but ultimate defeat, of a six-month strike. The colliery owners are shown as a new and more vicious breed than the old paternalists. They employ a spy, refuse to employ union members, and evict trade unionists from their homes. The working-class women in the play are represented as strong, and as politically knowledgeable, but also as too emotional for the business of political strategy. They have courage, but insufficient judgement. Joe Corrie's representation of working-class women in *In Time of Strife* is less ambiguous: his women are strong, courageous, and determined fighters for their class. Their sphere of influence is entirely domestic, but then so is the play.

The condition of working-class women was further explored in *The Street* by Alma Brosnan, which was one of the series of 'Plays for the People'. This play focuses on the ways in which poverty and unemployment drive women into prostitution. Notions of 'decency' are represented in this play as simply irrelevant in the face of imminent starvation.

In contrast to this series of naturalistic representations of working-class life and industrial struggle, there was also a developing practice of agit-prop theatre. Huntly Carter, who was closely acquainted with the work of Meyerhold and of Mayakovsky in the Soviet Union, was one of the key theorists of alternative forms of theatre. He argued, in the *Sunday Worker*, for the development of radically different forms of working-class theatre, which would be produced and performed by the working class themselves.[51] He criticized plays like *The Street* and *The Forge* for their defeatism, and their absence of political struggle. He advocated instead a theatre of short impromptu sketches and satires, a theatre of the street, without scenery or props, which relied on the immediacy and conviction of its arguments, on 'agitation' and 'propaganda'. Such theatrical performances were to be innovative, challenging, and spontaneous, to involve audience participation and to demonstrate eagerness and 'proletarian discipline'.

This was the position that was ultimately adopted as policy by the WTM. The WTM was initially founded in 1926, but quickly petered out. It was refounded in 1928, by Tom Thomas and the Hackney People's Players. The Hackney People's Players had performed various plays by Shaw, and Čapek's *RUR* at working men's clubs, for the Labour Party and the Communist Party. Frustrated by the lack of plays representing working-class lives and interests, they took to writing their own. Tom Thomas adapted Robert Tressell's *Ragged Trousered Philanthropists*, a novel which he describes as 'tragic realism', for the stage.[52] In 1930, by now as a branch of the WTM, they performed *Strike Up*, an agitational revue. This production was severely criticized in the *Daily Worker* as insufficiently political, as too close to traditional theatre, and for simply using available jazz tunes.[53] The implication was that it had failed to develop autonomous forms of workers' theatre, and was relying far too heavily on debased capitalist cultural forms. In 1931, the troupe went on a tour of Germany, where they saw large numbers of amateur agit-prop troupes. They returned determined to take their theatre to the streets, and to engage directly in working-class struggles. Their aim was to produce satire, rather than complex arguments, and the form of representation was to be an amalgam of the expressionist and constructivist techniques they had picked up in Germany. Their commitment to such forms of workers' theatre was strengthened by attendance at the International Workers' Theatrical Olympiad in Moscow in 1933.

The WTM troupes at this time determined to give up on complex staging, scenery and props, although the Hackney Group did, for example, possess a lighting board. They performed anonymously, and rejected all the trappings of the star system: 'our only star – the five pointed badge of the Soviet State'[54] They also performed in dungarees, a unisex badge of class affiliation. The WTM attempted to deny gender completely in its performances. Parts were taken up, irrespective of the gender of the actors. Class position rendered gender apparently irrelevant. This erosion of gender is related to the suspicion of sexuality. Sexuality was omnipresent in West End theatre and in commercial cinema, as an agent of class mystification. Sexuality was equated with the seductiveness of the dominant culture, and thus removed from the representations produced by the WTM. There is an emancipatory element in this denial of gender, in that women actors in the WTM were allowed a far greater range of parts than they would have been in any other theatre, although there was a continuing anxiety about the quality of their voices as representative of working-class strength: 'pretty girlish voices must be cut right out'.[55] It did also ensure, however, that sexual politics were subsumed completely under the banner of class.

Despite the aspiration to produce autonomous forms of workers' theatre, on and of the street, the actual practice of the WTM was quite diverse. As early as 1932, Tom Thomas was expressing doubts about the exclusivity of the project, and arguing for the need to forge links with ILP and Co-operative dramatic societies.[56] A critic of the WTM, in 1933, complained of its commitment to agit-prop, and argued for a return to naturalism, and to plays with a sympathetic member of the working class as hero.[57] In 1932 many WTM groups were doing outdoor performances for the first time, and, already by 1934, groups are arguing for the need to move back into halls and theatres.[58] Also, throughout this period, WTM groups continued to perform the repertoire of socialist plays outlined above.

There were also plays produced specifically for the WTM. One such was *Meerut*, a play arguing the case for solidarity with political prisoners in India. It was essentially a mass declamation, but with a clever visual effect produced by the actors holding poles in the form of prison bars. These were thrown aside and crashed to the ground with the final demand for international solidarity. WTM plays were generally short, and topical. They were produced for a particular event, such as May Day or a strike. The characters were basically types, the language very rhetorical, and the pace rapid. Plays were sent to all groups belonging to the WTM, and thus performed throughout the country.

Although I have looked mostly at the work of the Hackney branch of the WTM so far, there were branches throughout the country. Ewan MacColl was a member of the Red Megaphones, a branch of the WTM in Salford. He had joined the Clarion Players in 1929, for a performance of *Singing Jailbirds* by Upton Sinclair. However, finding the play defeatist, the rehearsals over-long and the audiences too small, he left and joined the WTM. The Red Megaphones had practically no experience of theatre. MacColl knew something about Brecht's work, and about agit-prop, through correspondence with a German pen-pal in the Young Communist League. Mostly, however, the troupe functioned on political priorities, and trial and error. They were very active during the Lancashire mill strikes of the early 1930s, performing outside mills and organizing support for strike action. Increasingly, however, they became dissatisfied with the theatrical limitations of agit-prop, and with the scripts they were sent by the national WTM. They began 'to doubt the efficacy of the endless sloganizing'.[59] They felt they were being patronized. So, they left the WTM. MacColl then pursued his theatrical work with Theatre of Action. Theatre of Action concentrated on developing theatrical technique, supported by the theories of Stanislavsky, and the practice of the New York Workers' Laboratory Theatre. They did a production of *Newsboy*, a satire on capitalist ideology as represented by the press.

It is perhaps worthy of note that MacColl cites both Brecht and Stanislavsky as theatrical influences, although we might now see them as representing fundamentally different positions on theatre and politics: Brecht advocating epic forms of theatre calculated to disturb, to challenge and to transform; Stanislavsky constructing naturalistic theatre aimed to provide insight and sympathetic identification. This difference was certainly perceived by Huntly Carter in the 1920s, at least in so far as he placed Stanislavsky on 'the right' and theatrical techniques which aimed to destroy illusion on 'the left'. It is quite common, however, to find theorists of popular theatre in the 1930s citing both Stanislavsky and Brecht: both are seen as part of 'taking theatre seriously.' Both offered techniques calculated to assure theatre's power and social effectiveness.

The history of popular theatre in Scotland demonstrates something of the principle of 'uneven development'. There was, indeed, a branch of the WTM in Glasgow in 1928, but it seems to

have had little success, and to have disappeared quite quickly.[60]
The Glasgow Workers' Theatre Group, founded in 1937, however,
seems to have used many of the techniques associated with the
WTM. Their style of performance was non-naturalistic, favouring
mass declamations and satirical sketches. Their uniform was
dungarees. Their performances were in halls, parks, and on the
street, although street performances were not very successful and
the group did much better at political rallies and meetings, where
they were assured of an interested audience.[61]

What the Glasgow Workers' Theatre Group aimed to be was

> A theatre that reflected the lives of the workers, that established a
> proletarian culture; and a theatre that exposed and explained the
> evils of society, an active, attacking, anti-capitalist and anti-fascist
> theatre.[62]

They were thus quite consciously struggling to create an alternative
culture. They wrote much of their own material, although they also
used scripts from Unity Theatre, which was, by now, well established.
UAB Scotland, a living newspaper by Harry Trott which involved a
confrontation between 'capital' and 'worker' about the origin of
wealth, an analysis of the workings of the Unemployed Assistance
Board in Scotland, and a mass declamation by 'typical Scotsmen
and Women', represented a significant development in the
representation of Scottish working-class life, but was also one of
their last performances.

The reasons for the demise of the WTM are complex, and
cannot be reduced to the statement that it was 'a casualty of the
Popular Front'.[63] In its strictly autonomous, workerist form, its
existence was always a little tenuous, and its effective role
somewhat constrained. In 1930, Huntly Carter expressed an anxiety
that the labour theatre movement was not popular with the
workers, and criticized the WTM for its 'purity of isolation'.[64]
Despite a commitment to agit-prop, many groups continued to
perform stage plays, indoors. Clearly, many within the movement
were worried by the notion that one technique was adequate to the
construction of a powerful and effective workers' theatre.

The idea that workers' theatre must be produced by the workers
alone was already undermined by the fact that in 1935 four WTM
groups were using professional directors, in order to enhance the
technical and theatrical power of their work. This tendency to seek
professional help, and to investigate alternative theatrical techniques,
certainly increased in response to the demands of the Popular Front
for the formation of a broad alliance of popular forces against

fascism. As Tom Thomas remarks, agit-prop was better suited to satirical attacks on the National Government, on behalf of the working class, than to the mobilization of different social forces round a complex political programme against capitalism, war and fascism.

Also, the equation between revolutionary politics and avant-garde cultural practice was being questioned in a number of spheres. Zhdanov's announcement of the Soviet commitment to a policy of socialist realism in literature, in 1934, led to renewed demands for realism in popular theatre. But all these responses had already been anticipated, for example, by the decision of the Rebel Players in 1933 to return to 'curtain plays', done before an audience of the labour movement, in halls and in theatres. They did a performance of *Newsboy*, and the first British performance of *Waiting for Lefty*, the play which is most powerfully evocative of the practice of Unity Theatre.

Although Unity theatre is the best-known initiative in socialist theatre of the 1930s, it is by no means the only one. The Group Theatre was also committed to the production of new socially con-scious writing, and to the defeat of fascism. Its best-known member was W. H. Auden, whose plays were frequently performed by the Group. Benjamin Britten, Tyrone Guthrie and Henry Moore were each, at some time, involved with the project. The Group Theatre worked with a concept of theatre as an art of the body. They produced highly stylized social dramas in verse. Their claim to the label 'popular', however, lies mostly in their political stance against fascism, since their audience was fairly limited, their membership was educated and middle-class and their plays were frequently patronizing in their representations of the working class. The Left Theatre began in 1934. It was an organization of professional actors, committed to the representation of working-class life, and to theatrical performances in working-class areas.

It was, however, the formation of Unity Theatre, and its growth into a national movement, which signalled the development of large-scale 'popular theatre' in the 1930s, involving far greater numbers, both in productions and as audience, than had ever been involved with the WTM. Unity was initially formed in 1937 by the Rebel Players, and members of Red Radio, the Hackney branch of the WTM. It began with sixty active and 300 associate members. At first, its practice was not significantly different from the WTM. Indeed, ironically in terms of the teleological history we have been offered, in 1937 Unity performed more often out of doors than in halls or theatres. It had both a play department and a propaganda squad, who were to perform short plays and sketches at political rallies and meetings. The play department, however, expanded massively throughout 1937 and 1938, whereas the propaganda squad became less and less active, and consequently was perceived as less significant.

Unity Theatre became a national organization, through the offices of the Left Book Club Theatre Guild (LBCTG). This was an offshoot of the Left Book Club, which had been formed for the publication and distribution of information and theoretical debate on the political priorities for the Left in the 1930s. It was organized, and initially funded, by Victor Gollancz. In the *Left News* of 1937, the formation of the LBCTG was announced, under the control of John Allen, and information was requested from any theatre groups performing political plays out in the streets.[65] The aim of the LBCTG was to provide information about, and support for, the formation of amateur socialist theatre groups, and to provide them with scripts. By the end of the 1930s, there were about 300 groups belonging to the Guild.

Unity Theatre expanded very quickly and, by the end of 1937, it had 7,000 individual members and 250,000 affiliated members from the labour movement. The London group moved into a converted Methodist hall in Goldington Street in 1937, which functioned not only as a theatre, but as a 'working-class cultural centre'.[66]

The plays they performed demonstrated the political priorities of the time. *Waiting for Lefty*, by Clifford Odets, was performed by all Unity groups, on numerous occasions. This play demonstrates the way in which individuals from various class positions, from Jewish doctor, to unemployed actor, come to realize their common interest in overthrowing capitalist social relations. It proceeds by a succession of short scenes, played out during a union meeting, demonstrating various individuals' experiences of oppression, and their politicization, and ends with the famous invocation to the audience to 'Strike! Strike! Strike!'.

Where's That Bomb?, by Herbert Hodge and Bob Buckley, two London taxi drivers, explored the various ways in which capitalism, and its ideological representations, pervade working-class lives. The narrative centres on the character of Joe Dexter, an engine fitter who has been sacked for writing subversive poetry. Joe is approached by the British Patriots' Propaganda Association and invited to earn some money by writing propaganda which will be printed on toilet paper, thus reaching the only place so far immune from capitalist ideology. Joe agrees, but is then confronted with the living realization of his own propaganda once he has fallen asleep.

The bolshevist, 'A Red Ferocialist', walks on, ready to destroy civilization, and carrying a bomb, hence the title. Joe, horrified by what he has created, refuses to sell it, and directs the gentleman instead to Fleet Street, where he will find all the lies he needs. The sexual politics of the play are dubious, for example, jokes are made about raping the boss's daughter, who is represented as relishing the prospect. It is, in other ways, however, an original and funny play, mixing a basic naturalism with extravagant set pieces reminiscent of pantomime.

These two plays attacking capitalist social relations were supported by plays such as Irwin Shaw's *Bury the Dead*, where war victims refuse to be buried, and the mass recitation of Jack Lindsay's *On Guard for Spain*, which rallied support for the anti-fascist struggle in Spain. Thus the priorities of political struggle, against capitalism, against war, and against fascism, were reflected in Unity's choice of plays.

Several of Unity's other productions are worthy of note. *Babes in the Wood* was a political pantomime: 'the babes' were Austria and Czechoslovakia and 'the robbers' were Hit and Muss. The production was seen by over 40,000 people. Unity's production of *Plant in the Sun*, by Ben Bengal, managed to attract Paul Robeson to act, turning down a lucrative West End part in favour of Unity. Brecht's *Señora Carrar's Rifles* was performed in 1938, and was the first production of a play by Brecht in Britain. Unity's production of *Crisis*, in September 1938, demonstrated that the group was still flexible, and willing to respond to political imperatives. This play, on the situation in Czechoslovakia was written and performed within twenty-four hours.

Finally, the production of *Busmen*, by André van Gyseghem and Herbert Marshall in 1938 was one of the earliest examples of a 'living newspaper' in Britain. André Van Gyseghem had worked with the WTM, and had studied in Moscow, and with Piscator, and had also visited various political theatre groups in the United States. The idea of a 'living newspaper' came from the Federal Theatre Project in the United States. The 'living newspaper' was an attempt to find a theatrical form for the representation of complex political argument, and the presentation of large numbers of facts. *Busmen* dealt with the reasons for the bus strike of 1937. A series of short scenes demonstrated the working conditions of drivers and conductors, and showed the ways in which their working conditions, and consequently their health, were being systematically under-mined in the interests of profit. Throughout the play, the 'Voice of the living newspaper' cites facts and statistics, details the conduct of

the strike, and advances the debate. The strike is eventually
defeated, and the activists are expelled from the union, but the
remaining members determine to continue the struggle.

London Unity was, thus, remarkably productive in the period
1937–8, producing the work of new playwrights, involving large
numbers of people, on an amateur basis, in their productions, and
bringing large sections of the labour movement into the theatre.
After this period of clear and urgent political priorities and
initiatives, however, the direction of the theatre bcame less clear.
The signing of the Nazi–Soviet Pact led to schisms within the Left
Book Club and the LBCTG. The ambiguity of rhetorics of 'the
people' analysed above began to have its effects, in terms of an
uncertainty about who Unity was speaking for, or to. Unity turned
more to productions of theatrical classics, and to the rediscovery of
popular theatrical initiatives of the past, particularly after the war.
Unity turned professional in London and Glasgow in 1946, but it
was, by then, more of an alternative space on the theatrical scene
than an innovative theatrical and political movement.

There were other Unity theatre groups apart from the one in
London. Merseyside Unity Theatre was not actually formed until
1944, but Merseyside Left Theatre, which preceded it, performed
many of the same plays as Unity, and belonged to the LBCTG.
Merseyside Left Theatre was formed in 1937, and, over the next
few years, performed plays by Jack Lindsay, Clifford Odets and
Joe Corrie, as well as mass declamations, and satirical sketches. In
1937 they did *Hunger March*, a 'living newspaper' about hunger,
poverty and unemployment. After the war Merseyside Unity
concentrated more on theatrical performances than on revues, or
on performances at political meetings and rallies. Its repertoire
consisted more of the 'classics of European socialist theatre':
Brecht, Shaw, O'Casey and Toller, than on contemporary writing.
It also undertook the production of large numbers of Elizabethan
and Jacobean plays, as part of a project of recovering theatrical
tradition and history for the people. Thus the emphasis was on
mediating, inflecting and reappropriating the dominant culture,
rather than on trying to construct or present alternative forms. In
so far as this emphasis involved a recognition, and transformation,
of cultural hierarchies, it does seem an inescapable part of any
project of constructing an oppositional popular culture. The danger
inherent in the developing practice of Merseyside Unity, however,
seems to lie in stultification: the acceptance of limited aesthetic and
political criteria as universal, and the failure to recognize or theorize
alternative theatrical forms. 'Popular theatre' thus becomes a polite

and well-meaning offspring of the theatrical establishment, rather than a space which challenges and undermines the definitions and assumptions of the dominant culture.

Glasgow Unity Theatre Group was founded in 1941, by an amalgamation of Glasgow Workers' Theatre Group, the Clarion Players, the Glasgow Players, the Transport Players, and the Jewish Institute Players. Its intention was to provide representations of Scottish working-class life, by and for the working class, whom it aimed to 'enlighten, encourage and enthuse'.[67] Glasgow Unity productions were generally socialist realist in form. Ena Lamont Stewart's *Men Should Weep* is typical of their work. It is set in an East End Glasgow tenement, and explores the double exploitation of women by unemployment and domestic labour. Maggie Morrison is shown struggling to bring up several children in the 1930s, while her husband is unemployed. The play speculates about whether marriage represents anything other than sanctified prostitution. The best-known of Glasgow Unity's productions, however, was undoubtedly *The Gorbals Story*, which was also performed on radio and made into a film. The play demonstrates the living conditions of families in the Gorbals: eight families sharing one kitchen. The characters, who all live in the same tenement, represent the various oppressed sections of the Glasgow working class: Irish, Indian, Highland, Catholic and female. The most powerful aspect of the play lay in its production of theatrical images of Scottish working-class life: unglamorous, oppressive, but humorous and strong, which produced strong identifications in its audience. It also attacked dominant notions of Scottish culture, as manifested by illustrations on shortbread tins. Such images of mystery and romance had little to do with the experience of the Gorbals.

The production of images that were recognized, and identified with, by a working-class audience was no small thing: there were few enough of them about. Still, as John Hill argues, Glasgow Unity Theatre failed to move beyond this fairly general project. Hill argues that Glasgow Unity was particularly disabled by the concept of 'popular theatre'. In the Scottish context, 'the people' readily became identified with a nationalist rhetoric, and lost the political 'bite' which had sustained its conceptualization in the 1930s. Thus, for Unity, 'the struggle for a "Scottish People's Theatre" became little more than that for a Scottish one'.[68]

Finally, it is important to analyse the role of women in popular theatre of the 1930s, since the construction of a popular culture which pays no attention to gender, and offers no creative role to women, must surely be a rather impoverished affair. The repression of gender implicit in the practice of the WTM disappeared with the emergence of plays which contained more fully developed characters. There were woman actors in Unity, a very small number of women playwrights, such as Ena Lamont Stewart, and of women directors such as Joan Littlewood of Manchester Theatre Union. On the whole, however, women were not in positions of power and influence over the development of popular theatre. There were, for example, no women on the General Council of Unity Theatre in the 1930s. This should be borne in mind in the assessment of claims that popular theatre in the 1930s accurately reflected working-class life, and actively involved large sections of the working class: some more actively than others.

The difficulty with producing a chronological account of any movement, or movements, is that it tends to become teleological. My intention has certainly not been to argue that all earlier initiatives were simply a distraction or an error, which led inevitably to the practices and theory of Unity Theatre.[69] It might perhaps be useful at this point, therefore, to attempt some more synthetic statement of the priorities and limitations of conceptions of popular theatre in the 1920s and 1930s.

The work of the WTM was theatrically and politically innovative. In placing cultural practice in the realm of the political, valorizing the culture of resistance, and refusing notions of 'folk' culture, the WTM represented an important challenge to the hegemony of definitions of popular culture as analysed in earlier chapters of this book. However, the WTM absolutely failed to engage with 'commercial culture'. It refused to pay any attention to the cultural forms being widely consumed by its audience, except to condemn them as 'seductive dope'. This seems like a lost opportunity to understand the power and the form of romantic, fantastical, or heroic narratives, which is reminiscent of the Chartist's suspicion, neglect and condemnation of penny fiction.

The WTM completely rejected the available forms of the dominant culture, and tried instead to construct alternative working-class forms of culture. That the attempt failed, or at least failed to construct cultural forms that were powerful and flexible enough to survive and develop, does not render the project without interest. The attempt to construct autonomous forms of workers' culture, enclaves of theatrical and political purity, at least demonstrated an understanding of the ease with which the dominant culture can appropriate the exotic and the different. It also led to the dissemination of important aesthetic and political arguments from Germany and the Soviet Union, and thus extended the range and nature of theatrical representation. It must be admitted, however, that in rejecting the dominant culture completely, the WTM did little to undermine it: there was simply no point of contact. It washed its hands of the history of Western theatre, and so could say nothing about it.

The WTM represents a departure from earlier theorizations of popular culture because of its insistence on the conscious agency of the working class. Folk singers were praised for their lack of consciousness, and peasant poets for their naturalness. For the WTM, however, 'workers' culture' only made sense if the working class both participated in, and were aware of, their role in its formation. This argument is not easily reconciled with the WTM's insistence on agit-prop as the only available form for the workers' theatre. To offer a cultural space, and then dictate the terms in which it is filled, is a curious practice, which suggests an excessive confidence in the absolute correctness of particular theoretical positions: in this case, the theatrical and political primacy of agit-prop.

Finally, the WTM did seem to operate with an impoverished conception of culture. Observing that it had functioned in the past as propaganda, the WTM tended to identify it as such. This identity makes cultural ambiguity or contradiction impossible, and largely fails to explain the desire of individuals to construct or consume cultural forms.

Popular theatre in the 1930s was less concerned with the autonomy and radical difference of its project. Instead it tended to mobilize notions of a continuous and coherent tradition of popular theatre. Like similar claims in relation to folk music, however, these arguments ignore the discontinuity of theatrical history and the different theatrical forms which have been privileged, and therefore sustained, by the dominant culture over the last 300 or 400 years. The claim for continuity and tradition often amounts to no more than a rhetorical refusal to analyse questions of power, and the facts of relative powerlessness. Such a refusal was certainly made easier by the slipperiness of the concept of 'the popular'. The ways in which theatre could be popular in 1600 and 1935 were not the same: the whole structure of cultural relations was different in each period. Yet, the undoubted power of the term rendered such differences invisible.

Theorists of the 1930s shared the earlier contempt for 'commercial culture'. Their reasons were, however, rather different. WTM writers dismissed commercial culture because it was ideological, misleading and seductive. In the 1930s, the argument was more likely to be about the trivializing and sordid aspects of commercial culture. Having argued for the emancipatory and human potential of culture, commercialized forms of culture were seen as degrading, and as diminishing this potential. The implications of this neglect of cinema, radio and popular fiction are, however, just as serious. It is thus to texts that have addressed 'commercial culture' as a constituent of 'popular culture', in the form of television, that I will turn in the next chapter.

6

As Seen on TV:
Technology and Cultural Decline

In this, the final chapter, I want to look at more recent analyses of popular culture. The potential field of study is obviously immense, and, as in earlier chapters, I have chosen one particular cultural form as a 'case study'. In this instance, I have chosen to look at the development of critical languages for the analysis of television. Obviously, had I looked at arguments about subcultures and style, about popular music, or about the culture of contemporary political movements, this chapter would have taken a different form.[1] I do not think, however, that this would have undermined the force of my claim for the importance of understanding the history of analyses of popular culture. Each of these areas of study tends to reproduce the sorts of arguments examined in previous chapters.

My reasons for opting to examine responses to television, however, are several. First of all, television is a new technology, and a new cultural form. It therefore might seem to offer the possibility of developing new categories of cultural analysis, of questioning the adequacy of received ideas about cultural and social relations. That critics of television have largely failed to produce such new concepts, or even to acknowledge that they might be required, is a measure of the difficulty of the problems addressed by this book. Also, television seems to offer the possibility of breaking down the rigid hierarchy that has characterized earlier discussions of popular culture. In the case of penny fiction, the difference between the dominant and the popular was visible at the point of consumption. This is not true of television, which makes the same representations available to members of different social classes. The erosion of rigid social categorizations turns out to be immensely worrying for critics of television. Those critics who reject the dismissal of all television as debased and corrupt try constantly to establish a hierarchy within forms of television, either in terms of different channels: ITV versus BBC, or in terms of different genres: soap opera versus current affairs. That such divisions cannot, actually, be related exactly to other social and cultural hierarchies is a problem for television critics, who constantly risk the ignominious slide into the domain of the popular. Finally, I am interested in the analysis of television because it is so widespread. Talking about television is something most people do. In the range of responses to television, in the press, by critics, or by cultural theorists, which will be examined in this chapter, we can find the energy of a cultural and social debate that is very much alive. To most people, television matters.

The discussion in this chapter will focus almost entirely on the responses to television by British critics and theorists. Given the vast amount of research on television undertaken, for example, in the United States, and the fact that television, as a technology and an institution, is becoming increasingly international, this may seem surprising. Yet, I must return to the proposition that the development of political, literary and theoretical languages with which to analyse popular culture has to be given the specificity of a national context. Accounts of popular culture have been related throughout this book to other debates within the dominant culture: debates about national identity, and about history, which themselves had to be related to the social and cultural relations within the British state. Even in moments where theorists of popular culture were most insistent in their denial of nationalism, such as in the case of the Workers' Theatre Movement, in order to understand the development of particular positions we had to turn to the political context of Britain in the 1920s and 1930s. Also, the specific history of broadcasting institutions within Britain has meant the development of recognizable and distinctive responses to the medium of television, characterized by patronage, paternalism and an obsessive return to the 'literary'.

Television, then, does allow us to look at responses to a new cultural form, to examine cultural hierarchies, and to see arguments about cultural decline in a wider context. It also presents particular, and interesting, problems for thinking about the relations between culture and national identity. It therefore seems to fit very productively into the argument of this book. There is, however, one remaining point of difficulty, which lies in the very identification of television as an aspect of popular culture.

Television has been described as a form of popular culture for several reasons: reasons which bring us back to the ambiguity of the concept of 'the popular' indicated in the first chapter of this book. First of all, television is seen as a popular form because of its difference from those forms favoured by the dominant culture. It is, thus, 'popular' culture by default: it does not meet the criteria for serious cultural significance. Critics of television constantly comment on its difference from literature. The experiences of reading and of watching television are frequently compared: reading is seen as offering free play to the imagination, while television is overly explicit, and thus produces passivity. Also, television is seen as too mediated, too technological, to allow of fruitful communication.[2] Reading, according to this theory, allows direct access to the thoughts and language of an author, whereas creative expression on television is constantly hampered by the industrial and technical constraints of the medium. Television is, therefore, described as a form of popular culture because it is seen as an impoverished form of culture. Once more, we have an equation of 'the popular' and 'the base'.

Television is also described as a 'popular' form because of its ephemeral nature. Dominant forms of culture are institutionalized in libraries or in galleries in ways that will ensure their preservation and their centrality to cultural debate. The institutions of television, on the other hand, are notorious for their reluctance to engage with any notion of the history of their medium. Thus, programmes which form part of the popular, or critical, memory of 'television' simply no longer exist: they have been destroyed. This ephemeral quality of television assures its exclusion from cultural discourses founded on notions of continuity and tradition. Television is thus largely denied the serious critical and theoretical attention given to other forms of communication.

Television is often described as a 'popular' cultural form simply because it is well liked. This observation can be made in relation to television as a whole, or in relation to particular sorts of programming. The power and popularity of television as a whole, the frequency with which people watch television, has generally been very problematic for television reviewers and critics, quite simply because the other, and negative, meanings of 'popular' are always present in the margins: for example, the meaning of 'popular culture', as 'suited to the tastes of the common people'. Television is seen as 'popular' in its pandering to mediocrity, in its general accessibility, in its bad taste. Thus the negative associations of 'popular' often win out over the descriptive, and the hierarchy of cultural forms is reintroduced. This is frequently accompanied by an explicit project of improving television, of elevating popular taste and of offering cultural leadership. Thus, critics joke about their own addiction, insist on their ordinariness, but nervously assert their discrimination and therefore their difference. Inclusion in the category of 'the popular' is an anxious affair.

In discussions of television, then, there is frequently an attempt to suggest cultural hierarchy and difference across what looks like similarity and continuity: all of us watch television, but not all in the same way. This argument is generally articulated in cultural terms, as if such differences were simply a matter of taste, and very rarely refers explicitly to the assumptions about class and gender which underpin them. At the same time as this attempt to reinstate difference at the level of the cultural, however, there is also a tendency to see the universal popularity of television as a symptom, or perhaps a source, of national homogeneity. Given that viewers are united by the fact of their watching television, critics and government committees have attempted to give more social and political substance to this unity. They assume that 'television viewers' form one coherent non-hierarchical group, who share cultural and political values. This is reminiscent of the shifts in the significance of 'the popular' discussed above: from a term of legal and political relations to a synonym for 'the general public'. Much discussion of television is concerned to establish this generality. We find, therefore, a very interesting tension within discussions of television as a form of popular culture. One set of arguments tends to reproduce existing social and cultural hierarchies, the other to repress them in the name of 'the audience' or 'the man in the street'. Difference and distinction can be acknowledged at the level of the cultural, where they can be represented as natural, but are insistently removed from discussions of the socal dimensions of television.

The tension between these two responses to television brings us to another way in which television is implicated in discourses of 'the popular'. This lies in the extent to which it is seen as itself constitutive of ideas of 'people' and 'nation'. Television is seen as offering a construction of social relations which makes a certain unified notion of 'the British people' possible. Critics frequently echo this sort of construction, either in their attempt to assert common cultural values, or in their suspicion towards foreign, and particularly US, television.

The identification of television as 'popular culture' can also, finally, represent a critique of the category of 'mass culture' as an adequate description of the cultural forms and relations of the twentieth century. The basis of such a critique lies in attempts to look at the complexity of the ways in which television is understood and the range of meanings it produces. Thus, instead of assuming that viewers are subjected, as a mass, to the representations of television, such an approach stresses the ways in which television engages differently with the experiences of viewers – such differences being related to factors such as class, age, race and gender.

Such accounts of television as popular culture point out the power and prevalence of the concept of 'mass culture' in relation to cultural forms which are highly technical, and susceptible of instant reproduction, while also trying to resist it. The particular significance of this identification of television as 'mass culture' will be examined further below, but it is important, at this point, to stress the actual difficulty of maintaining any rigid separation of these two terms, 'popular culture' and 'mass culture', in discussion of television. Even an article as theoretically aware as Laura Kipnis's recent '"Refunctioning" Reconsidered: Towards a Left Popular Culture' constantly slips between the concepts of 'mass' and 'popular' in relation to film and television.[3] We can, however, identify differences of emphasis. Theorists of television as popular culture tend to stress television as something favoured by the people; theorists of mass culture see it rather as a cultural form produced for the people. Or again, thinking in terms of 'popular culture' frequently leads to a concentration on the individual spectator whose subjectivity is constructed by the various systems of meaning in which he or she participates, while thinking in terms of 'mass culture' leads to a concentration on the audience as a social aggregate subjected to the representations of television.

The analysis of television thus raises exactly the sorts of questions about the relation between cultural forms and social and political structures which have been central to this book. The partiality of the models of television proposed, the difficulty of thinking social, technological and subjective determinants simultaneously, is a measure of the difficulty of breaking away from inherited debates about social and cultural relations. Available ways of talking about television represent a continuation, and an adaptation, of debates about the necessary relation between technological progress and cultural decline, about the corrupting effects of generally accessible forms of culture, about the possibility of cultural authenticity, about the use of cultural forms to maintain social control, about the relation between dominant and subordinate cultural forms, and about the role of women in cultural production and consumption.

TELEVISION: THE ENEMY WITHIN

We now take the form of, and sorts of programming on, television very much for granted. That it is a domestically consumed cultural form, showing documentary, light entertainment, news, drama and sport now seems like an inevitable part of its nature. This 'inevitability' is, however, a relatively recent phenomenon. Michael Egan wrote about television in the Independent Labour Party's *New Leader* in 1927, at a time when the technological possibilities of television had been discovered, but their social context remained unclear. He argued that 'there is a bigger future for it [television] *outside* the home than *in* the home'.[4] In the late 1930s, Selfridges had installed their own television studios to attract customers.[5] As recently as 1949, the Beveridge Committee was still discussing the possibility of television's being broadcast in cinemas.[6]

There is nothing inherent in the nature of television as a technology which dictated its development as a cultural form economically and institutionally linked to the family. Yet, from a very early stage, a particular and persistent equation was being made between television, the family, and the moral and spiritual health of the nation. The identification of television with the family is very clear in early advertisements for television sets, which insist that 'the whole family gets excited about a magnificent HMV TV receiver'.[7] The image that is offered is of a nuclear family, united in rapt attention to the television in the corner of the room. Television thus offers a new focus to family life, and signals both modernity and prosperity.[8]

The implications of this new cultural form, invading the bosom of the family, are not, however, as straightforward as such advertising images suggest. Television was very quickly perceived as a 'problem'. Discussion of television borrowed many of the terms developed in nineteenth-century responses to increasing literacy. The growth of a cultural form that was accessible and domestic was greeted with enthusiasm, as an indication of the triumph of values of individualism and self-improvement. At the same time, the home, because of its privacy, was a source of anxiety: how was control to be exercised over the consumption of such cultural forms? Once more, the family was seen as both the focal point, and the weak point, of social relations.

In the *Radio Times* of 1946, just before television recommenced broadcasting after the war, we can already find the elements that were to dominate the criticism of television: emphasis on technology, placing of television in the sphere of the domestic, and anxiety about its effects.[9] In an article entitled 'What is This Television?', Ernest Thomson began by discussing the technological achievements and limitations of television. He argued that television represented an advance over cinema in so far as it did not need to be watched in the dark: 'A reading lamp in the same room did not spoil things, and if you masked your screen you could have enough light for mother to sew by.'[10] Thus television is seen as an addition to the normal structure of family life, and not a disturbance. It is able to 'pluck pictures out of the air' and make them accessible to, and entertaining for, the general public. At the same time, however, Thomson registered a certain disquiet about its effects:

> Here we touch one of television's charms, which might also be considered a drawback. . . . You leave letters unwritten; you forget the income tax form. If people ring you are out – in another world.[11]

This is an early example of the anxiety about the addictive nature of television, its drug-like effects. Thomson has television sending us to 'another world'. It is interesting to note here the sites of Thomson's particular anxiety: that television will undermine the dominant culture by replacing the written word, and that it will make people forget their proper relation to society, in forgetting to fill in their tax forms.

Thomson's descriptions of television invoke many of the terms that have dominated attempts to think about television since the late 1950s. He begins by thinking about it as a technology. The technological elements of television are presented as both complex and unalterable: they have been determined by the inevitable march of scientific progress. When Thomson comes to think about the ways in which television will be used, he offers us an image of the patriarchal family, untouched by this new technology: mother can still carry on with her sewing. At the same time, however, Thomson worries about the possibility of addiction, the possibility that television could send us all to 'another world'.

The emphasis on television as a technology is echoed in early government reports about broadcasting. The Television Committee of 1943 was almost entirely concerned with technological aspects of the medium.[12] Its members included an engineer, a representative from the Scientific and Industrial Research Department and a representative from Air Defence Research and Development. Witnesses included Marconi, the General Electrical Company, and the Board of Trade. Although there were also submissions from the BBC and the Ministry of Education, the Committee's report dealt almost entirely with the technological needs and potential of the medium, and scarcely at all with decisions about the sort of programming television should carry, or with the social context of television's growth and development.

Discussion of technological aspects of television is, of course, unavoidable. The regulation of broadcasting is closely related to the need to control the scarce resource of available wavelengths for transmission. The problem, however, lies in the split between discourses which address television in its technological aspects and those which address its social implications and potential. The technological argument, because it neglects questions of social needs and cultural potential, assumes a sort of objectivity and inevitability.

This separation of accounts of television as a technology from considerations of it as a cultural form has been dealt with in two different ways. The first response has been to ignore the specificity of television as a technical form and talk about its output as a series of discrete creative works, generally focusing on the artistic role of the writer or the director. The second response has been to assume a direct link between the technological, mass-produced form of television and cultural decline or audience passivity: thus television is considered purely in terms of its consumption, and dismissed as either trivial or ideological. These responses amount to either repressing the implications of cultural and political transformations, as in the case of folk song collectors, or equating such transformations necessarily with cultural decline, as in many responses to penny fiction. Indeed, critics often follow both strategies at once: analysing television as if it were continuous with earlier cultural forms of fiction or drama, but assuming that its development necessarily signals cultural impoverishment and social decline.

TELEVISION AND 'AUTHENTICITY'

Such a contradictory set of attitudes to television is expressed in Denys Thompson's book, *Discrimination and Popular Culture*.[13] Thompson's writing about popular culture shares many of the anxieties about changing cultural relations expressed by F. R. Leavis in *Mass Civilisation and Minority Culture*. Leavis's work has been very influential for many critics of television. Leavis's articulation of the role of the literary intellectual in preserving society from a slide into complete cultural and social trivialization has proved very attractive. His writings offer a confident justification of cultural values as expressed in a 'great tradition'. At the same time, however, he advances the importance of thinking seriously about the 'culturally trivial'. Like Fanny Mayne, Leavis argues that society cannot afford to ignore vast areas of cultural production and consumption, however impoverished and inauthentic. Leavis saw the capitalization of cultural forms as disastrous for the spiritual and intellectual well-being of the nation. His indictment was particularly aimed at advertising, as a glib and exploitative form of communication. Leavis insisted on the importance of a cultured minority, who would be the guardians of tradition, and the 'consciousness of the race'.[14] Leavis's position is not dissimilar to that of Matthew Arnold, except that Leavis's sense of cultural decline is not linked to perceptions of ignorance, but rather to an anxiety about partial knowledge. Arnold was making a case for the potential of culture, while Leavis was trying to safeguard that potential in the face of the democratization and perceived mediocrity of most cultural forms.

Denys Thompson, then, developed many of F. R. Leavis's concerns about cultural decline and the possibility of cultural authenticity, when he turned his attention to the mass media as 'the expression and mouthpiece of a particular type of civilization'.[15] He criticized television's tendency to blandness, to the production of representations that were so general as to be of no particular interest to anyone. He thus seemed to argue against the tendency of television to unify and homogenize its audence. This was not done in the interests of making television more representative of cultural and political diversity, however, but rather in an attempt to win television over to a particular set of cultural values, as represented by cultural experts: 'Experts are needed in the sphere of "cultural" health as much as they are for bodily health.'[16] This amounts to an attempt to recreate an Arnoldian confidence in the existence of a recognizable, and universal, set of cultural values, a confidence that is continually undermined by the facts of television programming. Thompson insists on the existence of cultural authenticity, of representations that will express the truth about human relationships, and seeks only to discover how such representations can be offered by television.

Philip Abrams, writing in *Discrimination and Popular Culture*, is quite clear that television's departure from authenticity and excellence is due to its technological nature: 'I would argue that the process of trivialization . . . is to a large extent integral to the technical nature of the media.'[17] This is an interesting attempt to think through the causes of perceived cultural decline without resorting to theories of 'conspiracy' or 'bad taste'. Abrams develops an argument to the effect that television is bound to be mediocre as long as it tries to offend, or disturb, no one: that is, to assume homogeneity in its audience. Thus, he insists on the falsity of attempts to construct all television viewers as politically and culturally identical.

Abrams does not develop these perceptions, however, but falls back, once more, on the solid ground of 'authenticity'. He counterposes 'authenticity' and 'intelligibility', arguing that any representation that is generally accessible cannot be an authentic cultural expression. This position is very similar to that of nineteenth-century folk song collectors, who saw themselves as uniquely placed to recognize authenticity, while the contemporary working class were doomed to the debased form of Music Hall. Abrams bases his description of cultural authenticity in the sphere of the literary, arguing that only television which respects individual personality can be good. Thus, television is measured against the forms of narrative and characterization found in the novel, and found wanting. This attempt to represent the particular, historically specific, modes of representation which have character-ized the novel as a guarantor of the worth of all cultural forms cannot but be partial. Once more, it is a testament to the importance of the 'literary' as an articulation of agreed cultural values: an articulation whose origins have been examined in earlier chapters.

The greatest threat to authenticity, for Abrams, lies in the home. Women, and domesticity, once more upset the confident cultural categories of authenticity and significance: 'the domesticity of broadcasting, combining with its universality and continuity, opens a primrose path along which the audience has an open invitation to be led towards addiction'.[18] A cultural form so clearly placed in the family, in the private rather than the public sphere, cannot avoid contamination, and a lack of critical judgement. Both Thompson and Abrams assume a model of cultural decline. They compare television to a set of cultural values derived from literature, and find it wanting. They can find no way to respond to the democratization, or accessibility, represented by television, except in terms of decline, and loss of authenticity. Abrams does concede that, as a medium for information and education, television may represent some sort of progress. In the realm of fiction, however, the realm of imaginative engagement, he declares television a failure.

In all of the contributions to *Discrimination and Popular Culture*, 'decline' is conceived in purely cultural terms. It is, of course, implicit in such descriptions of cultural impoverishment and decay that the cultural is symptomatic of the state of civilization: that social relations are best perceived and understood in terms of their cultural effects. Nonetheless, the emphasis on the state of culture means that there is very little explicit discussion of history, or of changing social relations. History is absent from most texts on television except as the possibility of a recently lost moment of authenticity and cultural well-being. The history of the medium is not discussed at all, and the political and economic choices that led to the appearance of television in the home are taken for granted. Television is perceived as symptomatic of social decline, but the terms of, and reasons for, such perceived decline are not discussed. As with the folk song collectors, the interest is rather in the construction of an imaginary space where cultural forms remain untouched by capitalist social relations, and not in the development of a sustained cultural history.

The perception of cultural change as the erosion of 'authenticity' was also the theme of Richard Hoggart's *The Uses of Literacy*. Hoggart published this text in 1958. In it, he began by describing the lived experience and shared cultural and social values of the British working classes of the 1920s and 1930s. He did so in explicit opposition to the tendency either to despise, or to romanticize, such experiences. His account is intensely personal, offering both detail and emotional response. He describes the world where father and son 'share the real world of work and men's pleasures', and 'the mother is the working centre'.[19] He tries to render the texture of daily life in cramped, but not alienating, houses: 'The iron thumps on the table, the dog scratches and yawns or the cat miaows to be let out; the son, drying himself on the family towel near the fire, whistles, or rustles the communal letter from his brother in the army which has been lying on the mantelpiece behind the photo of his sister's wedding.'[20]

Hoggart argues that the experience of living in working-class communities in the 1920s and 1930s produced a variety of cultural forms and social attitudes which were relevant and valuable: a sense of the concrete; a fundamental stoicism; a sense of social hierarchy, understood in terms of 'them' and 'us'; an awareness of common interests; and an attachment to the homely and the ordinary. It must be said that in his representation of the social relations of the 1920s and 1930s, Hoggart demonstrates an evasion of the long history of social and cultural change that preceded this period: he suggests a kind of timelessness, the security of an unchanging tradition. He also drifts towards a form of essentialism, as he talks of the features that 'are indeed part of the outlook of the "common people" in any generation and in almost any land': an essentialism which seems to render critique impossible.[21] Hoggart's writing, thus, has much in common with cultural analyses discussed in earlier sections of this book. At the same time, however, *The Uses of Literacy* represented a departure from much cultural criticism in that the values it sought to defend were not those of the dominant culture, but rather those of social groups explicitly excluded from the dominant.

Hoggart's intention is thus clearly different from much of the criticism examined in this book. His methodology, and his conclusions, however, are remarkably similar. Having set up the 1920s and 1930s as a Golden Age of working-class authenticity in social and cultural relations, he proceeds to analyse the dangers implicit in the 'newer mass art'. He sees the mass-produced cultural forms of the 1950s as insidious in their appropriation of particular aspects of working-class life: their recreation of the cultural values and experiences of the working classes. Thus 'tolerance' is reproduced as irresponsible hedonism; 'tradition' is debunked in favour of modernity; and history is repressed in the glorification of youth.

Hoggart compares such cultural forms to the values represented by the literary. The description of social life in contemporary magazines is seen as trivial and impoverished when compared to the complexities of *Adam Bede*. Spillane is compared unfavourably to Faulkner. In contrast to this, Hoggart had argued that the best of the authentically popular songs could stand comparison, in terms of emotional effect, with an aria from an Italian opera. He does not challenge the cultural values of the dominant culture, but rather seeks to include selected elements of popular culture within such values.

The new cultural developments which Hoggart criticizes take many forms: from commercial popular music, through conspicuous consumption and milk bars, to cinema and television. He sees televison as offering a superficial pleasure: 'a pleasure in simply sharing the unifying object'.[22] But the values represented by television he sees as entirely negative and dangerous: a continual living in the present, a glorification of progress, and an uncritical celebration of youth. Having repressed the contradictions inherent in older social and cultural relations in the name of authenticity, Hoggart then sees the cultural developments of the 1950s as equally monolithic: as corrupting, and as a threat to critical thought and class identity.

Stuart Hall and Paddy Whannel's discussion of television in 1964, on the other hand, insisted on the need to recover television from critical disdain while still retaining the possibility of judging it against 'some whole human standard'.[23] In *The Popular Arts*, Hall and Whannel discussed the question of violence on television, and succeeded in challenging the poverty of most responses to the problem. They argued that 'violence' was not something that could be readily identified, or simply assessed. The analysis of violence on television was not just a question of counting acts of violence and measuring their effects, but rather of considering how violence was treated on television, and how its portrayal related to the whole programme in which it appeared. They therefore developed a much more careful and historically specific response to the isssue of television violence than many of the other writers who will be examined below.

When Hall and Whannel came to find models for the successful representation of violent conflict, however, they turned immediately to the sphere of the literary. They argued that the murder of Nancy by Bill Sykes, in the television adaptation of *Oliver Twist*, 'stemmed naturally from the story and was not gratuitously introduced', and that this offered a standard against which other representations of violence on television could be measured.[24] Their assessment of the power of television representations was made in relation to the imaginative impact of Shakespearean drama. The importance of Shakespearean drama lay in its offering an entry to another order of life, through the power of imaginative representation: the importance of television as a popular art could therefore be measured by the extent to which it succeeded in offering such stimulation. This attempt to examine television explicitly in terms of the norms and values of literary representation was bound to leave many of its forms simply unexamined, or silently condemned. Hall and Whannel's condemnation of the false and unchallenging naturalism of *Coronation Street* was quite explicit. Yet, more recent critics have found different spaces from which to respond to these texts: the space of the woman viewer, or the space of the semiologically sophisticated family, which measure their narrative and representational strategies against a different set of norms.[25] Such accounts reveal the ways in which the stereotypical but strong representations and unending narratives of soap-opera are of particular significance, precisely because of their difference from dominant literary representations. Instead of assuming that the departure from literary structures and characterization represents cultural decline, such critiques argue that it offers the possibility of recognizing the range of cultural needs to be found across society, and within the individual.

Hall and Whannel are also profoundly suspicious of US programming, and its effects on British television. They see US programmes as cheap and commercial, and as threatening the style and content of British television. There is, indeed, an argument to be made about US cultural imperialism, and its economic effects on indigenous cultural production. Hall and Whannel, however, seem to use 'American' as a synonym for the trivial and repetitive: 'low-level dramatized series – many of them American in origin or feeling'.[26] This amounts to identifying the inauthentic with the 'American', regardless of whether or not the programme concerned was produced in the United States. Hall and Whannel thus tend to construct a sphere of authentic British culture, which is under attack from forces outside it, rather than trying to analyse the complexity of social and cultural relations within Britain which lead to a variety of different sorts of programmes.

TELEVISION AND ITS 'EFFECTS'

The Pilkington Committee, which reported on the state of television in 1962, was clearly uneasy about certain sorts of television programming. They were anxious about the damaging effects of the repetition of representations of violence and immorality:

> . . . the way television has portrayed human behaviour and treated moral issues has already done something . . . to worsen the moral climate of the country.[27]

Generally, they blamed this perceived decline on commercial television, which was neglecting its responsibilities of leading and transforming public taste. The very accessibility and popularity of commercial television was the source of its danger:

> The disquiet and the dissatisfaction are, in our view, justly attributed very largely to the service of independent television. This is so despite the popularity of the service.[28]

The advent of commercial television is thus seen as making the project of developing a critical and discriminating discourse about television more urgent. This shifting of unease about declining standards onto commercial television is a frequent strategy. It involves moving the focus of anxiety from the technology itself, to the social relations that determine its reception. Such arguments set in play a range of very powerful discourses about the relation between working-class cultural consumption and depravity or mediocrity. The forms of television that are most despised are blamed on the bad taste of the working-class audience. Yet, in fact, the forms of television that arouse most critical disdain, the quiz shows, the variety performances, the wrestling, were established forms of television in 1946, when television, because of the cost of receivers, was a thoroughly middle-class form. The assumption that commercial television is a reflection of working-class bad taste, while the BBC embodies the more refined critical judgements of the middle classes, is thus insupportable. The frequency with which it is mobilized, however, shows the power of the equation between mass production and market forces on the one hand and cultural decline on the other.

Much discussion about television as a cultural form concentrates on its effects on moral and political values. To some extent, such questions are clearly unavoidable, since television is such a widely consumed source of political and dramatic representations. It is notable, however, as Denis McQuail has pointed out, that we do not ask such questions of other major institutions of communication such as the Church, or the law, whose legitimacy and responsibility seem to be taken for granted.[29] Still, it does not seem unreasonable to look at such a culturally powerful medium as television in terms of the ways in which it contributes to our conception of social and cultural relations, or to try to think about the types of experience or knowledge which television either enhances or marginalizes. To frame such problems in terms of an assessment of television's measurable 'effects' on an otherwise stable political and cultural structure is, however, to risk both simplifying the process of communication and displacing a complex of social transformations onto the single institution of television. Just as Fanny Mayne's anxiety about penny fiction was also an anxiety about industrialization, working-class organization, and Chartism, many effects theorists seem to be talking about something other than television.

This is particularly clear in Marie Winn's book *The Plug-In Drug*. Although this book is actually American, its influence on ways of talking about television in Britain has been very significant. This influence is clearly visible, for example, in the strategies and arguments adopted by the TV Action Group.[30] A report in the *Guardian* in 1979 describes how the TV Action group aims to stop children watching television. The group argue that the mere fact of watching television is bad, regardless of what is being watched; that television blunts the senses; and that children should be kept away from television completely.

These arguments are taken directly from Winn's book. Winn argued that television, because it was a one-way form of communication, and because it was a highly technological medium, produced a drug-like stupor in children. The effort of continually defocusing the eyes, when confronted by fast moving images, apparently disoriented and exhausted children. Winn insisted that the content of television was irrelevant: television was bad, purely as a result of its technological nature. She argued that television retarded brain development because it required no interaction. She classified children who perpetually watched television as zombies, or addicts. She also criticized the visual explicitness and mediation of television drama, which she argued tended to constrain children's responses, and contrasted this with the immediate and imaginative access to the world of fiction as offered by writing.

Winn's method is fairly anecdotal, and her language is frequently inflated. The significance of her book lies not in the strength of its argument, but rather in its identification of the ways in which television constitutes a 'problem', and her investigation of 'the *power* of the new medium to dominate family life'.[31] These are the issues which Winn addresses through her analysis of television. She is talking about television in order to talk about the family, and the forces which seem to threaten its stability. She is quite explicit about her focus on the middle-class family, and its attitudes and behaviour. She explains this concentration in terms of the power and resources of the middle classes to change society. Yet her narrative is essentially one of powerlessness in the face of the institution of television. Winn's concentration on the middle class can be explained, rather, in terms of the success of earlier identifications of television as the mark of the social and financial stability of the middle-class home. The power of this equation in the 1950s and 1960s means that television can now provide a metaphor for the erosion of cultural and economic confidence within the middle class: a shorthand for social and political transformations which threaten consensus.

Winn's assessment of the damaging effects of television, of its erosion of proper and fulfilling relations between parents and children, is made in terms of a contrast between the isolation and alienation of the nuclear family in the 1970s, and the strength and vigour of the Victorian family. She invokes the family games, long leisurely meals and large families, apparently characteristic of

Victorian middle-class life, as a counterpoint to the lack of communication characteristic of families in the age of television. Once more, cultural debate proceeds on the basis of an imaginary history of organic social relations. Television is then held responsible for the erosion of the secure and self-confident patriarchal family into social powerlessness and cultural confusion. Television thus not only comes to stand for the social, economic and political transformations of the last hundred years, but is also held responsible for them.

This displacement of social problems onto the institution of television is also clear in the work of H. J. Eysenck and D. K. B. Nias on the effects of sex and violence in the media.[32] *Sex, Violence and the Media* is a 'scientific' and mostly psychological study of the effects of television: that is to say, it describes the changes of behaviour and attitudes measurable in individuals as a result of their exposure to images of sex and violence in an experimental situation. It argues that a small percentage of individuals are clearly adversely affected by violent and pornographic images in the media, and that such effects are sufficiently significant to warrant censorship of certain sorts of representations. They concede that not all viewers react in the same way, and that many viewers' behaviour is unaffected by watching television, but insist that the problem of television's effects is a serious social problem.

The identification of their research as 'scientific' is central to Eysenck and Nias's argument, and is the strategy they use to legitimize their pronouncements on television. They describe their work as objective and verifiable, contrasting it with the well-meaning muddled thinking which has characterized many studies of television and violence. They expose subjects, in 'laboratory' conditions, to representations of violence, quantify their responses, draw up graphs of 'predispositions to violence', and offer precise figures for the social effects of television.

What they do not question, however, are the assumptions they have brought to bear on the very categories of their research. In the first chapter of the book, they state that, 'the civilization in which we live may be in danger of being submerged under a deluge of crime, violence and sexual perversion'.[33] The perception of cultural decline and social disintegration therefore overdetermines their whole study. Also, they do not examine the history of the concepts of 'sex' and 'violence', in order to understand the cultural and historical specificity of identifying particular images or acts as 'sexual' or 'violent'. Within any society there is a complex set of legitimate and illegitimate acts of violence, and the meanings of any particular representation can only be assessed in terms of such social norms. Eysenck and Nias ignore the fact that the meanings people derive from particular representations are to some extent culturally specific. Their confusion is particularly clear in relation to representations of sexuality. At certain points they discuss pornographic images as demeaning to women, and therefore as socially irresponsible and damaging. The category of pornography is stretched, however, to include the representation of attempted seduction, and an argument that exposure to pornography induces violence is used to prove that increasing sexual liberty leads to a more violent society. Eysenck and Nias signal 'the problem' of television by citing not just an increase in rape and sexual perversion, but also in pre- and extramarital sex.[34] At one point in the book, they even condemn sex education as offering information that can lead to sexual activity between children. Their arguments are not confined to representations on television. They also criticise sex and violence in literature:

> Our point would be, not only that art does not need the explicit portrayal of sex and violence . . . but that such portrayal is entirely counterproductive, destroying whatever artistic intentions the author may have had.[35]

What Eysenck and Nias's project amounts to is an eradication of all images of sexuality and violence. They do not consider how violence is represented in a particular programme, its relation to a particular narrative, or the extent to which certain forms of violence, such as war, are culturally sanctioned while others, such as vandalism, are condemned. They merely assume that sex and violence are bad, and their representation dangerous. They argue that pornography and violence in the media are 'symptoms of . . . a general loss of values', which can be overcome only by 'a more positive assertion of traditional values'.[36] The 'problem' is thus social decay, the 'cause' is television, and the 'solution' is the imposition of one common set of social and moral values: all this in the name of science.

William Belson's project in investigating television violence and the adolescent boy is, to some extent, more modest. He sets out to demonstrate that 'high exposure to television violence increases the degree to which boys engage in serious violence'.[37] Once more, Belson assumes 'violence' as an unproblematic and measurable category. He then seeks to establish a relation between exposure to violent images on television and subsequent acts of violence. He does not look at the ways in which representations of violence interact with discourses of class and masculinity. Nor does he consider the extent to which violent behaviour might be explicable in terms of environment and class.[38] Once again, television is seen as expressive of social decline but, in the process of analysis, is removed from the social relations that constantly inflect its meaning and use.

Belson's concentration on adolescent boys is interesting, because it seems to him so self-evident. He assumes that violence is innate, and that television reduces inhibitions in relation to violent behaviour: exposure to television thus leads to acts of violence. He does not, however, analyse why girls, when exposed to such images, do not resort to acts of violence on the same scale. An earlier study, by Himmelweit, had established that 'unexpectedly' girls were as interested as boys in crime and detective series.[39] If this interest among girls does not transform itself into violent behaviour in female adolescents, perhaps we need to examine more closely the relationship between the formation of social and sexual identity and acts of violence. If, as Belson argues, television is responsible for increasing violence, why is this increase so gender-specific?

Studies about the 'effects' of television seem to be caught in something of a contradiction. Images on television are held to stimulate individuals to commit acts of violence, but television as a whole is held responsible for engendering passivity and withdrawal. This contradiction can be resolved, however, by observing that these assessments are made in relation to different segments of the television audience. The anxiety about violence is an anxiety about the possibility of social control: whether the general consumption of televisual representations will lead to uncontrollable and 'anti-social' behaviour, particularly by working-class adolescent males. It is a fear about consequences of television from which critics and analysts feel themselves personally exempt. Such anxiety can thus usefully be compared to the worries about penny fiction explored in chapter 3. The worry about passivity, on the other hand, is one in which critics feel themselves much more seriously implicated. It is a worry about the cultural and spiritual health of television viewers, a fear about the erosion of cultural and social values and judgements. It thus has more in common with the interest in peasant poetry or in folk song, which were also symptomatic of concerns about the erosion of the power and significance of the dominant culture.

Such complexity of response to the social effects of television is also visible in the coverage given to television by the press: at one level they chastise television for its damaging effects, at another they review it as an art form. Responses to the 'dangers' of television in the press have a long history. In the *Daily Telegraph* of 1954, we can find a report about excessive violence in children's television programming.[40] The MP who raised the matter said that he himself had not seen the programme concerned, but had decided to protest after the twelve-year-old child of one of his constituents had had hysterics, caused by watching it. Just as Dixon Hepworth did not have to read penny fiction in order to know it was a source of evil, television is here assumed to be responsible for corruption, without any consideration of the nature of the programme concerned.

The press show a great fascination with reporting television's harmful consequences. Any particular event, like the formation of the TV Action Group, or the publication of a Report by teachers on the ways in which television's representations inflect children's perceptions of reality, releases a predictable set of headlines of the 'Teachers Slam TV Smut and Sex' type.[41] This sort of image of television as damaging and dangerous might seem strange in a paper such as the *Daily Express*, with its hedonist populism. Yet, this image is part of the process of organizing that populism, through a fear of violence and a suspicion of intellectuals. TV executives are ordered to, 'make sure that smart alec trendy producers are not alowed to abuse their power, to the injury of the innocent'.[42]

This anger and unease about television as an institution is, however, completely absent from television reviewing in the press. The commonest response of reviewers to television is not to treat it as television at all. The economic, technological and cultural transformations represented by television are ignored, and it is treated as just another, though inferior, form of literature. Mike Poole has noted the strong literary bias in television reviewing: Julian Barnes, Martin Amis and Dennis Potter have all worked as television reviewers.[43] Such frequent movement between the realm of literary criticism and the analysis of popular culture has tended to hamper the development of a specific language for the analysis of television. The conception of the job of a television reviewer was clearly expressed by Hugh Greene in 1970, when he insisted that the critic should 'set standards of excellence and . . . record the ebb and flow of inspiration'.[44] This judgement assumes that the standards are unproblematic, and that television merely expresses the inspiration of a particular artistic creator. It therefore looks at television purely as an expressive medium, and does not consider the ways in which the technical, economic or programming structures of television affect the meanings it can produce. Again, this response echoes the ways in which cultural critics looked to both peasant poetry and folk song to provide unmediated expressions of universal perceptions, and were reluctant to consider the social and formal constraints which characterize cultural production.

The power of this expressive metaphor of television is clear in the writing of T. C. Worsley, a theatre critic turned television reviewer. Worsley, in his collection of television reviews, published as *Television: The Ephemeral Art*, insists that he is merely an ordinary, though critical, viewer. No special expertise is required for the analysis of television. Worsley's reviews, like Clive James's, concentrate very markedly on the 'prestige' elements of television: drama, documentary, and literary adaptations. Worsley does not attempt to deal with the specificity, or the industrial nature, of the medium of television, and indeed seems to find these something of a nuisance:

> are we blaming the author for distortions which are really the fault of the producer, the director, the story editor (the list of interlopers has grown with television) or the actors?[45]

He thus represses the technical dimensions of mass-produced representations, and struggles to construct a continuity between forms of the dominant culture and forms of popular culture. The price of such denials of historical change and of cultural hierarchy, however, is the marginalization of huge segments of television production, which serves, in the end, to reinforce, with all the weight of history and the dominant culture, the absolute difference between 'serious' and 'popular' culture.

Clive James's discourse about television is equally wedded to the critical practices and discourses of the literary. He compares television, negatively, to the triumphal march in *Aida* or to a medieval allegorical display: amusing, but scarcely informative.[46] James uses television to write, wittily, about the 'real world' it offers to us, but has no interest whatsoever in developing any theoretical or historical approaches to the medium: 'All politico-sociological or socio-political surveys of British television can safely be dismissed as moonshine.'[47] James places himself, with only a glance over his shoulder at television, within the dominant culture.

TELEVISION AS MASS CULTURE

The response of the Left in Britain to television has been powerfully structured by the concept of 'mass culture'. As a form of 'mass' culture, television is seen as part of the complex of social transformations which have led to the alienation, atomization and false consciousness of the working class. The problem is twofold. Traditional social structures have been undermined by developments within international capitalism, leaving the working class particularly vulnerable to ideological manipulation by the mass media. Also, the commodification of culture has led to inauthenticity and trivialization of cultural forms, including television. Such perceptions of television as mass culture tend to lead to a concentration on the ways in which it manipulates, or offers false representations. It also tends to focus critics' attention on the structure of ownership and control of television, since its commodity form is seen as being the root of the problem. Finally, the identification of television as 'mass' culture leads once more to a refusal to engage with many of its forms or representations. Just as many Chartists refused to examine penny fiction, seeing it simply as a distraction from political struggle, many theorists of television demonstrate an extreme reluctance to discuss fictional forms of television, concentrating instead on the 'political heartland' of news and current affairs.

In 1927 Michael Egan, however, writing in the *New Leader*, was still cautiously optimistic about the potential of television. He argued that its documentary power could have significant political implications: 'Television could thus be used for the purpose of stimulating active, intelligent sympathy for those upon whom the prosperity of the community rests.'[48] Yet, he concluded that if television were to fall into private hands this would not happen. It would undoubtedly prove more profitable to produce images of the rich for consumption by the poor than vice versa. Television, in private hands, would become an instrument of ideological oppression, a means for the promotion of war. The Labour Research Department's 1959 report on the 'Men and Money behind TV' came to the same conclusions.[49] The report argued that television was a powerful medium for the dissemination of ideas, and should not be controlled by people with such an obvious interest in the maintenance of the status quo. The report described the business interests and political affiliations of the owners of independent television companies. It illustrated that only three out of 150 members of the Boards of the BBC and the independent companies were from the labour movement. It further described the BBC as simply a part of the apparatus of government, and one very remote from democratic influence or control. Clearly, such criticisms are pertinent and important. They do not, however, engage at all with the confident cultural judgements about television, such as 'British television is the best in the world' or the construction of notions of a unified television audience which have been explored above. Like the Workers' Theatre Movement, they aim their theoretical and political assault elsewhere. They thus produce powerful criticisms of the structure of ownership of British television, but leave 'common-sense' judgements about the nature and significance of television untouched.

Anxiety about ownership and control of television generally focuses on its status as a source of information, rather than as a source of entertainment: the fictional representations on television are treated as irrelevant to the political argument. Brian Groombridge's analysis of 'television and the people' invoked the slogan used by the *Poor Man's Guardian*: 'Knowledge is Power'.[50] Groombridge argued that television, as a source of information, should have a vital role in the construction of a participatory democracy. Yet, for Groombridge, television failed in this task, by providing too much information which was both distorted and distracting, and thus leaving people feeling simply powerless. Television was thus a 'merchandising form of sub-communication'.[51]

The Birmingham Centre for Contemporary Cultural Studies has been responsible for much important theoretical and historical research on popular culture over recent years. Its members have drawn on the work of a number of European social and literary theorists, in order to develop more powerful accounts of social and cultural relations, and to specify the interaction between different cultural forms. Thus, for example, in analysing the ways in which television affects perceptions of social reality they reject a model of 'direct influence' and look instead at the ways in which television functions to organize discourses about social reality. They analyse the way in which current affairs programmes construct the 'unity' of national political life, and both reproduce and reinforce the existing field of the poltical struggle.[52] Despite such attention to the specificity of televisual representation, something earlier critics on the Left had not engaged with, members of the Birmingham Media Group still focus almost exclusively on the partiality of media representations, and on news as the 'heartland of political communications'.[53] They impose a very clear hierarchy of programmes worthy of serious critical attention, and have little to say about other, more trivial, forms of television. There is, of course, a gender dimension to this emphasis. Public affairs are seen as serious and political, while forms such as soap-opera or quiz shows, which are widely consumed by women viewers, are seen as trivial, and as irrelevant to the business of political analysis. This emphasis has been challenged by writers like Tania Modleski or Dorothy Hobson, but it remains pervasive.[54] It leaves a lot of television unaccounted for, and thus unaccountable.

Work by the Birmingham Media Group, has, however, served to put in question the identification of television as an agent of ideological manipulation: or at least to think more precisely about the ways in which television's representations of social reality are affected by the social realities of its audience.[55] Such work on the relative autonomy of the audience, can, however, develop into a sort of wishful positing of authentic class consciousness: mythification is never far away in analyses of popular culture. Such is the implication, for example, of Ian Connell's defence of the political potential of commercial television. He attacks the Left's assumption that commercial television must be 'hard-core ideology, especially if the ratings are high', and seeks to demonstrate the multiplicity of representations on commercial television.[56] He pins this analysis, however, on the claim that commercial television expresses 'popular structures of feeling' better than the BBC.[57] He thus seems to accept 'popular structures of feeling' as a given, as something that exists outside cultural forms, and is then more or less adequately expressed by them. He does not consider the role that commercial television might have in constructions of notions of 'the popular', nor does he seem to believe that 'the popular' is a site of contradiction, and therefore susceptible to critical analysis. He thus calls on the Left to suspend judgement and evaluation in relation to commercial television: but this, surely, would be to suspend political analysis.

For many theorists on the Left, then, the explanation of television's power tends to be articulated in terms of conspiracies. If television is controlled by the agents of capitalism, it is argued, its representations will be ideological. The implication is that if it were controlled by the people it would provide images of 'the real': but television is not so transparent, nor so easily appropriated. The only alternative to television as agent of ideological domination, therefore, lies in positing a space beyond the reach of ideology: a space of authenticity where the dominant culture will hold no sway. As we have discovered throughout this book, however, such spaces are produced by the terms of cultural analysis, and have no existence outside them.

TELEVISION AND HISTORY: THOUGHTS FOR THE FUTURE

The emphasis on the measurable effects of television, whether as moral corruption or as ideological manipulation, has been challenged in more recent critical treatments. Work such as that in *Popular Film and Television* or *Television Mythologies* tries to challenge the split between discourses which treat television as 'art', and therefore ignore its specificity, and those which treat it as 'mass culture' and thus susceptible only of economic or sociological analysis.[58] By equating television with 'popular' rather than 'mass' culture, and examining the specific ways in which television structures its representations and constructs its audience, such studies consider questions of subjectivity and pleasure, and their relation to textual structures, rather than seeing television as the bearer of already constituted ideologies. In their close attention to the mechanisms of televisual representation, and to the specificity of television as a cultural form, such studies represent an attempt to develop a critical language which will address television as institution, as text, as source of pleasure and as politicized discourse. They are thus able to discuss forms of television which had been completely despised, such as situation comedy or soap-opera, and to unravel their relation to the constitution of social and sexual identity.

Such approaches are not, however, without their limitations, which are, once more, related to the continuities in cultural analysis detailed throughout this book. Such limitations are perhaps best specified by looking at one particular, and very influential, debate about the political effectivity of television. Colin MacCabe's criticism of realist representation, specifically as manifested in the television drama-documentary *Days of Hope*, was a powerful attempt to think through the relation between politics and cultural form.[59] He argued that the television series *Days of Hope*, despite its representations of a period of political struggle, and of the politicization of a working-class man, was compromised by its realist form. The series represented political struggle, but did not politicize representation. MacCabe argued that *Days of Hope* offered its audience a coherent historical narrative, told from a particular, and consistent, point of view. It thus did not allow them to question the version of history represented by the series, but tended instead to reinforce an understanding of history as linear and as coherent. Instead, MacCabe argued for the importance of finding forms for the representation of history as contradictory, and of demonstrating to the audience the historically specific conventions which lie behind any form of representation.

MacCabe's position was criticized as formalist, as paying too little attention to the political implications of *Days of Hope*'s positive representation of the development of class consciousness, and also as advocating a cultural practice that would be largely inaccessible.[60] MacCabe conceded that any other form of representation of history was likely to be less accessible, but insisted that it must be developed. The terms of this debate are reminiscent of struggles within the Workers' Theatre Movement: the need to provide completely new representations, to break with all existing theatrical forms. They also demonstrate very clearly the continuing importance of literary debates for the analysis of popular culture: MacCabe made his argument about James Joyce as well as about *Days of Hope*. MacCabe produced a politicized theory of representation, which offered radically different strategies for the representation of historical change. In doing so, however, he refused absolutely to engage with the dominant form of televisual representation, to grant it even a contingent power and effectivity. MacCabe rejected realism absolutely, and offered either theoretical and political purity or reactionary compromise. Against identification and recognition he placed textual productivity, and insisted on its political primacy.

Tania Modleski has criticized this theoretical schism between production and consumption.[61] She argues that 'production' has always been a metaphor of male industrial and cultural labour, and sees the suspicion of consumption, understood as pleasurable recognition, as a suspicion of the role of women in political and cultural structures. Modleski's attention to the language, the metaphors, of theoretical discourse is important, and her critique of the unquestioning primacy of production over consumption is timely.

It is clearly not enough, however, to replace 'production' with 'consumption' as the focus of theoretical and political debates about popular culture. Jane Root's *Open the Box*, for example, comes close to doing just this.[62] Root's book is a lucid and very powerful attack on the sociological paradigms which have dominated the study of television. Root demonstrates the untenability of theories of television addiction, insists on the complexity of uses of and responses to television, and challenges the 'hierachy' of forms of television. The work of challenging the dominant ways of talking about, and theorizing, television absorbs the book to such an extent, however, that it is left with very little critical edge. She seems, finally, to be saying: this is television, this is how and why people watch it, and we must be content with it. The popular is popular: no more to be said.

In order to say any more than that, we need to recover the history of the concept of 'popular culture'. We have to understand the origins of certain sorts of judgements about popular culture: as debased, as bastion of authenticity, or as irrelevant. We have to see popular culture in its historically shifting relation to dominant cultural forms, in order to avoid the temptation to naturalize existing social and cultural relations. Above all, we must not lose sight of the fact that popular culture matters: it has clearly mattered to those who have sought to classify it or to control it, and should also matter to those who seek to challenge existing social, sexual and cultural relations.

Conclusion

My object in this book has been to open out the history of the concept of 'popular culture': to see it as a developing concept, which has served as a focus for struggles over the relationship between culture and society. This has meant considering the analysis of popular culture in relation to a wide range of cultural forms and practices, and over an extended historical period. Each chapter has examined a different set of responses to popular cultural forms, in order to identify the relation between theorization of the 'dominant' and of the 'popular', and also in order to construct a more coherent history of the analysis of popular culture.

The relationship between 'the dominant' and 'the popular' has emerged as very complex. Thus, for example, peasant poets understood the significance of their writing largely in terms of texts derived from the dominant culture, at the same time as the fact and the nature of their writing was being used as a demonstration of 'the natural', and as a critique of elements of the dominant culture. The struggles of individual writers to find a poetic voice which could mediate between the realms of the popular and the dominant, and the contradictory economic and social relationships within which they found themselves caught, all serve to demonstrate the historically changing relation between popular and dominant culture. Similarly, folk singers found their repertoire of songs valorized as the locus of continuity and tradition, and then appropriated by composers and arrangers in the name of Englishness or of authenticity. Folk music thus moved, to some extent, into the dominant culture, as did traditional pottery, and the poetic expression of Ossian.

It is important to understand each of these moments as part of the history of the analysis of popular culture. It is often assumed that an interest in popular culture is a very recent phenomenon: dating at the earliest from the beginning of this century. As we have seen, however, an interest in marginalized cultural forms, in the cultural forms of 'the people', goes back as far as the early eighteenth century. If we are to understand more recent accounts of popular culture, and to realize their limitations, we must first understand their historical origins. We must analyse the ways in which critics of popular culture in the past have talked about social and cultural change, about history, about technological progress, about increasing democracy in both cultural and political spheres, or about cultural authenticity.

The difficulty, throughout the book, has obviously been to do justice to the specificity of each moment examined, while also seeing it in relation to issues raised by the book as a whole. In order to understand what was at stake in discussions of popular theatre, of television, or of pottery, it has been necessary to go into considerable detail about the ways in which such cultural forms emerged, developed, and were made sense of. To some extent, these discussions of popular culture have to be presented 'in their own terms', in order that their assumptions and implications can be made clear. This has meant quoting quite extensively from the work of folk song collectors, reproducing the terms in which peasant poetry was presented to potential patrons, looking at journalistic and critical accounts of penny fiction or of television, following the changes in conceptions of popular theatre as articulated in newspapers or pamphlets, and reproducing the various arguments about Ossian's poetry as they developed throughout the eighteenth century.

Given the volume and diversity of the analyses of popular culture examined throughout this book, it has also been important to return constantly to the central questions which motivated this whole study: how can we think of cultural diversity and plurality without accepting uncritically existing cultural hierarchies; what has been the historical relationship between social power and cultural prestige; what are the theoretical terms and research practices which have led to the disappearance of women from histories of popular culture; how can we develop a critical language which will not simply reconfirm the marginality of popular culture; and to what extent have critics been able to challenge the assumptions about class, gender and history which have structured so many discussions of popular culture? Thus, for example, in looking at responses to penny fiction in the nineteenth century, I looked not only at the range of these responses as articulated in the periodical press, but also at the assumptions about cultural value and significance that lay behind such responses. I demonstrated the ways in which critics from different social and political positions all shared an investment in the poetic and a fear of the fictional. I analysed the relation between penny fiction and the changing political and social structures of the early nineteenth century. I also, finally, looked at numerous recent accounts of nineteenth-century popular culture, in order to demonstrate the ways in which they have consistently marginalized the cultural experiences of women, and have thus worked with very partial theories of social class.

The major reason for writing this book was an unease about the language of contemporary cultural criticism. Arguments about popular culture can now be found in a number of different disciplines: anthropology, literary studies, history, music, sociology, communications, and the relatively new discipline of 'cultural studies'. In every case the assumption seems to be that all that needs to be done is to bring a theoretical language to bear on that unproblematic entity: 'popular culture'. In each of these disciplines, however, discussions of popular culture seem to end up reproducing one of a very limited number of explanations, or descriptions, of popular culture, while straining after specificity and novelty. For example, if theorists of popular culture consistently see themselves as witnessing a period of cultural decline, while pointing to a Golden Age so recently past, we might begin to conclude that this says more about the language of cultural analysis than it does about culture. When we hear a major, and theoretically sophisticated, cultural critic reproduce exactly this argument, claiming that the 1960s represents a Golden Age of television, against which we must measure the cultural decay and trivialization of present-day television, the need to challenge such arguments becomes even more pressing.[1]

The point here is not that it is necessarily wrong to identify particular cultural forms as being in decline. Developments in the social and economic relations of cultural production can, indeed, lead to a diminishing in particular cultural forms: clearly it is true, for example, that the role and significance of traditional song is different, and arguably less central, now, compared to one hundred years ago. The significance and extent of such 'decline', however, can only be measured through an understanding of the long and complex history of traditional song in Britain: its relation to other forms of music and song, and its role in the construction of regional or class identities. To set up a largely imaginary 'Golden Age', against which all developments will be measured as decline, is not helpful to the historical specificity such an analysis would require.

Similarly, if it is assumed, as in the case of penny fiction or of television, that greater cultural accessibility inevitably leads to trivialization and addiction, any assessment of the ways in which individuals from different social groups negotiate their relationship to a range of cultural texts and practices becomes difficult. The equation of 'the popular', understood as the generally accessible, with manipulation and distortion has a long history. It has been used in discussions of political strategy, of penny fiction, of commercial theatre and of television. It is important, however, to identify the interests that those who make such an equation are advancing: to deny it the weight of inevitability and certainty. Questions of the power of particular cultural forms, the economic interests of those who produce them, or the ways in which cultural commodification has altered the cultural relations of Britain are important. To assign them simply to a discourse of 'manipulation' and 'addiction', however, is to trivialize.

The other side of this immediate assumption of popular culture as being in decline, as the site of trivialization and manipulation, lies in the desperate search for an example of cultural authenticity. Here, the object is to repress historical change in the name of tradition, or to ignore technology in the name of unmediated expression. Thus the Arts and Crafts Movement sought to undo the developments in social and industrial relations which characterized the nineteenth century by creating a space for unalienated labour. Yet, the movement remained fragmented in terms of class and gender, and, necessarily, caught within the relations of commodity production: their products were very expensive. Folk song collectors, too, tried to locate examples of authentic national and popular expression. This desire so overdetermined their theorizing and their collecting, however, that they ignored the range of music which was both produced and consumed by the people they studied. They also removed these people from their real historical circumstances, by placing them resolutely, and unchangingly, as 'the folk'. Even in relation to television, this search for 'authenticity' has been clear, and damaging. It leads to a refusal to consider television as a technology, or as an industrially produced cultural form, and an attempt to see it as an essentially literary form. Once more, this insistence on 'authenticity' involves the repression of cultural and social change, and a denial of the complex, and sometimes contradictory, ways in which individuals live their cultural and social identities.

Thus, all of these judgements about popular culture, as in decline, as leading to addiction, as the last bastion of authenticity, are misleading to the extent that they are automatic. The very significant continuities revealed throughout this book, from the eighteenth century to the present day, and from apologist for Victorian capitalism to theorist of revolutionary change, reveal the power of these sorts of assessments of popular culture. They represent a set of attitudes towards culture and society, but they do not represent an analysis of cultural relations at a given historical moment. If we are to be able to imagine cultural plurality, to understand the possible relations between cultural production and social power, and to see the historical dimensions of particular cultural developments, then the concepts which we bring to bear on the analysis of popular culture need to be much more carefully considered. This can only be done through an attention to the history of analyses of popular culture, a critical reappraisal of 'obvious' judgements about the nature and potential of 'the popular', and a constant questioning of the power and significance of the dominant culture.

Notes

INTRODUCTION

1 Judith Williamson, 'The Problems of Being Popular', *New Socialist*, 41 (September 1986), 14–15.
2 See, for example, Marie Winn, *The Plug-In Drug* (Harmondsworth, 1977).
3 See, for example, Jame Root, *Open The Box: About Television*, Comedia Series, 34 (London, 1986) and David Morley, *The 'Nationwide' Audience: Structure and Decoding*, BFI Television Monograph 11 (London, 1980).
4 For a discussion of developments in the concept of 'culture' see the introduction to Raymond Williams, *Culture and Society 1780–1950* (Harmondsworth, 1958).
5 See, for example, Pierre Bourdieu, *Distinction: A Social Critique of the Judgement of Taste*, trans. Richard Nice (London, 1984).
6 Pierre Bourdieu and Jean-Claude Passeron, *Reproduction in Education, Society and Culture*, trans. Richard Nice, Sage Studies in Social and Educational Change, 5 (London, 1977), p. 76.
7 See Antonio Gramsci, *Selections from the Prison Notebooks*, ed. Quintin Hoare and Geoffrey Nowell Smith (London, 1971), esp. pp. 55–60 and 160–1.
8 Gramsci, *Prison Notebooks*, p. 57.
9 Stuart Hall, Bob Lumley and Gregor McLennan, 'Politics and Ideology: Gramsci', in Centre for Contemporary Cultural Studies, *On Ideology* (London, 1977), 45–76 (p. 49).
10 Raymond Williams, *Marxism and Literature* (Oxford, 1977), p. 123.

CHAPTER 1   A HISTORY OF CHANGING DEFINITIONS OF 'THE POPULAR'

1 Henry Cockeram, *The English Dictionarie* (1623).
2 Nathan Bailey, *A Pocket Dictionary* (1753).
3 Allon White, '"The Dismal Sacred Word"', *LTP*, 2 (1983), 4–15 (p. 8).

4   J. Rastell, *An Exposition of Certaine Difficult and Obscure Words, and Termes of the Lawes of this Realme* (1592), p. 8.
5   William Blackstone, *Commentaries on the Laws of England*, 2 vols (Oxford, 1766), II, 438.
6   William Lambard, *Eirenarcha*, 1st edn 1581 (London, 1599), p. 126.
7   Rastell, *An Exposition*, p. 8.
8   *OED*, 'popular', definition 2.
9   W. Strype, *Ecclesiastical Memorials*, 3 vols (London, 1721), II, 91.
10 ibid., p. 100.
11 ibid., Appendix 'S', p. 65.
12 ibid., p. 65.
13 ibid., p. 66.
14 ibid., p. 67.
15 Plutarch, *Lives*, trans. by Sir Thomas North (London, 1676), p. 223.
16 Archibald Alison, *History of Europe from the Commencement of the French Revolution to the Restoration of the Bourbons in 1815*, 14 vols (London, 1849–50), II, 110.
17 ibid., p. 110.
18 ibid., p. 111.
19 ibid., pp. 112 and 111.
20 ibid., p. 110.
21 *OED*, 'popular', definition 2/b.
22 Nicholas Harpsfield, *A Treatise on the Pretended Divorce between Henry VIII and Catherine of Aragon*, Camden Society (London, 1878), p. 42.
23 Michel de Montaigne, *The Essayes*, trans. John Florio, 1st edn 1603 (London, 1632), p. 624.
24 Sir Robert Naunton, *Fragmenta Regalia* (1641), pp. 3 and 9.
25 ibid., p. 9.
26 B. Jonson, *Every Man out of His Humour*, reprinted from the Holmes Quarto of 1600 (London, 1907), Act 1, sc. i, p. 19.
27 J. Milton, *Paradise Regain'd and Samson Agonistes* (London, 1671), *Samson Agonistes*, lines 15–17.
28 James Kirkton, *The Secret and True History of the Church of Scotland, from the Restoration to the Year 1678* (Edinburgh, 1817), p. 217.
29 E. Dorrington, *The Hermit: Or the Unparalleled Sufferings and Surprising Adventures of Mr Philip Quarll, An Englishman* (London, 1727), p. 16.
30 ibid., p. ix.
31 ibid., p. 47.
32 *OED*, 'popular', definition 4.
33 *Letter Book of Gabriel Harvey*, ed. Edward John Long Scott, Camden Society (London, 1884), pp. 10–11.
34 Thomas Babington Macaulay, *The History of England*, 5th edn, 2 vols (London, 1849), II, 108.
35 J. S. Mill in *London Review*, 2 (1835), p. 273.

36 *Encyclopaedia Britannica*, 35 vols (London, 1902), XXIX, 751.

37 Samuel Taylor Coleridge, *Biographia Literaria*, 2 vols (1817), I, 253.

38 *OED*, 'popular', definition 5/a.

39 Francis Bacon, *The Historie of the Raigne of King Henry the Seventh* (London, 1622), p. 165.

40 J. Swift, *A Discourse on the Contests and Dissensions between the Nobles and the Commons in Athens and Rome, with the Consequences they had upon both those States* (London, 1701), p. 25.

41 ibid., p. 36.

42 *OED*, 'popular', definition 6.

43 *The Tatler: The Lucubrations of Isaac Bickerstaff Esq.*, ed. Richard Steele, 4 vols (London, 1711), IV, 5.

44 Samuel Bamford, *Passages in the Life of a Radical*, 2 vols (London, 1844), I, 200.

45 Carl Engel, *Introduction to the Study of National Music* (London, 1866), p. 168.

46 Aldous Huxley, *Beyond the Mexique Bay* (London, 1934), p. 267.

47 H. F. Chorley, *The National Music of the World* (London, 1911), p. 201.

48 *Saturday Review of Literature*, 10 May 1947, p. 9.

49 David Jenkins, *The Educated Society* (London, 1966), p. 58.

50 Montaigne, *The Essayes*, p. 432.

51 *Medical and Physical Journal*, 9, (1803), 422.

52 B. Jonson, *The Divell is an Asse* (London, 1631), Act 1, sc. ii. p. 101.

53 Sir David Lyndsay, *The Monarch and Other Poems*, English Early Text Society (London, 1865), lines 4965–6.

54 Sir Thomas Smith, *The Commonwealth of England* (London, 1633), p. 5.

55 ibid., p. 64.

56 *Saturday Review of Politics, Literature, Science and Art*, 8 November 1884, p. 590.

CHAPTER 2 'PEASANT POETS' 1730–1848: CONSISTENCY IN DIFFERENCE

1 See E. P. Thompson, 'Eighteenth Century English Society: Class Struggle Without Class?', *Social History*, 3: 2 (May 1978), 133–65.

2 H. Gustav Klaus, *The Literature of Labour: Two Hundred Years of Working-Class Writing* (Brighton, 1985), ch. 1.

3 Brian Maidment, 'Essayists and Artizans – The Making of Nineteenth-Century Self-Taught Poets', *Literature and History*, 9 (Spring 1983), 74–91, and Martha Vicinus, *The Industrial Muse: A Study of Nineteenth Century British Working-Class Literature* (London, 1974).

4 See John Barrell, *The Idea of Landscape and the Sense of Place 1730–1849: An Approach to the Poetry of John Clare* (Cambridge, 1972), ch. 1.

5 Terry Eagleton, *The Function of Criticism* (London, 1984), p. 9.

6 Richard Steele, in *The Englishman*, no. 7, 20 October 1713, p. 32.

7 For discussions of pastoral poetry in the eighteeth century, see, J. E. Congleton, *Theories of Pastoral Poetry in England 1684–1798* (Gainesville, Florida, 1952) and Raymond Williams, *The Country and The City* (London, 1985), ch. 3.

8 Alexander Pope, *The Guardian*, no. 40, 27 April 1713.

9 See *The Guardian*, 6–17 April 1713.

10 T. Tickell, *The Guardian*, no. 22, 6 April 1713.

11 John Hughes, 'Remarks on The Shepherd's Calendar', in *The Works of Mr Edmund Spenser*, ed. J. Hughes, 6 vols (London, 1715), I, ci–cii.

12 For discussion of the ideological stake of different social groups in the concepts of 'nature' and 'the country' see Williams, *The Country and the City*.

13 J. Husbands, Preface to *A Miscellany of Poems by Several Hands* (Oxford, 1731).

14 Samuel Johnson, *The Rambler*, no. 36, 21 July 1750.

15 For the importance of the *Georgics* in the eighteenth century, see Richard Feingold, *Nature and Society: Later Eighteenth Century Uses of the Pastoral and Georgic* (Brighton, 1978).

16 J. Addison, 'An Essay on the Georgics', in *The Works of Virgil*, trans. J. Dryden (London, 1792), pp. 241–251.

17 For a discussion of Thomson in relation to descriptive poetry, see Ralph Cohen, *The Art of Discrimination: Thomson's 'The Seasons' and the Language of Criticism* (London, 1964).

18 J. W. and Anne Tibble (eds), *The Prose of John Clare* (London, 1951), p. 78.

19 Barrell, *The Idea of Landscape*, ch. 1.

20 James Thomson, *The Seasons* (London, 1730), 'Spring', lines 211–16.

21 ibid., 'Spring', lines 72–5.

22 ibid., 'Summer', lines 546–8.

23 ibid., 'Autumn', lines 163–8.

24 ibid., 'Autumn' lines 177–86.

25 Leslie Stephen, *History of English Thought in the Eighteenth Century*, 2 vols (London, 1962), II, 379 and 386.

26 Robert Southey, *The Lives and Works of the Uneducated Poets*,1st edn 1831 (London, 1925), p. 183.

27 Hannah More, 'A Prefatory Letter' to *Poems on Several Occasions* by Ann Yearsley (London, 1785), pp. iii–xii (p. viii).

28 ibid., p. vii.

29 See Olivia Smith, *The Politics of Language 1791–1819* (Oxford, 1984).

30 Rayner Unwin, *The Rural Muse: Studies in the Peasant Poetry of England* (London, 1954), p. 34.

31 Octavius Gilchrist, 'Some Account of John Clare, An Agricultural Labourer and Poet', *The London Magazine*, 1: 1 (January 1820), 8.

32   Mary Leman Gillies, 'The People their own Patrons', *The People's Journal*, 1 (1846), 83–4.

33   Joseph Spence, 'An Account of the Author' in Stephen Duck, *Poems on Several Occasions*, (London, 1736), pp. xi–xx.

34   See also Maidment, 'Essayists and Artizans'.

35   Addison, 'An Essay on the Georgics', p. 242.

36   Duck, 'The Thresher's Labour', *Poems on Several Occasions*, p. 13.

37   ibid., pp. 24–5.

38   ibid., p. 14.

39   ibid., p. 20.

40   ibid., 'On Poverty', p. 7.

41   R. G. Furnival, 'Stephen Duck: The Wiltshire Phenomenon, 1705–1756', *Cambridge Journal*, 6: 8 (May 1953), 486–96.

42   See, for example, Samuel Johnson, 'An Account of the Life of Mr Richard Savage', *The Lives of the English Poets*, 2 vols (London, 1972), I, 156.

43   Furnival, 'Stephen Duck', p. 489.

44   *Memoirs of the Viscountess Sundon, Mistress of the Robes to Queen Caroline*, published by Mrs K. Thomson (London, 1847), p. 192.

45   Arthur Duck, *The Thresher's Miscellany* (London, 1730).

46   Stephen Duck, *Poems on Several Occasions*, p. xx.

47   ibid., 'A Description of a Journey', p. 209.

48   *The Gentleman's Magazine*, 9 (1739), p. 500.

49   Mary Collier, 'The Woman's Labour', *Poems on Several Occasions* (Winchester, 1762), p. 8.

50   ibid., pp. 12 and 14.

51   ibid., p. 9.

52   Collier, 'Some Remarks on the Author's Life Drawn by Herself', in *Poems on Several Occasions*, pp. iii–v (p. iv).

53   Collier, 'The Woman's Labour', p. 6.

54   ibid., p. 6.

55   Unwin, *The Rural Muse*, p. 73.

56   Collier, 'Some Remarks', p. v.

57   Collier, 'A Gentleman's Request', *Poems on Several Occasions*, p. 41.

58   Robert Tatersal, title page to *The Bricklayer's Miscellany: Or Poems on Several Subjects* (London, 1734).

59   ibid., 'To Stephen Duck', p. 24.

60   ibid., 'The Bricklayer's Labours', p. 27.

61   ibid., p. 29.

62   ibid., 'To the Honourable John King Esq.', p. 20.

63   Mary Leapor, 'The Beauties of the Spring', *Poems Upon Several Occasions* (London, 1748), p. 17.

64   ibid., p. 16.

65   ibid., 'On Winter', p. 257.

66   *The Gentleman's Magazine*, 54 (December 1784), p. 897.

67 More, 'A Prefatory Letter' p. xi.
68 J. M. S. Tompkins, *The Polite Marriage* (Cambridge, 1938), p. 82.
69 Yearsley, 'Night', *Poems on Several Occasions*, lines 219–22.
70 ibid., 'Clifton Hill', lines 15–16.
71 ibid., lines 20–1.
72 ibid., lines 37–8.
73 ibid., 'To Mr R— on His Benevolent Scheme for Rescuing Poor Children From Vice and Misery by Promoting Sunday Schools', lines 120–2.
74 ibid., 'To Mr R—', lines 67–9.
75 Ann Yearsley, *A Poem on the Inhumanity of the Slave-Trade* (London, 1788), pp. 5 and 7.
76 Richard Polwhele, 'The Unsex'd Females', *Poems*, 5 vols (London, 1810), II, p. 40.
77 Ann Yearsley, 'On Genius Unimproved', *Poems on Various Subjects* (London, 1787), p. 80.
78 See John Frederick Bryant, *Verses* (London, 1787).
79 ibid., p. 53.
80 ibid., p. 42.
81 ibid., p. 54.
82 Tibble, *The Prose of John Clare*, pp. 51 and 78.
83 George Dyer on *The Farmer's Boy*, cited in Unwin, *The Rural Muse*, p. 103.
84 Robert Bloomfield, *Works* (London, 1864), p. 17.
85 ibid., p. 18.
86 ibid., p. 31.
87 ibid., p. 31.
88 Unwin, *The Rural Muse*, p. 107.
89 John Clare, 'Letter to Richard Newcomb', in Mark Storey (ed.), *The Letters of John Clare* (Oxford, 1985), p. 4.
90 Octavius Gilchrist, 'Some Account of John Clare, An Agricultural Labourer and Poet,' *The London Magazine* 1: 1 (January 1820), 8.
91 John Taylor, Introduction to John Clare, *Poems Descriptive of Rural Life and Scenery* (London, 1820).
92 For a discussion of the patronage of John Clare, see Roger Sales, *English Literature in History 1780–1830: Pastoral and Politics* (London, 1983).
93 John Clare, Preface to *The Shepherd's Calendar* (London, 1826).
94 Cited in M. Storey, *The Poetry of John Clare* (London, 1974), p. 25.
95 J. W. and Anne Tibble (eds), *The Letters of John Clare* (London, 1951), p. 254.
96 Extracts are taken from BM *Egerton MSS* 2245, fols 39–40, 94–7, 118–21, 239–42.
97 Elaine Feinstein (ed.), *John Clare: Selected Poems* (London, 1968), Introduction.
98 Eric Robinson and Geoffrey Summerfield, 'John Taylor's Editing of

Clare's "The Shepherd's Calendar"', *Review of English Studies*, NS, 14: 56 (1963), 359–69 (p. 367).

99   ibid.
100 Eric Robinson and David Powell (eds), *John Clare* (Oxford, 1984), p. 4, lines 127–30.
101 Oliver Goldsmith, *The Deserted Village* (London, 1770), p. vi.
102 ibid., p. 7.
103 Robinson and Powell, *John Clare* p. 5, lines 173–8.
104 'Impromptu on Winter', in J. W. Tibble (ed.), *The Poems of John Clare*, 2 vols (London, 1935), I, 19.
105 ibid., cited on p. vi.
106 'The Parish', in Robinson and Powell, *John Clare*, p. 98.
107 Barrell, *The Idea of Landscape*, Appendix.
108 Eric Robinson and Geoffrey Summerfield (eds), *The Shepherd's Calendar* by John Clare (London, 1964), p. 61.
109 ibid, p. 99.
110 John Clare, *The Shepherd's Calendar* (London, 1826), p. 72.
111 Tibble, *The Prose of John Clare*, p. 44.
112 J. W. and Anne Tibble, *John Clare: A Life* (London, 1932), p. 89.
113 Feinstein, Introduction to *John Clare: Selected Poems*, p. 4.
114 Robinson and Powell, *John Clare*, p. 309, lines 1020–1 and 1034–5.
115 ibid., p. 361, lines 13–15.
116 J. A. Gordon, Pamphlet (1841), citing *Aberdeen Weekly Journal*, Aberdeen University Library, MSS 2304/4, p. 4.
117 William Thom, *Rhymes and Recollections of a Hand-Loom Weaver*, (London, 1847), p. 54.
118 ibid., p. 45.
119 *Edinburgh Weekly Chronicle*, February 1841, cited in J. A. Gordon, 'Pamphlet', p. 11.
120 Thom, *Rhymes and Recollections*, p. 42.
121 See Douglas Jerrold, 'Letter to Forster', Victoria and Albert Museum, *Forster Collection*, MSS ix, no. 19, press mark 48.F.66.
122 R. Bruce, *William Thom: The Inverurie Poet – A New Look* (Aberdeen, 1970), p. 87.
123 Review of *Rhymes and Recollections of a Hand-loom Weaver*, in *Banffshire Journal*, 27 January 1880, Aberdeen University Library, MSS 2497/4.
124 Thom, *Rhymes and Recollections*, p. 73.
125 Letter from James Bruce to editor of *Aberdeen Free Press*, February 1888, Aberdeen University Library MSS 2304/7, p. 6.
126 Cited in J. A. Gordon, 'Pamphlet', p. 14.

CHAPTER 3   POPULAR CULTURE AND THE PERIODICAL PRESS 1830–1855

1   Louis James, *Fiction for the Working Man, 1830–50* (London, 1963), p. 12.
2   Tony Bennett, *Popular Culture: Themes and Issues (2)* (Milton Keynes, 1981), p. 10.
3   Eileen Yeo, 'Culture and Constraint in Working Class Movements, 1830–50', in E. and S. Yeo (eds), *Popular Culture and Class Conflict 1590–1914: Explorations in the History of Labour and Leisure* (Brighton, 1981), p. 160.
4   See, for example, Bennett, *Popular Culture*; Yeo, *Popular Culture and Class Conflict*; and A. P. Donajgrodzki (ed.), *Social Control in Nineteenth Century Britain* (London, 1977).
5   See Anthony Delves, 'Popular Recreation and Social Conflict in Derby, 1800–1850', in Yeo, *Popular Culture and Class Conflict*.
6   J. M. Golby and A. W. Purdue, *The Civilisation of the Crowd: Popular Culture in England 1750–1900* (London, 1984).
7   Gareth Stedman Jones, 'Class Expression versus Social Control? A Critique of Recent Trends in the Social History of Leisure', *History Workshop*, 4 (Autumn 1977), 162–70.
8   David Vincent, 'Reading in the Working Class Home', in J. K. Walton and J. Walvin (eds), *Leisure in Britain 1780–1939* (Manchester, 1983), pp. 207–26.
9   *Chambers's Edinburgh Journal*, 10 April 1841, p. 91.
10 R. K. Webb, *The British Working Class Reader 1790–1848: Literacy and Social Tension* (London, 1955), p. 157.
11 ibid., p. 105.
12 Richard Johnson, 'Educating the Educators: "Experts" and the State 1833–39', in Donajgrodzki, *Social Control*.
13 Golby and Purdue, *The Civilisation of the Crowd*, pp. 11, 12 and 13.
14 ibid., p. 195.
15 ibid., p. 27.
16 ibid., pp. 14 and 9.
17 J. F. C. Harrison, *Learning and Living 1790–1960* (London, 1961), p. 29.
18 ibid., p. 55.
19 ibid., p. 30.
20 ibid., p. 36.
21 For one account of the relation between class, gender and the consumption of literature, see Darko Suvin, 'The Social Addresses of Victorian Fiction: A Preliminary Enquiry', *Literature and History*, 8 (1982), 11–41.
22 Dixon J. Hepworth, 'The Literature of the Lower Orders,' *Daily News*, 26 October 1847, p. 3.
23 Vincent, 'Reading in the Working Class Home', pp. 219–20.
24 Delves, 'Popular Recreation', p. 94.

25 Vincent, 'Reading in the Working Class Home', p. 212.
26 For discussion of these technological developments in relation to the history of the press, see Stanley Harrison, *Poor Men's Guardians* (London, 1974).
27 James, *Fiction for the Working Man*, p. 27.
28 Matthew Arnold, *Culture and Anarchy*, ed. J. Dover Wilson (Cambridge, 1967), pp. 27, 93, 69 and 11.
29 ibid., p. 108.
30 ibid., p. 70.
31 Chris Baldick, *The Social Mission of English Criticism 1848–1932* (Oxford, 1983), p. 63.
32 Arnold, *Culture and Anarchy*, p. 43.
33 ibid., p. 96.
34 ibid., p. 203.
35 Samuel Taylor Coleridge, *On the Constitution of the Church and State*, The Collected Works of S. T. Coleridge, vol. 10, ed. John Colmer (London, 1976), pp. 42–3.
36 Central Society of Education, *Second Publication* (London, 1838), p. ix.
37 B. F. Duppa, 'Industrial Schools for the Peasantry', in Central Society of Education, *First Publication* (London, 1837), p. 174.
38 James Augustus St John, *The Education of the People* 1st edn 1858, (London, 1970), p. 146.
39 John Churton Collins, *The Study of English Literature* (London, 1891), p. 4.
40 Mildred Ellis, 'The Education of Young Ladies of Small Pecuniary Resources for other Occupations than that of Teaching', in Central Society of Education, *Second Publication*, pp. 192–8.
41 Vincent, 'Reading in the Working Class Home', p. 216.
42 Mary Smith, *The Autobiography of Mary Smith* (London, 1892), p. 128. For discussion of this, and other autobiographical texts of the nineteenth century, see Julia Swindells *Victorian Writing and Working Women*, (Cambridge, 1985).
43 *The Penny Magazine of the Society for the Diffusion of Useful Knowledge*, 31 March 1832, p. 1; and 11 August 1832, p. 187.
44 ibid., 17 November 1832, p. 326.
45 Barry Cornwall (pseud.), *English Songs* (London, 1851), p. 119.
46 'Popular Literature', *Saturday Magazine*, 12 January 1833, pp. 12–13 (p. 13).
47 *Saturday Magazine*, Preface to vol. 25, 1844, p. v.
48 ibid., 12 January 1833, p. 12.
49 *The London Review*, 1 (April–July 1835), 188.
50 See title page of *Poor Man's Guardian*.
51 *Poor Man's Guardian*, 27 August 1831, p. 59.
52 *Crisis*, 19 July 1834, p. 118.
53 ibid., 18 August 1832, p. 95.
54 *Pioneer*, 4 January 1834, p. 143.

55   ibid.
56   See Brian E. Maidment, 'Magazines of Popular Progress and the Artisans', *Victorian Periodicals Review*, 17 (1984), 83–94.
57   Mrs Percy Sinnett, 'What is Popular Literature?', *People's Journal*, 5 (1848), 7.
58   ibid.
59   Maidment, 'Magazines of Popular Progress', p. 93.
60   *Daily News*, 26 October 1847, p. 3.
61   ibid.
62   ibid., 3 November 1847, p. 3.
63   For details of circulation see Anne Humphreys, 'G. W. M. Reynolds: Popular Literature and Popular Politics', *Victorian Periodicals Review*, 16 (1983), 79–89.
64   Fanny Mayne, 'The Literature of the Working Classes', *English-woman's Magazine and Christian Mother's Miscellany*, October 1850, pp. 620–1.
65   ibid., pp. 621–2.
66   ibid., p. 620.
67   *True Briton*, 8 July 1852, p. 30.
68   ibid.
69   ibid., 20 January 1853, p. 471.
70   *Chambers's Edinburgh Journal*, 7 August 1852, p. 95.
71   'Ballads of the People', *Westminster Review*, 1 January 1855, pp. 25–52 (p. 26).
72   ibid., p. 49.
73   *Blackwood's Edinburgh Magazine*, March 1852, p. 373.
74   ibid., p. 374.
75   *Notes to the People* (1851/52), p. 385.
76   ibid., p. 411.
77   ibid., p. 20.
78   Alexander Bell, 'Education for the People', *Friend of the People*, 25 January 1851, p. 51.

CHAPTER 4   POETRY, POTTERY AND SONG: THE MEDIATION OF 'POPULAR FORMS'

1   See Tony Bennett, 'Popular Culture: A "Teaching Object"', *Screen Education*, 34 (Spring 1980), 17–29.
2   For discussion of this concept see Dave Harker, *Fakesong: The Manufacture of British 'Folksong' 1700 to the Present Day* (Milton Keynes, 1985), ch. 11.
3   See, for example, John Harland and T. T. Wilkinson (eds), Preface to *Lancashire Folk-Lore*, 1st edn 1867 (East Ardsley, 1972).
4   James Macpherson (trans.), *Fragments of Ancient Poetry, Collected in the Highlands of Scotland, and Translated from the Galic or Erse Language* (Edinburgh, 1760).

5   James Macpherson (trans.), *Fingal, an Ancient Epic Poem, in Six Books: Together with Several Other Poems, Composed by Ossian the Son of Fingal. Translated from the Galic Language* (Edinburgh, 1762); and *Temora* (Dublin, 1763).

6   James Grant, *Thoughts on the Origin of the Gael* (Edinburgh, 1814), p. 379.

7   Davd Hume, 'Of Commerce' and 'Of Refinement in the Arts', in *Essays, Moral, Political and Literary*, ed. T. H. Green and T. H. Grose, 2 vols (London, 1875), I, 287–309.

8   Adam Ferguson, *An Essay on the History of Civil Society* (Edinburgh, 1767), p. 126.

9   Margaret Mary Rubel, *Savage and Barbarian: Historical Attitudes in the Criticism of Homer and Ossian in Britain, 1760–1800* (Amsterdam, 1978).

10 Donald Macdonald, 'The Letter', *Three Beautiful and Important Passages Omitted by the Translator of Fingal* (London, 1762).

11 Malcolm Laing, *The History of Scotland*, 2 vols (London, 1800), I, 388.

12 ibid., p. 453.

13 ibid., p. 390.

14 Hugh Blair, 'A Critical Dissertation on the Poems of Ossian', in *The Poems of Ossian* (Edinburgh, 1819), pp. 57–172 (pp. 58, 133 and 135).

15 Macdonald, 'The Letter'.

16 See A. Gillies, *Herder* (Oxford, 1948), ch. 4.

17 *Howitt's Journal of Literature and Popular Progress*, 17 April 1847, p. 212.

18 Henry Mackenzie (ed.), *Report of the Committee of the Highland Society of Scotland, Appointed to Inquire into the Nature and Authenticity of the Poems of Ossian*, (Edinburgh, 1805), p. 152.

19 Laing, *History of Scotland*, p. 391.

20 See Derick S. Thomson, *The Gaelic Sources of Macpherson's 'Ossian'* (Edinburgh, 1952), pp. 85–90.

21 Thomas Percy, 'An Essay on the Ancient English Minstrels', *Reliques of Ancient English Poetry*, 3rd edn (London, 1775), pp. xix–xxxix (p. xxix).

22 Harker, *Fakesong*, p. xiii.

23 Apart from the use by Mary Howitt mentioned above, the first recorded example in the *Oxford English Dictionary* is in *The Cornhill Magazine* in November 1871.

24 Sir Walter Scott, *Minstrelsy of the Scottish Border* (London, 1931) and William Motherwell, *Minstrelsy: Ancient and Modern* (Glasgow, 1827).

25 Carl Engel, *An Introduction to the Study of National Music* (London, 1866).

26 Scott, *Minstrelsy*, p. 53.

27 See Harker, *Fakesong*, p. 40.

28   Sir Hubert Parry, 'Inaugural Address', *Journal of the Folk Song Society*, 1 (1899), 3.
29   Motherwell, *Minstrelsy*, p. ix.
30   Cecil Sharp, *English Folk Song: Some Conclusions*, ed. Maud Karpeles, 4th edn (London, 1965), p. 113.
31   Alfred Williams (ed.), *Folk Songs of the Upper Thames* (London, 1923), p. 19.
32   A. L. Lloyd, 'The Revolutionary Origins of English Folk Song', in *Folk: Review of People's Music*, ed. Max Jones (London, 1945), pp. 13–15 (p. 13).
33   See R. Vaughan Williams, 'Cecil Sharp: An Appreciation', in Sharp, *English Folk Songs*, pp. vii–ix (p. vii).
34   Sharp, *English Folk Songs*, p. 5.
35   Robert Stark Thomson, 'The Development of the Broadside Ballad Trade and its Influence upon the Transmission of English Folk Songs' (unpublished doctoral thesis, University of Cambridge, 1974).
36   See George Deacon, *John Clare and the Folk Tradition* (London, 1983).
37   Michael Pickering, *Village Song and Culture* (London, 1982).
38   A. L. Lloyd, *Folk Song in England* (London, 1967), p. 72.
39   Sharp, *English Folk Song*, pp. 152–3.
40   Harland and Wilkinson, *Lancashire Folk-Lore*, p. 2.
41   See Charlotte Burne's Essay in G. L. Gomme (ed.), *The Handbook of Folklore* (London, 1890), pp. 162–72.
42   Sharp, *English Folk Song*, p. 133.
43   Kate Lee, 'Some Experiences of a Folk-Song Collector', *Journal of the Folk-Song Society*, 1 (1899), pp. 7–13 (p. 7).
44   ibid., p. 9.
45   Cited in Vic Gammon, 'Folk Song Collecting in Sussex and Surrey, 1843–1914', *History Workshop*, 10 (Autumn 1980), 61–89 (pp. 68–69).
46   R. S. Thomson, 'The Development of the Broadside Ballad Trade', p. 216.
47   Gammon, 'Folk Song Collecting', p. 70.
48   See Harker, *Fakesong*, p. 190.
49   Motherwell, *Minstrelsy*, p. xii.
50   Harker, *Fakesong*, ch. 5.
51   Williams, *Folk Songs of the Upper Thames*, p. 17.
52   A. L. Lloyd, *Folk Song in England* p. 61.
53   ibid., p. 137.
54   Motherwell, *Minstrelsy*, p. iv.
55   Gammon, 'Folk Song Collecting', p. 71.
56   Harker, *Fakesong*, ch. 7.
57   Deacon, *John Clare and the Folk Tradition*, p. 42.
58   Sharp, *English Folk Song*, p. xx.
59   ibid., p. 133.
60   Robert Bell (ed.), *Early Ballads Illustrative of History, Traditions*

and Customs, Also Ballads and Songs of the Peasantry of England (London, 1877), p. 5.

61 R. S. Thomson, 'The Development of the Broadside Ballad Trade', p. 145.
62 ibid., p. 226.
63 ibid., p. 265.
64 A. L. Lloyd, *The Singing Englishman; An Introduction to Folksong*, Workers' Music Association (London, n.d. [1944]), p. 35.
65 ibid., p. 48.
66 A. L. Lloyd, *Folk Song in England*, p. 405.
67 Motherwell, *Minstrelsy*, p. iv.
68 Bell, *Early Ballads*, p. 227.
69 Parry, 'Inaugural Address', p. 1.
70 ibid., p. 2.
71 Sir Hubert Parry, *Style in Musical Art* (London, 1924), p. 112.
72 Sharp, *English Folk Song*, p. 44.
73 Williams, *Folk Songs of the Upper Thames*, p. 16.
74 A. L. Lloyd, *Folk Song in England*, pp. 5, 394 and 401.
75 Ginette Dunn, *The Fellowship of Song: Popular Singing Traditions in East Suffolk* (London, 1980), ch. 2.
76 Vic Gammon discusses the significance of such songs in 'Song, Sex, and Society in England, 1600–1850', *Folk Music Journal*, 4 (1982), 208–45, an article which is unusual in its raising of questions about the ways in which gender, as well as class, affect responses to folk music.
77 Vaughan Williams, 'Cecil Sharp', pp. vii–viii.
78 ibid., p. viii.
79 A. L. Lloyd, *The Singing Englishman*, p. 3.
80 A. L. Lloyd, *Folk Song in England*, p. 19.
81 ibid., p. 31.
82 Pickering, *Village Song and Culture*, p. 4.
83 Richard Dorson, *The British Folklorists: A History* (London, 1968), p. 279.
84 ibid., p. 104.
85 ibid., p. 152.
86 Sharp, *English Folk Song*, p. 42.
87 Harker, *Fakesong*, p. 178.
88 Sharp, *English Folk Song*, p. 45.
89 See G. L. Gomme, 'What Folk-Lore is', in *The Handbook of Folklore*, pp. 1–7.
90 A. L. Lloyd, 'Revolutionary Origins', p. 13.
91 See *Marxism Today*, 10: 1 (January 1966); 10: 3 (March 1966); and 10: 7 (July 1966).
92 *Scottish Folk Notes*, 1 December 1967, p. 34.
93 Harker, *Fakesong*, p. 254.
94 William Morris, 'How I Became a Socialist' (1894), in Asa Briggs (ed.), *William Morris: Selected Writings and Designs* (Harmondsworth, 1977), pp. 33–7 (p. 36).

95　William Morris, 'Popular Art', extract from 'Some Hints on Pattern Designing' (1881), in Briggs, *William Morris*, pp. 106–7 (p. 106).

96　J. Bruce Glasier, 'Towards England: Was There Once a Merry England?', *Labour Leader*, 21 August 1908, p. 529.

97　ibid.

98　Morris, 'Popular Art', p. 106.

99　William Morris, 'Useful Work Versus Useless Toil' (1885), in Briggs, *William Morris*, pp. 117–36, (p. 117).

100　Ray Watkinson, 'Morris the Designer: Art, Work and Social Order', in Peter Lewis (ed.), *William Morris: Aspects of the Man and His Work* (Loughborough, 1978), pp. 75–105 (p. 93).

101　Morris, 'Useful Work Versus Useless Toil', p. 118.

102　Anthea Callen, *Angel in the Studio: Women in the Arts and Crafts Movement 1870–1914* (London, 1979), p. 26.

103　ibid. p. 17.

104　Bernard Leach, *A Potter's Book*, 1st edn 1940 (London, 1948), p. 33.

105　ibid., p. 13.

106　ibid., p. 15.

107　Carol Hogben (ed.), *The Art of Bernard Leach* (London, 1978), Introduction, p. 12.

108　Leach, *A Potter's Book*, p. 9.

109　ibid., p. 14.

110　ibid., p. 10.

111　ibid., p. xxv.

112　Oliver Watson, 'Studio Pottery: New and Traditional', in *Carol McNicoll Ceramics* (London, 1985), pp. 9–11 (p. 9).

113　Hugh Wakefield, 'The Leach Tradition', *Crafts*, 6 (January/February 1974), 16–20 (p. 18).

114　Brian Moeran, 'Yanagi, Morris and Popular Art', *Ceramic Review* (November/December 1980), 25–6.

115　Peter Dormer, 'Familiar Forms', in *Fast Forward: New Directions in British Ceramics* (London, 1985), pp. 5–8 (p. 6).

116　ibid., p. 5.

CHAPTER 5　WORKERS'/POPULAR THEATRE

1　See Tom Thomas, 'A Propertyless Theatre for the Propertyless Class', in R. Samuel, E. MacColl and S. Cosgrove (eds), *Theatres of the Left 1880–1935*, (London, 1985), pp. 77–98 (p. 94).

2　See, for example, Jon Clark, 'Agitprop and Unity Theatre: Socialist Theatre in the Thirties', in J. Clark, M. Heinemann, D. Margolies and C. Snee (eds), *Culture and Crisis in Britain in the Thirties* (London, 1979), pp. 219–39; and *Busmen*, Nottingham Drama Texts (Nottingham, 1984).

3　See, for example, 'The Cinema: An Instrument of Class Rule', *Plebs*,

23: 4 (April 1931), 90–1; and 'The Theatres', *Plebs*, 21: 3 (March 1929), 53–5.

4 This correlation is also made in Valentine Cunningham's brief discussion of the WTM in *British Writers of the Thirties* (Oxford, 1988), pp. 324–6, although Cunningham does admit that the 'purity' of WTM practice was in doubt as early as 1931.

5 R. Samuel, Introduction to Samuel et al., *Theatres of the Left*, pp. xiii–xx (p. xvii).

6 R. Samuel, 'Theatre and Socialism in Britain', in Samuel et al., *Theatres of the Left*, pp. 3–73, (p. 48).

7 ibid., p. 61.

8 This observation comes from a paper delivered by Jerry Dawson at the Conference on Unity Theatre held at Edge Hill College, February 1986.

9 Samuel, 'Theatre and Socialism in Britain', p. 50.

10 ibid., p. 44.

11 ibid., p. 53.

12 See Norman Veitch, *The People's: Being a History of the People's Theatre, Newcastle Upon Tyne, 1911–1939* (Gateshead, 1950), for discussion of the centrality of George Bernard Shaw.

13 Ness Edwards, Foreword to *The Workers' Theatre* (Cardiff, 1930).

14 D. H. Lawrence, Preface to *Touch and Go* (London, 1920), p. 8.

15 M. R. Adamson, 'A People's Theatre', *New Leader* 15 June 1923, p. 12.

16 John Arnott, 'Factories and Footlights: Leeds Industrial Theatre', *Labour Magazine*, 1: 11 (March 1923), 489–91.

17 See Lena Ashwell, 'Drama and the State', *Clarion*, no. 1868, NS no. 24 (April 1929), 10; and Amabel Williams-Ellis, 'Winning Beauty for the Masses', *New Leader*, 30 January 1925, pp. 10–11.

18 For criticism of *The Forge* as despairing, see 'Will the WTM Make up its Mind?' *Sunday Worker*, 8 January 1928, p. 8.

19 Miles Malleson, *The ILP Arts Guild: The ILP and its Dramatic Societies. What They Are and Might Become* (London, 1925), p. 14.

20 R. Gore Graham, 'Socialism and the Theatre', *Socialist Review*, 25 (April 1925), 166–78.

21 Edwards, *The Workers' Theatre*, p. 4.

22 ibid., p. 10.

23 R. Palme Dutt, 'The Workers Theatre', *Labour Monthly*, 8: 8 (August 1926), 503–510 (p. 509).

24 Stuart Macintyre, *A Proletarian Science: Marxism in Britain 1917–1933* (Cambridge, 1980).

25 Palme Dutt, 'The Workers Theatre' p. 503.

26 This quotation from Karl Marx's *Theories of Surplus Value* was reproduced in *International Literature* 5 (1934), p. 101.

27 Stuart Macintyre, *A Proletarian Science*, ch. 3.

28 Leon Trotsky, *Literature and Revolution*, trans. R. Strunsky (London, 1925), p. 130.

29   Charles Ashleigh, 'Plays Needed, Now is the Time', *Sunday Worker*, 11 July 1926, p. 8.

30   *Red Stage*, 2 (January 1932), 1; and 5 (May 1932), 7.

31   *Plebs*, 21: 3 (March 1929), 51–8.

32   See František Deák, 'Blue Blouse', *Drama Review*, 17: 1, (March 1973), 35–46.

33   *Red Stage*, 3 (February 1932), 1.

34   *Bulletin* of The Organization Committee of the International Workers Theatrical Olympiad (*International Theatre*), 1 (1932), 1.

35   Tom Thomas, 'Workers Drama That Can Be', *Sunday Worker*, 1 January 1929, p. 4.

36   Veitch, *The People's*, p. 48.

37   Maurice Dobb, 'The Theatres', *Plebs*, 21: 3 (March 1929), 53–5 (p. 54).

38   Charles Mann, '"Sex-Appeal" is Dope for the Masses', *Red Stage*, 6 (June/July 1932), 2.

39   Dobb, 'The Theatres', p. 55.

40   T. Ashcroft, 'The Theatre and Socialism', *Plebs*, 27: 12 (December 1935), 295–6.

41   See Joe Corrie, *Plays, Poems and Theatre Writing*, ed. Linda Mackenney (Edinburgh, 1985), pp. 174, 177 and 181.

42   Barbara Nixon, 'Theatre Now', *Left Review*, 3 (December 1935), 105–7 (p. 107).

43   John Allen, 'The Left Book Club and the Fight for Democracy', *Left News*, February 1939, p. 1179.

44   Oscar Lewenstein, *Unity Theatre Presents – The Story of a People's Movement* (London, n.d.), p. 5.

45   John Allen, 'Theatre', *Fact*, 4 (July 1937), 30–8 (p. 32).

46   See Lewenstein, *Unity Theatre Presents*, p. 15; and Malcolm Page, 'The Early Years at Unity', *Theatre Quarterly*, 1: 4 (October–December 1971), 60–6 (p. 61).

47   *New Theatre*, 1 (December 1945), 8.

48   Ralph Bond, 'Cinema in the Thirties', in Clark et al., *Culture and Crisis*, pp. 241–56 (p. 245).

49   J. Symons, *The Thirties. A Dream Revolved* (London, 1975), ch. 6.

50   See Howard Goorney, *The Theatre Workshop Story*, (London, 1981), ch. 1.

51   Carter's articles on workers' theatre appear in the *Sunday Worker* throughout 1926 and 1927.

52   See Thomas, 'A Propertyless Theatre for the Propertyless Class', p. 83.

53   *Daily Worker*, 10 February 1930, p. 10.

54   *Red Stage*, 1 (November 1931), 1.

55   Charles Mann, 'How to Produce *Meerut*', in Samuel et al., *Theatres of the Left*, pp. 106–8 (p. 106).

56   Tom Thomas, 'The Workers' Theatre in Britain', *International Theatre*, 1 (1934), 22–4.

57 Extract from *Bulletin* (September/October 1933), in Samuel et al., *Theatres of the Left*, pp. 167–70 (p. 168).

58 See, for example, *New Red Stage* (June/July 1932), p. 3.

59 Ewan MacColl, 'Some Origins of Theatre Workshop', in Samuel et al., *Theatres of the Left*, pp. 205–55 (p. 231).

60 See Douglas Allen, 'Political Culture in Scotland: The Glasgow Workers' Theatre Group, 1937–40' (unpublished thesis, University of Glasgow), Scottish Theatre Archive.

61 See Linda Mackenney, 'Working Class Theatre in Glasgow 1900–1950: Catalogue of Plays' (1981); 'Legends', *Scottish Theatre News*, April 1983, 11–14; and 'Interview with Vincent and Ann Flynn': all in Scottish Theatre Archive.

62 Douglas Allen, 'Political Culture in Scotland', p. 22.

63 Samuel, 'Theatre and Socialism in Britain', p. 58.

64 Huntly Carter, 'Labour and the Theatre', *Plebs*, 22: 9 (September 1930), 206–9 (p. 207).

65 *Left News*, May 1937, p. 329.

66 *Left Review*, 9 (October 1937), 510.

67 John Hill, 'Towards a Scottish People's Theatre: The Rise and Fall of Glasgow Unity', *Theatre Quarterly*, 7: 27 (August 1977), 61–70 (p. 61).

68 John Hill, 'Glasgow Unity Theatre. The Search for a "Scottish People's" Theatre', *New Edinburgh Review*, 40 (February 1978), 31.

69 Such a teleological account is offered, for example, by Len Jones, 'The Workers' Theatre Movement in the Thirties', *Marxism Today*, 18: 9 (September 1974), 271–80.

CHAPTER 6   AS SEEN ON TV: TECHNOLOGY AND CULTURAL DECLINE

1 I have discussed the theoretical assumptions behind theories of 'subcultures' in *The Concept of 'The Popular' in Cultural Analysis*, McGill University Working Papers in Communications (Montreal, 1986).

2 For an account of the tension between approaches to television as a technology and accounts of it as a cultural form, see Raymond Williams, *Television, Technology and Cultural Form* (London, 1974).

3 Laura Kipnis, '"Refunctioning" Reconsidered: Towards a Left Popular Culture', in Colin MacCabe (ed), *High Theory/Low Culture: Analysing Popular Television and Film* (Manchester, 1986) pp. 11–36.

4 Michael Egan, 'Television for the Masses: Its Effects on Social Progress and War', *New Leader*, 15 April 1927, p. 11.

5 See Jeanne Allen, 'The Social Matrix of Television: Invention in the United States', in E. Ann Kaplan (ed.), *Regarding Television: Critical Approaches – An Anthology* (Frederick, Maryland, 1983), pp. 109–19 (p. 112).

6 See *Report of the Broadcasting Committee 1949* (Beveridge Committee), HMSO, cmnd. 8116, 1951.
7 Advertisement in the *Daily Mail*, 20 September 1963, p. 11.
8 For a discussion of the varied and complex ways in which families actually use the medium of television, see Philip Simpson (ed.), *Parents Talking Television: Television in the Home*, Comedia Series, 46 (London, 1987).
9 Ernest Thomson, 'What is This Television?', *Radio Times*, 17 May 1946, pp. 3 and 23.
10 ibid., p. 23.
11 ibid., p. 23.
12 *Report of the Television Committee 1943* (London, 1945).
13 See Denys Thompson (ed.), *Discrimination and Popular Culture* (Harmondsworth, 1964).
14 F. R. Leavis, *Mass Civilisation and Minority Culture*, Minority Pamphlet 1 (Cambridge, 1930).
15 Thompson, Introduction to *Discrimination*, pp. 9–22 (p. 9).
16 ibid., p. 18.
17 Philip Abrams, 'Radio and Television', in D. Thompson *Discrimination*, pp. 50–73 (p. 51).
18 ibid., p. 60.
19 Richard Hoggart, *The Uses of Literacy* (Harmondsworth, 1958), pp. 26 and 46.
20 ibid., p. 22.
21 ibid., p. 11.
22 ibid., p. 154.
23 Stuart Hall and Paddy Whannel, *The Popular Arts* (London, 1964), p. 141.
24 ibid., p. 115.
25 See, for example, Dorothy Hobson, *Crossroads: The Drama of a Soap Opera* (London, 1982); and Ken Worpole, 'Reduced to Words', in Simpson, *Parents Talking Television*, pp 80–9.
26 Hall and Whannel, *The Popular Arts*, p. 111.
27 *Report of the Committee on Broadcasting 1960* (Pilkington Committee) HMSO cmnd. 1753, 1962, p. 31.
28 ibid., p. 68.
29 Denis McQuail, 'The Influence and Effects of Mass Media', in James Curran, Michael Gurevitch and Janet Woollacott (eds), *Mass Communication and Society* (London, 1977), pp. 70–94.
30 For a report of this group's activities, see Anne Karpf, 'A Touch of the TTs', *Guardian*, 13 March 1979, p. 9.
31 Marie Winn, *The Plug-In Drug* (New York, 1977), p. 106.
32 H. J. Eysenck and D. K. B. Nias, *Sex, Violence and the Media* (London, 1978). For a discussion of various approaches to the 'problem' of violence on television, see Bob Hodge and David Tripp, *Children and Television* (Cambridge, 1986), ch. 7.
33 Eysenck and Nias, *Sex, Violence and the Media*, p. 17.

34 ibid., p. 9.

35 ibid., p. 264.

36 ibid., pp. 273 and 271.

37 William A. Belson, *Television Violence and the Adolescent Boy* (Farnborough, 1978), p. 15.

38 For discussion of this point see Graham Murdock and Robin McCron, 'The Television and Delinquency Debate', *Screen Education*, 30 (Spring 1979), 51–67.

39 Hilde T. Himmelweit et al., *Television and the Child: An Empirical Study of the Effect of Television on the Young* (London, 1958), p. 14.

40 'Children's TV Film a Mistake', *Daily Telegraph*, 15 January 1954, p. 9.

41 *Daily Express*, 22 June 1983, p. 1.

42 'Opinion', *Daily Express*, 22 June 1983, p. 6.

43 See Mike Poole, 'The Cult of the Generalist: British Television Criticism 1936–83', *Screen*, 25: 2 (March–April 1984), 41–61.

44 Hugh Greene, Introduction to T. C. Worsley, *Television: The Ephemeral Art* (London, 1970), p. 9.

45 Worsley, *Television*, p. 33.

46 Clive James, *The Crystal Bucket: Television Criticism from 'The Observer' 1967–79* (London, 1981), p. 20.

47 ibid., p. 13.

48 Egan, 'Television for the Masses', p. 27.

49 Labour Research Department, *Men and Money Behind TV* (London, 1959).

50 Brian Groombridge, *Television and the People: A Programme for Democratic Participation* (Harmondsworth, 1972), p. 123.

51 ibid., p. 128.

52 Stuart Hall, Ian Connell and Lydia Curti, 'The "Unity" of Current Affairs Television', in *Culture and Domination*, Working Papers in Cultural Studies, 9 (Birmingham, 1976), pp. 51–93.

53 Stuart Hall, 'Introduction to Media Studies at the Centre', in Stuart Hall et al. (eds), *Culture, Media, Language: Working Papers in Cultural Studies 1972–79* (London, 1980) pp. 117–21 (p. 119).

54 See Hobson, *Crossroads*; and Tania Modleski, 'Femininity as Mas(s)querade: A Feminist Approach to Mass Culture', In MacCabe, *High Theory/Low Culture*, pp. 37–52.

55 See, for example, David Morley, *The 'Nationwide' Audience*, BFI Television Monograph 11 (London, 1980).

56 Ian Connell, 'Commercial Broadcasting and the British Left', *Screen*, 24: 6 (November–December 1983), 70–80 (p. 74).

57 ibid., p. 76.

58 Tony Bennett et al. (eds), *Popular Television and Film* (London, 1980) and Len Masterman (ed.), *Television Mythologies: Stars, Shows and Signs*, Comedia Series, 24 (London, 1984).

59 For the 'debate' over *Days of Hope*, see Bennett et al., *Popular Television and Film*, pp. 282–352.

60 See ibid., pp. 288–301 and 305–9; and Colin McArthur, *Television and History*, BFI Television Monograph 8 (London, 1980).
61 Modleski, 'Femininity as Mas(s)querade'.
62 See Jane Root, *Open the Box: About Television*, Comedia Series, 34 (London, 1986); and, in response, Judith Williamson, 'The Problems of Being Popular', *New Socialist*, 41 (September 1986) 14–15.

CONCLUSION

1 This argument was advanced by Colin MacCabe in a lecture on 'Television' broadcast in 1988.

Select Bibliography

THE RECEPTION OF OSSIAN'S POETRY AND THE WORK OF THE PEASANT POETS

Addison, J., 'An Essay on the *Georgics*', in *The Works of Virgil*, trans. J. Dryden (London, 1792), pp. 241–51

Barrell, John, *The Dark Side of the Landscape: The Rural Poor in English Painting 1730–1840* (Cambridge, 1980)

——, *English Literature in History 1730–80: An Equal, Wide Survey* (London, 1983)

——, *The Idea of Landscape and the Sense of Place 1730–1849: An Approach to the Poetry of John Clare* (Cambridge, 1972)

Beattie, James, *The Minstrel, or The Progress of Genius*, 4th edn (London, 1774)

Bloomfield, Robert, *Works* (London, 1864)

Bruce, R., *William Thom: The Inverurie Poet – A New Look* (Aberdeen, 1970)

Bryant, John Frederick, *Verses* (London, 1787)

Clare, John, *Poems Descriptive of Rural Life and Scenery* (London, 1820)

——, *The Shepherd's Calendar* (London, 1826)

Cohen, Ralph, *The Art of Discrimination: Thomson's 'The Seasons' and the Language of Criticism* (London, 1964)

Collier, Mary, *Poems on Several Occasions* (Winchester, 1762)

——, *The Woman's Labour: An Epistle to Mr Stephen Duck* (London, 1739)

Congleton, J. E., *Theories of Pastoral Poetry in England 1684–1798* (Gainesville, Florida, 1952)

Davis, Rose Mary, *Stephen Duck: The Thresher Poet*, University of Maine Studies, Series 2, 8 (Orono, Maine, 1926)

Dodsley, Robert, *A Muse in Livery: or the Footman's Miscellany* (London, 1732)

Duck, Stephen, *Poems on Several Occasions* (London, 1736)

Feingold, Richard, *Nature and Society: Later Eighteenth Century Uses of the Pastoral and Georgic* (Brighton, 1978)

Feinstein, Elaine, ed., *John Clare: Selected Poems* (London, 1968)

Furnival, R. G., 'Stephen Duck: The Wiltshire Phenomenon, 1705–1756', *Cambridge Journal*, 6: 8 (May 1953), 486–496

Goldsmith, Oliver, *The Deserted Village* (London, 1779)

Grant, James, *Thoughts on the Origin of the Gael: with an Account of the Picts, Caledonians and Scots and Observations Relevant to the Authenticity of the Poems of Ossian* (Edinburgh, 1814)

Graves, Robert, 'Peasant Poet', *Hudson Review*, 8: 1 (Spring 1955), 99–105

Husbands, J., *A Miscellany of Poems by Several Hands* (Oxford, 1731)

Johnson, Samuel, 'The Reasons Why Pastorals Delight', *Rambler*, no. 36, 21 July 1750

Laing, Malcolm, *The History of Scotland, from the Union of the Crowns on the Accession of James VI to the Throne of England to the Union of the Kingdoms in the Reign of Queen Anne*, 2 vols (London, 1800)

Leapor, Mary, *Poems Upon Several Occasions* (London, 1748)

Macdonald, Donald, *Three Beautiful and Important Passages Omitted by the Translator of 'Fingal'* (London, 1762)

Mackenzie, Henry, ed., *Report of the Committee of the Highland Society of Scotland, Appointed to Inquire into the Nature and Authenticity of the Poems of Ossian* (Edinburgh, 1805)

Macpherson, James, trans., *Fingal, an Ancient Epic Poem, in Six Books: Together with Several Other Poems, Composed by Ossian the Son of Fingal. Translated from the Galic Language* (London, 1762)

——, trans., *Fragments of Ancient Poetry, Collected in the Highlands of Scotland, and Translated from the Galic, or Erse Language* (Edinburgh, 1760)

——, trans., *The Poems of Ossian* (Edinburgh, 1819)

——, trans., *Temora. An Ancient Epic Poem Translated from the Galic Language* (Dublin, 1763)

Maidment, Brian, 'Essayists and Artizans – The Making of Nineteenth-Century Self-Taught Poets', *Literature and History*, 9 (Spring 1983), 74–91

Robinson, Eric and David Powell, *John Clare* (Oxford, 1984)

—— and Geoffrey Summerfield, 'John Taylor's Editing of Clare's "The Shepherd's Calendar"', *Review of English Studies*, NS 14, no. 56 (1963) 359–69

—— and Geoffrey Summerfield, eds., *The Shepherd's Calendar* by John Clare (London, 1964)

Rubel, Margaret Mary, *Savage and Barbarian: Historical Attitudes in the Criticism of Homer and Ossian in Britain, 1760–1800* (Amsterdam, 1978)

Sales, Roger, *English Literature in History 1780–1830: Pastoral and Politics* (London, 1983)

Smith, Olivia, *The Politics of Language 1791–1819* (Oxford, 1984)

Southey, Robert, *The Lives and Works of the Uneducated Poets*, 1st edn 1831 (London, 1925)

Storey, Mark, *The Letters of John Clare* (Oxford, 1985)

——, *The Poetry of John Clare: A Critical Introduction* (London, 1974)

Tatersal, Robert, *The Bricklayer's Miscellany: or Poems on Several Subjects* (London, 1734)

Thom, William, *Rhymes and Recollections of a Hand-Loom Weaver* (London, 1847)

Thomson, Derick S., *The Gaelic Sources of Macpherson's 'Ossian'* (Edinburgh, 1952)

——, '"Ossian" Macpherson and the Gaelic World of the Eighteenth Century', *Aberdeen University Review*, 40: 129 (Spring 1963), 7–20

Thomson, James, *The Seasons* (London, 1730)

Tibble, J. W., ed., *The Poems of John Clare* (London, 1935)

—— and Anne Tibble, *John Clare: A Life* (London, 1932)

—— and Anne Tibble, eds, *The Letters of John Clare* (London, 1951)

—— and Anne Tibble, eds, *The Prose of John Clare* (London, 1951)

Tompkins, J. M. S., *The Polite Marriage* (Cambridge, 1938)

Unwin, Rayner, *The Rural Muse: Studies in the Peasant Poetry of England* (London, 1954)

Vicinus, Martha, *The Industrial Muse: A Study of Nineteenth-Century British Working-Class Literature* (London, 1974)

Williams, Raymond, *The Country and the City* (London, 1985)

Yearsley, Ann, *A Poem on the Inhumanity of the Slave Trade* (London, 1788)

——, *Poems on Several Occasions* (London, 1785)

——, *Poems on Various Subjects* (London, 1787)

——, *The Royal Captives: A Fragment of Secret History Copied from an Old Manuscript* (Dublin, 1795)

——, *Stanzas of Woe* (1790)

FOLK SONG COLLECTING, THE ARTS AND CRAFTS MOVEMENT AND NINETEENTH-CENTURY POPULAR CULTURE

Altick, Richard D., *The English Common Reader* (London, 1957)

Arnold, Matthew, *Culture and Anarchy*, 1st edn 1869, ed. J. Dover Wilson (Cambridge, 1967)

Baldick, Chris, *The Social Mission of English Criticism* (Oxford, 1983)

Bell, Robert, ed., *Early Ballads Illustrative of History, Traditions and Customs, Also Ballads and Songs of the Peasantry of England* (London, 1877)

Bennett, Tony, *Popular Culture: Themes and Issues (2)* (Milton Keynes, 1981)

Briggs, Asa, ed., *William Morris: Selected Writings and Designs* (Harmondsworth, 1977)

Bryant, Margaret, *The Unexpected Revolution*, Studies in Education, 10 (London, 1979)

Buchan, David, *The Ballad and the Folk* (London, 1972)

Callen, Anthea, *Angel in the Studio: Women in the Arts and Crafts Movement 1870–1914* (London, 1979)

Central Society of Education, *First Publication* (London, 1837)

——, *Second Publication* (London, 1838)

Child, Francis James, *English and Scottish Ballads*, 8 vols (Boston, 1857–9)

Coleridge, Samuel Taylor, *On the Constitution of the Church and State*, The Collected Works of S. T. Coleridge, Bollingen Series, 75 (London 1969–), X, ed. John Colmer (1976)

Collins, John Churton, *The Study of English Literature* (London, 1891)

Deacon, George, *John Clare and the Folk Tradition* (London, 1983)

Donajgrodzki, A. P., ed., *Social Control in Nineteenth Century Britain* (London, 1977)

Dormer, Peter, 'Familiar Forms' in *Fast Forward: New Directions in British Ceramics* (London, 1985), 5–8

Dorson, Richard, *The British Folklorists: A History* (London, 1968)

Dunn, Ginette, *The Fellowship of Song: Popular Singing Traditions in East Suffolk* (London, 1980)

Engel, Carl, *An Introduction to the Study of National Music* (London, 1866)

Gammon, Vic, 'Folk Song Collecting in Sussex and Surrey, 1843–1914', *History Workshop*, 10 (Autumn 1980), 61–89

——, 'Song, Sex, and Society in England, 1600–1850', *Folk Music Journal*, 4 (1982), 208–245

Golby, J. M. and A. W. Purdue, *The Civilisation of the Crowd: Popular Culture in England 1750–1900* (London, 1984)

Gomme, G. L., ed., *The Handbook of Folklore* (London, 1890)

Harker, Dave, *Fakesong: The Manufacture of British 'Folksong' 1700 to the Present Day* (Milton Keynes, 1985)

Harland, John and T. T. Wilkinson, eds, *Lancashire Folk-Lore*, 1st edn 1867 (East Ardsley, 1972)

Harrison, J. F. C., *Learning and Living 1790–1960* (London, 1961)

Harrison, Stanley, *Poor Men's Guardians* (London, 1974)

Hogben, Carol, ed., *The Art of Bernard Leach* (London, 1978)

Hollis, Patricia, *The Pauper Press: A Study in Working Class Radicalism of the 1830s* (London, 1970)

——, ed., *Class and Conflict in Nineteenth Century England 1815–1850* (London, 1973)

Houghton, Walter E., ed., *The Wellesley Index to Victorian Periodicals 1824–1900*, 3 vols (Toronto, 1979)

Humphreys, Anne, 'G. W. M. Reynolds: Popular Literature and Popular Politics', *Victorian Periodicals Review*, 16 (1983), 79–89

James, Louis, *Fiction for the Working Man 1830–50* (London, 1963)

——, ed., *Print and the People* (London, 1976)

Kelvin, Norman, *The Collected Letters of William Morris*, (Princeton, 1984–), vol. 1.

Leach, Bernard, *A Potter's Book* (London, 1948)

Lewis, Peter, ed., *William Morris: Aspects of the Man and His Work* (Loughborough, 1978)

Lloyd, A. L., *Folk Song in England* (London, 1967)

——, *The Singing Englishman: An Introduction to Folksong* (London: Workers' Music Association, (London, n.d. [1944])

——, 'The Revolutionary Origins of English Folk Song', in *Folk: Review of People's Music*, ed. Max Jone (London, 1945), pp. 13–15.

Lloyd, Edward, ed., *Lloyd's Penny Weekly Miscellany of Romance and General Interest* (London, 1843–46)

Maidment, Brian E., 'Magazines of Popular Progress and the Artisans', *Victorian Periodicals Review*, 17 (1984), 83–94

Marshall, Roderick, *William Morris and the Earthly Paradise* (Tisbury, Wiltshire, 1979)

Mayhew, Henry, *London Labour and the London Poor*, 4 vols (London, 1861–2)

Mitchell, Sally, 'Sentiment and Suffering: Women's Recreational Reading in the 1860s', *Victorian Studies*, 21: 1 (Autumn 1977)

Moeran, Brian, 'Yanagi, Morris and Popular Art', *Ceramic Review* (November/December 1980), 25–6

Motherwell, William, *Minstrelsy: Ancient and Modern* (Glasgow, 1827)

Neuburg, Victor E., *Popular Literature: A History and Guide* (Harmondsworth, 1977)

Parry, Sir Hubert, *Style in Musical Art* (London, 1924)

Percy, Thomas, *Reliques of Ancient English Poetry, Consisting of Old Heroic Ballads, Songs and Other Pieces of our Earlier Poets* (London, 1765)

Pickering, Michael, *Village Song and Culture* (London, 1982)

Reynolds, G. W. M., *Miscellany* (London, 1846–69)

——, *The Mysteries of London*, 2 vols (London, 1846)

——, *Political Instructor* (London, 1849–50)

Rymer, J. M., *Varney the Vampire, or The Feast of Blood*, 3 vols (New York, 1970)

St Ives 1939–64: Twenty Five Years of Painting, Sculpture and Pottery, Tate Gallery (London, 1985)

St John, James Augustus, *The Education of the People*, 1st edn 1858 (London, 1970)

Scott, Sir Walter, *Minstrelsy of the Scottish Border* (London, 1931)

Sharp, Cecil, *English Folk Song: Some Conclusions*, ed. Maud Karpeles, 4th edn (London, 1965)

Shattock, Joanne and Michael Wolff, *The Victorian Periodical Press: Samplings and Soundings* (Leicester, 1982)

Stedman Jones, Gareth, *Language of Class: Studies in English Working Class history 1832–1982* (Cambridge, 1983)

——, 'Class Expression versus Social Control? A Critique of Recent Trends in the Social History of Leisure', *History Workshop*, 4 (Autumn 1977), 162–70

Stewart Hunter, J. V. B., 'George Reynolds, Sensational Novelist and Agitator', *Book Handbook*, 4 (1947), 225–36

Suvin, Darko, 'The Social Addressees of Victorian Fiction: A Preliminary Enquiry', *Literature and History*, 8 (1982), 11–41

Swindells, Julia, *Victorian Writing and Working Women* (Cambridge, 1985)

Thompson, E. P., *William Morris: Romantic to Revolutionary* (London, 1955)

Thompson, Paul, *The Work of William Morris* (London, 1977)

Vann, J. Don, and Rosemary T. Van Arsdel, eds, *Victorian Periodicals: A Guide to Research* (New York, 1978)

Vaughan Williams, R., 'Cecil Sharp: An Appreciation', in Cecil Sharp, *English Folk Song: Some Conclusions*, ed. Maud Karpeles, 4th edn (London, 1965), pp. vii–ix

Wakefield, Hugh, 'The Leach Tradition', *Crafts*, 6 (January/February 1974), 16–20

Walton, John K. and James Walvin, eds, *Leisure in Britain 1780–1939* (Manchester, 1983)

Watson, Oliver, 'Studio Pottery: New and Traditional', in *Carol McNicoll Ceramics*, Crafts Council (London, 1985), pp. 9–11.

Webb, R. K., *The British Working Class Reader 1790–1848: Literacy and Social Tension* (London, 1955)

Williams, Alfred, ed., *Folk Songs of the Upper Thames* (London, 1923)

Wolff, M. et al., *Waterloo Directory of Victorian Periodicals 1824–1900* (Waterloo, Ontario, 1976)

Yeo, Eileen and Stephen eds, *Popular Culture and Class Conflict 1590–1914: Explorations in the History of Labour and Leisure* (Brighton, 1981)

POPULAR THEATRE

Allen, John, 'The Left Book Club and the Fight for Democracy', *Left News*, February 1939, p. 1179

——, 'Theatre', *Fact*, 4 (July 1937), 30–8

Ashcroft, T., 'The Theatre and Socialism', *Plebs*, 27: 12 (December 1935), 295–6

Ashleigh, Charles, 'Plays Needed, Now is the Time', *Sunday Worker*, 11 July 1926, p. 8

Ashwell, Lena, 'Drama and the State', *Clarion*, no. 1868, NS 24 (April 1929), 10

Auden, W. H. and C. Isherwood, *The Ascent of F6* (London, 1936)

——, and C. Isherwood, *The Dog Beneath the Skin* (London, 1935)

Bergonzi, Bernard, *Reading the Thirties: Texts and Contexts* (London, 1978)

Bernard, Heinz, 'Working Class Theatre', *Prompt*, 2 (Spring 1963), 22–4

Branson, Noreen and Margot Heinemann, *Britain in the Nineteen Thirties* (London, 1971)

Brecht, Bertolt, *Brecht on Theatre*, trans. J. Willett (London, 1964)

Brosnan, Alma, *The Street* (London, 1926)

Čapek, Karel, *Rossum's Universal Robots (RUR)* (New York, 1923)

—— and Josef Čapek, *The World We Live In (The Insect Comedy)* (London, 1933)

Carter, Huntly, *The New Spirit in the Russian Theatre 1917–28* (London, 1929)

——, *The New Theatre and Cinema of Soviet Russia* (London, 1924)

——, 'Labour and the Theatre', *Plebs*, 22: 9 (September 1930), 206–9

Clark, Jon, M. Heinemann, D. Margolies and C. Snee, eds, *Culture and Crisis in Britain in the Thirties* (London, 1979)

Corrie, Joe, *Plays, Poems and Theatre Writings*, ed. Linda Mackenney (Edinburgh, 1985)

Cunningham, Valentine, *British Writers of the Thirties* (Oxford, 1988)

Dawson, Jerry, *Left Theatre: Merseyside Unity Theatre, A Documentary Record* (Liverpool, 1985)

Deák, František, 'Blue Blouse', *Drama Review*, 17: 1 (March 1973), 35–46

Dobb, Maurice, 'The Theatres', *Plebs*, 21: 3 (March 1929), 53–5

Dodds, Ruth, *The Pitman's Play* (London, 1923)

Edwards, Ness, *The Workers' Theatre* (Cardiff, 1930)

Fyfe, Hamilton, *The Kingdom, The Power and The Glory* (London, 1920)

Goldring, Douglas, *The Fight For Freedom* (London, 1919)

Goorney, Howard, *The Theatre Workshop Story* (London, 1981)

Gore Graham, R., 'Socialism and the Theatre', *Socialist Review*, 25: 138 (April 1925), 166–78

Gullan, Roger and Buckley Roberts (Herbert Hodge and Bob Buckland), *Where's That Bomb?* (London, 1937)

Hill, John, 'Glasgow Unity Theatre. The Search for a "Scottish People's" Theatre', *New Edinburgh Review*, 40 (February 1978)

——, '"Scotland Doesna Mean Much to Glesca:" Some Notes on 'The Gorbals Story', in *Scotch Reels*, ed. Colin McArthur (London, 1982), pp. 100–11

——, 'Towards a Scottish People's Theatre: The Rise and Fall of Glasgow Unity', *Theatre Quarterly*, 7: 27 (August 1977), 61–70

Houghton, Stanley, 'Hindle Wakes', in *The Works of Stanley Houghton*, ed. H. Brighouse, 3 vols (London, 1914), III

Jacobs, Nicholas and Prudence Ohlsen, *Bertolt Brecht in Britain* (London, 1977)

Jones, Len, 'The Workers' Theatre Movement in the Thirties', *Marxism Today*, 18: 9 (September 1974), 271–80

Lawrence, D. H., *Touch and Go* (London, 1920)

Lenin, V. I., 'Draft Resolution on Proletarian Culture', *On Literature and Art*, (Moscow, 1967), pp. 154–5

Lewenstein, Oscar, *Unity Theatre Presents – The Story of a People's Movement* (London, n.d.)

Lewis, Edwin, *The Forge* (London, 1926)

Lewis, John, *The Left Book Club: An Historical Record* (London, 1970)

Lindsay, Jack, 'On Guard For Spain! A Mass Recitation', *Left Review*, 3: 2 (March 1937), 79–86

Lucas, John, ed., *The 1930s: A Challenge to Orthodoxy* (Brighton, 1978)

Lunacharski, A. V., *Three Plays*, trans. L. A. Magnus and K. Walter (London, 1923)

McGrath, John, *A Good Night Out: Popular Theatre: Audience, Class and Form* (London, 1981)

Macintyre, Stuart, *A Proletarian Science: Marxism in Britain 1917–1933* (Cambridge, 1980)

Mackenney, Linda, 'Legends', *Scottish Theatre News* (April 1983), 11–14

——, 'Popular Theatre in Scotland 1900–1950', in *Clydebuilt: Souvenir Programme*, 7:84 Publications (Edinburgh, 1982)

Malleson, Miles, *'D' Company and Black 'Ell* (London, 1916)

——, *The ILP Arts Guild: The ILP and its Dramatic Societies. What They Are and Might Become* (London, 1925)

—— and H. Brooks, *Six Men of Dorset* (London, 1934)

Mann, Charles, '"Sex Appeal" is Dope for the Masses', *Red Stage*, 6 (June/July 1932), 2

Marshall, Norman, *The Other Theatre* (London, 1947)

Nixon, Barbara, 'Theatre Now', *Left Review*, 3 (December 1935), 105–7

Odets, Clifford, 'Waiting for Lefty', in *Theatres of the Left 1880–1935*, ed. R. Samuel, E. MacColl and S. Cosgrove (London, 1985), pp. 326–52

Palme Dutt, R., 'The Workers Theatre', *Labour Monthly*, 8: 8 (August 1926), 503–10

Samuel, Raphael, E. MacColl and S. Cosgrove, eds, *Theatres of the Left 1880–1935* (London, 1985)

Symons, Julian, *The Thirties: A Dream Revolved* (London, 1975)

Thomas, Tom, 'Workers Drama That Can Be', *Sunday Worker*, 1 January 1929, p. 4

——, 'The Workers' Theatre in Britain', *International Theatre*, 1 (1934), 22–4

Trotsky, Leon, *Literature and Revolution*, trans. R. Strunsky (London, 1925)

Unity Theatre, *Busmen*, Nottingham Drama Texts (Nottingham, 1984)

Unity Theatre Society, *Unity Theatre Handbook* (London, 1940)

Veitch, Norman, *The People's: Being a History of the People's Theatre, Newcastle Upon Tyne, 1911–1939* (Gateshead, 1950)

TELEVISION

Arato, Andrew and Eike Gebhardt, *The Essential Frankfurt School Reader* (Oxford, 1978)

Beharrell, Peter, and Greg Philo, *Trade Unions and the Media* (London, 1977)

Belson, William A., *Television Violence and the Adolescent Boy* (Farnborough, 1978)

Bennett, Tony et al., *Popular Television and Film* (London, 1981)

Brunsdon, Charlotte, and David Morley, *Everyday Television: 'Nationwide'*, BFI Television Monograph 10 (London, 1978)

Connell, Ian, 'Commercial Broadcasting and the British Left', *Screen*, 24: 6 (November–December 1983), 70–80

Curran, James, Michael Gurevitch and Janet Woollacott, eds., *Mass Communication and Society* (London, 1977)

Dyer, Richard et al., *Coronation Street*, BFI Television Monograph 13 (London, 1981)

Egan, Michael, 'Television for the Masses: Its Effects on Social Progress and War', *New Leader* 15 April 1927, p. 11

Ellis, John, *Visible Fictions* (London, 1982)

Eysenck, H. J. and D. K. B. Nias, *Sex, Violence and the Media* (London, 1978)

Fiske, John and John Hartley, *Reading Television* (London, 1978)

Gardner, Carl, 'Populism, Relativism and Left Strategy', *Screen*, 25: 1 (January/February 1984), 45–51

—— and Julie Sheppard, 'Transforming Television: Part One, The Limits of Left Policy', *Screen*, 25: 2 (March/April 1984), 26–38

Garnham, Nicholas, *Structures of Television*, BFI Television Monograph 1 (London, 1980)

——, 'Public Service versus the Market', *Screen*, 24: 1 (January/February 1983), 6–27

Glasgow University Media Group, *Bad News* (London, 1976)

Groombridge, Brian, *Television and the People: A Programme for Democratic Participation* (Harmondsworth, 1972)

Hall, Stuart, 'Encoding/Decoding', in Stuart Hall et al., eds, *Culture, Media, Language: Working Papers in Cultural Studies 1972–79* (London, 1980), pp. 128–139

——, 'Introduction to Media Studies at the Centre', in Stuart Hall et al., eds, *Culture, Media, Language: Working Papers in Cultural Studies 1972–79* (London, 1980), pp. 117-121

——, Ian Connell and Lydia Curti, 'The "Unity" of Current Affairs Television', in *Culture and Domination*, Working Papers in Cultural Studies, 9 (Birmingham, 1976), pp. 51–93

——, and Paddy Whannel, *The Popular Arts* (London, 1964)

Halloran, J., ed., *Effects of Television* (London, 1970)

Higgins, A. P., *Talking About Television* (London, 1966)

Himmelweit, H. T. et al., *Television and the Child: An Empirical Study of the Effect of Television on the Young* (London, 1958)

Hobson, Dorothy, *Crossroads: The Drama of a Soap Opera* (London, 1982)

Hodge, Bob and David Tripp, *Children and Television* (Cambridge, 1986)

Hoggart, Richard, *The Uses of Literacy* (Harmondsworth, 1958)

Hood, Stuart, *On Television* (London, 1980)

James, Clive, *The Crystal Bucket: Television Criticism from 'The Observer'
1976–79* (London, 1981)

Kaplan, E. Ann, ed., *Regarding Television: Critical Aproaches – An
Anthology* (Frederick, Maryland, 1983)

Labour Research Department, *Men and Money Behind TV* (London,
1959)

Leavis, F. R., *Mass Civilisation and Minority Culture*, Minority Pamphlet
1 (Cambridge, 1930)

Lusted, David and Phillip Drummond, *TV and Schooling* (London, 1985)

McArthur, Colin, *Television and History*, BFI Television Monograph 8
(London, 1980)

MacCabe, Colin, ed., *High Theory/Low Culture: Analysing Popular
Television and Film* (Manchester, 1986)

—— and Olivia Stewart, eds, *The BBC and Public Service Broadcasting*
(Manchester, 1986)

McQuail, Denis, ed., *Sociology of Mass Communication* (Harmondsworth,
1972)

Masterman, Len, ed., *Television Mythologies: Stars, Shows and Signs*,
Comedia Series, 24 (London, 1984)

Mills, Adam and Phil Rice, 'Quizzing the Popular', *Screen Education*, 41
(Winter/Spring 1982), 15–25

Morley, David, *The 'Nationwide' Audience*, BFI Television Monograph 11
(London, 1980)

Murdock, Graham and Peter Goldring, 'For A Political Economy of Mass
Communications', in *The Socialist Register 1973*, ed. R. Miliband and
J. Saville (London, 1974), pp. 205–234

Murdock, Graham and Robin McCron, 'The Television and Delinquency
Debate', *Screen Education*, 30 (Spring 1979), 51–67

Poole, Mike, 'The Cult of the Generalist: British Television Criticism
1936–83', *Screen*, 25: 2 (March–April 1984), 41–61

Report of the Broadcasting Committee 1949 (Beveridge Committee),
HMSO, cmnd. 8116, 1951

Report of the Committee on Broadcasting 1960 (Pilkington Committee),
HMSO, cmnd. 1753, 1962

Report of the Committee on Financing the BBC (Peacock Committee),
HMSO, cmnd. 9824, 1986

Report of the Committee on the Future of Broadcasting (Annan
Committee), HMSO, cmnd. 6753, 1977

Report of the Television Committee 1943 (London, 1945)

Root, Jane, *Open The Box: About Television*, Comedia Series, 34
(London, 1986)

Simpson, Philip, ed., *Parents Talking Television: Television in the Home*,
Comedia Series, 46 (London, 1987)

Thompson, Denys, ed., *Discrimination and Popular Culture*
(Harmondsworth, 1964)

TUC Media Working Group, *Media Coverage of Industrial Disputes,
January and February 1979: A Cause for Concern* (London, 1979)

Tumber, Howard, *Television and the Riots* (London, 1982)

Williams, Raymond, *Television: Technology and Cultural Form* (London, 1974)

Winn, Marie, *The Plug-In Drug* (New York, 1977)

Woollacott, Janet, 'Class, Sex and The Family in Situation Comedy', in *Politics, Ideology and Popular Culture (2)* (Milton Keynes, 1982), pp. 61–92

Worsley, T. C., *Television: The Ephemeral Art* (London, 1970)

GENERAL HISTORICAL AND THEORETICAL WORKS

Bennett, Tony, 'Popular Culture: A "Teaching Object"', *Screen Education*, 34 (Spring 1980), 17–29

Birmingham University Centre for Contemporary Cultural Studies, *On Ideology* (London, 1977)

——, *Resistance Through Rituals*, Working Papers in Cultural Studies, 7–8 (Birmingham, 1975)

Bourdieu, Pierre, *Distinction: A Social Critique of the Judgement of Taste*, trans. Richard Nice (London, 1984)

—— and Jèan-Claude Passeron, *Reproduction in Education, Society and Culture*, trans. Richard Nice, Sage Studies in Social and Educational Change, 5 (London, 1977)

Burke, Peter, *Popular Culture in Early Modern Europe* (London, 1978)

Certeau, Michel de, *La culture au pluriel* (Paris, 1974)

Chambers, Ian, 'Rethinking "Popular Culture"', *Screen Education*, 36 (1980), 113–17

Clarke, J., et al, eds, *Working Class Culture: Studies in History and Theory* (London, 1979)

Gans, Herbert J., *Popular Culture and High Culture: An Analysis and Evaluation of Taste* (New York, 1974)

Gramsci, Antonio, *Selections from Cultural Writings*, ed. David Forgacs and Geoffrey Nowell-Smith (London, 1985)

——, *Selections from the Prison Notebooks*, ed. Quintin Hoare and Geoffrey Nowell Smith (London, 1971)

Grealy, Jim, 'Notes on Popular Culture', *Screen Education*, 22 (1977), 5–11

Kaplan, Steven L., ed., *Understanding Popular Culture* (Berlin, 1984)

Klaus, H. Gustav, *The Literature of Labour: Two Hundred Years of Working Class Writing* (Brighton, 1985)

Laclau, Ernesto, *Politics and Ideology in Marxist Theory* (London, 1977)

Modleski, Tania, *Loving With a Vengeance: Mass Produced Fantasies For Women* (London, 1984)

Samuel, Raphael, ed., *People's History and Socialist Theory* (London, 1981)

Shiach, Morag, *The Concept of 'The Popular' in Cultural Analysis*, McGill University Working Papers in Communications (Montreal, 1986)

Swingewood, Alan, *The Myth of Mass Culture* (London, 1977)

Taylor, Barbara, *Eve and the New Jerusalem: Socialism and Feminism in the Nineteenth Century* (London, 1983)

Thompson, E. P., *The Making of the English Working Class* (London, 1963)

——, *Whigs and Hunters: The Origin of the Black Act* (London, 1975)

——, 'Eighteenth Century English Society: Class Struggle Without Class', *Social History*, 3: 2 (May 1978), 132–65

Women's Studies Group, Birmingham University Centre for Contemporary Cultural Studies, *Women Take Issue: Aspects of Women's Subordination* (London, 1978)

Williams, Raymond, *Culture and Society 1780–1950* (Harmondsworth, 1958)

——, *Keywords: A Vocabulary of Culture and Society* (Glasgow, 1976)

——, *The Long Revolution* (Harmondsworth, 1961)

——, *Marxism and Literature* (Oxford, 1977)

Williamson, Judith, 'The Problems of Being Popular', *New Socialist*, 41 (September 1986), 14–15

ARCHIVAL AND UNPUBLISHED MATERIAL

Allen, Douglas, 'Political Culture in Scotland: The Glasgow Workers' Theatre Group 1937–40' (unpublished thesis, University of Glasgow), Scottish Theatre Archive (University of Glasgow), STA.A.t.Box 3

Harker, David Ian, 'Popular Song and Working Class Consciousness in North-East England' (unpublished doctoral thesis, University of Cambridge, 1976)

Jerrold, Douglas, 'Letter to Forster', Victoria and Albert Museum, Forster Collection, MSS ix, no. 19, press mark 48.F.66

Letters and Papers by or concerning William Thom, Aberdeen University Library, MSS 2304 and 2497

Letters to John Clare, British Library, Egerton MSS 2245, fols 90–1, 94–9, 118–21 and 239–42

Mackenney, Linda, 'Interview with Vincent and Ann Flynn', tape in Scottish Theatre Archive, STA.TR.I(Fly).1(3)

——, 'Working Class Theatre in Glasgow 1900–1950: Catalogue of Plays' (1981), Scottish Theatre Archive, STA.A.t.4

McLeish, Robert, *The Gorbals Story*, tape of radio performance in Scottish Theatre Archive, STA.A.r.Box 9

Stewart, Ena Lamont, *Men Should Weep* (1947), Scottish Theatre Archive, STA.A.r.Box 10

Thomson, Robert Stark, 'The Development of the Broadside Ballad Trade and its Influence upon the Transmission of English Folk Songs' (unpublished doctoral thesis, University of Cambridge, 1974)

Trott, Harry, *UAB Scotland* (1940), Scottish Theatre Archive, STA.A.t. Box 3

Index

238   INDEX